THE KENNEDY CHILDREN

The Kennedy Children

TRIUMPHS & TRAGEDIES

BY BILL ADLER

Franklin Watts
New York/London/Toronto/Sydney
1980

Library of Congress Cataloging in Publication Data

Adler, Bill.
The Kennedy children.

1. Kennedy family. I. Title.

E843.A33   973.92'092'2 [B]   80–17460
ISBN 0–531–09933–4

CONTENTS

THE KENNEDY CHILDREN

CHAPTER 1
The Kennedy Mystique

You see one of them waiting to be seated at a restaurant, tall and self-assured, handsome, with that freckled face, that long curly brown hair, and that *something* that makes your eye move directly to him, and you know, without being told, who he is.

You see another of them walking down a dusty, boiling hot southwestern street, studying the beat-down hovels sheltering undernourished citizens, pausing to chat with wizen-faced oldsters forced to live in poverty on the reservation because there is no other place to live, and you know, without being told, who she is.

You see yet another of them laughing and living it up inside a fevered disco in the middle of Manhattan, arm around a half-dressed girl, cigarette tilted in the mouth Bogart-style, playing it laid back and macho in the midst of total Western decadence, and you know, without being told, who he is.

A Kennedy.

The name Kennedy has come to mean so much to the world in the past few decades that there is virtually nowhere it is not known. Conjured up by the name itself are various familiar images:

John Fitzgerald Kennedy, who leads the long list. He revived Camelot in Washington, held on for three glorious years, and gave his life for it.

Robert Francis Kennedy, who came second. He sought the same status as his brother, and was on his way, when he was denied the sceptre by a bullet.

Edward Moore Kennedy (Ted), third in line. He too wanted to take up where his older brother had left off. And his future is still in the hands of the gods.

And then the younger generation:

Caroline Bouvier Kennedy. She escaped death by seconds when an Irish Republican Army terrorist's bomb exploded under the car she was about to enter on her way to Sotheby's in London.

John Fitzgerald Kennedy, Jr. He was the target of a fantastic abduction plot by Greek terrorists who dreamed of holding him for ransom to bring down the junta government and raise the wages of the working people.

Joseph Patrick Kennedy III. He turned over a car he was driving, crippled a young woman for life, leaving her paralyzed from the waist down, and injured two others of the seven passengers, one of whom was his brother David, whom he almost killed.

Robert Francis Kennedy, Jr. He has been busted on a pot charge, arrested for "loitering" and fined $50 after spitting ice cream at a policeman, and has also been arrested for speeding in New Hampshire.

David Anthony Kennedy. He was mugged and robbed in a Harlem "shooting gallery" and was later admitted to Massachusetts General Hospital suffering from a condition frequently associated with drug addiction.

Michael LeMoyne Kennedy. He was fined $35 for speeding through a New Hampshire town, and has been seen constantly in discos and entertainment spots with various representative beautiful people.

Mary Kerry Kennedy. She jumped out of a window into a snow bank "just for kicks" and broke her leg, and has also been arrested for speeding after running into a snowplow clearing a wintry road.

Christopher George Kennedy. He began squiring actress Tatum O'Neal around town when he was only sixteen years of age, much to the distress of his mother, Ethel Kennedy.

Kara Anne Kennedy. She ran away from home twice, rebelling against the Kennedy lifestyle, and suffered so many emotional problems she was put under a doctor's care to help her keep up her grades in school.

Edward Moore Kennedy, Jr. (Ted). He lost his right leg to cancer and learned to ski, swim, and play other games with an artificial leg.

Christopher Lawford. He was arrested and ordered to appear in Aspen, Colorado, after having obtained a prescription for a narcotic by fraud or deceit, the charge calling for a fine of up to $1,000 and a jail sentence of up to one year.

Maria Owings Shriver. She dated muscleman Arnold Schwarzenegger, the retired "Mr. Universe" and "Mr. Olympus," and actor of *Pumping Iron* fame, much to the distress of her mother and father.

And that is only a partial listing of the foibles, follies, and frivolities of the twenty-nine grandchildren of the family patriarch, Joseph Patrick Kennedy, and the matriarch, Rose Fitzgerald Kennedy.

There are now twenty-nine third-generation Kennedys. Joe Kennedy began the line. He planned its every move. He gave it power with the millions of dollars he is said to have made in his long career involving stock manipulations, liquor-industry machinations, and wheeler-dealer operations in the motion picture business.

The reasons why he did what he did lie buried in his background and in the past of the immigrant Kennedy family as it struggled, survived, and then finally prospered in Boston.

Joseph Patrick Kennedy grew up as one of the hated in a Boston dominated at the time by American blue bloods, who formed an aristocracy of wealthy families we would now call WASPS—White Anglo-Saxon Protestants.

Kennedy was Catholic and Irish. The centuries-old hatred between Irish Catholics and Protestants raged not only in Ireland but in America as well—particularly in Boston. Kennedy grew up scorned and detested by neighbors who considered themselves his social superiors.

His father was a saloonkeeper and had become a power locally as a politician. He was ward boss of East Boston and a state representative. Joe Kennedy understood from birth that politics was power, and that money was the be-all and the end-all of power, the wellspring from which flowed clout and influence.

With the two—political power and money to back up that power—a man could call himself king of the mountain. Without both, he was a pawn for the movers and shakers to do with what they would.

Somewhere in his formative years Joe Kennedy decided that he would devote himself to building a citadel of influence from which he could wield political and financial power. In that way he would not even have to think about getting back at the hated WASPS. He would be above them; they might even have to come to him for permission to operate.

Whether he consciously made those decisions or not is beside the point. His desire to make money and wield power was always there from the start, deep inside him.

From the beginning, he discovered that he had no patience with academic impedimenta. He was too restless, too concerned with movement and action to sit still with books and contemplate the world from afar. His way to power would not be through the accepted paths of academic pursuit, upward mobility in the corporate structure, and final acceptance.

In spite of his lack of genius in academic pursuits, he forced himself to concentrate on his school work and was just shrewd enough to get by with what he could remember and whom he could bluff with his agile mind.

He was always one step ahead of his teachers. Because of his ability to anticipate and flank his mentors intuitively, he got himself into Boston Latin School—the most prestigious of all Boston private schools of the day and a school known for its scholars.

But he was hardly the top student there. True to form, he flunked out one year and had to repeat. Nevertheless, he did finish.

From Boston Latin, Joe Kennedy got into Harvard, where he was still by no means a scholar, but where he distinguished himself by excelling at sports. His cocky, belligerent manner helped. Everyone had to admit Joe Kennedy was great at playing any kind of game—and always playing it to win.

A strangely sour man on the outside, he nevertheless had the ability to make friends readily when he wanted to and when it suited his purpose.

At the same time, he was developing a remarkable ability to make money through all the means known to young people of his day. Joe Kennedy always had three jobs when his competitors had one. It was easy for him to make money. He sold candy on sightseeing boats, pushing the price so high that it strained credulity. He caught pigeons and conned the less knowledgeable into purchasing them as pets.

But he knew that making money in itself was not really enough for him. He had to use the money to raise himself in the world.

He chose his wife, Rose Fitzgerald, from a successful Boston political line, to further his own instinctive ends. Her father, Major John Fitzgerald ("Honey Fitz"), didn't think much of his prospective son-in-law, but the marriage came off nevertheless, because Rose was his favorite daughter. In the years that passed, Rose Fitzgerald proved to be another intuitively shrewd choice of Joe Kennedy's.

The Boston Brahmins still wouldn't accept the Kennedys, no more than the Harvard clubs had invited him to join. As the children kept coming, Kennedy began making big money. Soon he decided to pull up stakes.

"We're never going to get anywhere in this town," he told Rose. "We're going where true Americans can live in style." And he moved from Massachusetts to New York, where the family lived in the posh Riverdale section of the Bronx.

By now Joe Kennedy was beginning to amass the fortune that eventually became one of the largest family fortunes in the country. Details of his business dealings are shrouded in secrecy.

For five decades he continued to make money during periods when others made something and lost everything. He traded in stocks on Wall Street. He bought and sold motion picture companies in Hollywood. He produced movies. He bought and sold real estate—some of the deals small, some unbelievably large. He bought and sold banks and ran them for a time. He purchased oil wells, oil fields, oil stocks, and ran oil companies.

There was very little in the business world that he failed to do. In some instances he lost money, but he made so much that the percentage of his successes was staggering.

With his growing family, Joe Kennedy decided that he would prepare them for all the good things of the American way of life by setting them up as wealthy individuals even before they grew up.

He set up his first trust fund in 1926 for his family. The income tax wasn't as stringent nor as large then as it is now, but when a rich man died, his money was stiffly taxed by the government before it could be passed on to his offspring. Kennedy sensed that with the country moving into a booming prosperity the government would begin to take more and more of a man's money from him.

The trust was a tried-and-true way for the affluent of that era to avoid the inheritance tax. Joe Kennedy was avoiding the inheritance tax bite when he created that first trust fund for his sons and daughters.

In 1929 his instincts told him that the stock market was hopelessly overextended. He sold out every piece of stock he had and put it into other holdings.

The worldwide Depression that followed the bursting of the giant Wall Street bubble was the luckiest of breaks for Joe Kennedy. He had money, he had opportunity, and he had experience in making money. He plunged into the completely chaotic situation, and began amassing a fortune in profits.

In 1936 he set up eight trusts, one for each of his children (except Rosemary). To fund these trusts, he endowed more than $100 million dollars. In 1949 and 1959, Joe Kennedy once again set up more trust funds for his family, but it was the 1926 and 1936 funds that established the fortunes for his children.

Little is actually known about these sources of wealth: secrecy has always been the modus operandi of Kennedy's financial dealings. As a result, researchers have been unable to measure the exact dimensions and holdings of the Kennedy wealth. In addition, many of these businesses are held under assumed names.

Example: The title on the door of the family business headquarters in New York today—Joseph P. Kennedy Enterprises—is actually an illusion. No company of that name exists at all!

The actual name of the business that controls the Kennedy fortune is an inconspicuous, low-profile label: Park Agency, Inc. In an office on the thirtieth floor of the Pan Am Building about a dozen employees sit in seclusion and administer all the paper work that is needed.

Overall manager of the Kennedy fortune is Stephen E. Smith, married to Joe Kennedy's daughter Jean. For twenty-seven years a former accountant named Thomas J. Walsh has supervised the operation, which ranges from multi-million-dollar stock transactions to the preparation of tax returns for all members of the Kennedy family.

Even the amount of the Kennedy fortune is uncertain. Estimates range from $300 to $500 million.

"The family fortune is an integral part of the Kennedy mystique," *The New York Times* wrote in an appraisal recently. "The money and the secrecy that surrounds it lend an aura of power and influence to family members; to critics of the Kennedys, the money inspires suspicion and distrust."

The trustees of the fortune come from a very tight circle of Kennedy family and friends. One of the family is Stephen Smith, another is Robert Sargent Shriver, husband of Eunice Kennedy. A family friend is Robert S. McNamara, president of the World Bank and secretary of defense for President John F. Kennedy.

Still, the trust funds are in no way the bulk of the family fortune. Once Joe Kennedy had put his money into these trusts and created lifetime affluence and ease for his offspring, he invested his remaining millions in many more sometimes precarious, albeit more profitable, holdings. These include four "legs" on which the fortune stands: real estate; oil holdings; stocks and bonds; and family foundations.

In the 1950s, for example, he bought heavily into Manhattan's real estate market. Estimates are that he got out with over $100 million in profit in something less than ten years.

An earlier real estate acquisition was the Merchandise Mart in Chicago—a building with over 4.2 million square feet of space in it. Joe Kennedy bought the building just after the end of World War II for $13 million, putting up only $1 million in cash. The building is now worth from $150 to $200 million. The Mart also produces annual rent revenues of about $23 million, was pre-tax profits estimated at $7 million.

Kennedy divided ownership of the Mart into twelve unequal shares, and distributed these shares throughout the trusts he had created in 1926 and 1936. Each of the eight offspring received an equal percentage of the total.

Recently, the Kennedy family opened a $55 million apparel center next door to the Mart, which is located just outside the Loop on the north bank of the Chicago River. That building is about 95 percent filled and is not yet a moneymaker, but it will be soon.

Joe Kennedy bought into oil heavily during his lifetime, although most of his oil acquisitions were made late in his financial life, and some of them were viewed as good tax write-offs rather than good investments.

During the 1950s, he invested in oil royalty properties and oil leases in Texas and nearby states. Two companies were formed to handle the businesses: Mokeen Oil, headquartered in Corpus Christi, and Kenoil Company, incorporated in Delaware. These are said to be "small operations," primarily exploration and development companies.

Mokeen, for example, is a holding company for oil and gas leases. The company does frequently drill and produce oil on a small scale. Mokeen operates about nineteen natural gas wells, of which eight are active, producing about 600,000 cubic feet of gas. It operates fifteen oil wells, of which seven are active, producing about 12,000 barrels of crude.

Kenoil produces money from oil royalties and from the payments received from drillers and developers to whom the company leases mineral rights.

Kenoil owns mineral rights to dozens of pieces of property in the Texas-Oklahoma area, leasing the rights to developers and retaining a one-eighth royalty interest on any oil production.

Secrecy surrounds the actual amount of money made by the Kennedy oil interests. Some Texas oilmen, however, have been quoted as saying that these two Kennedy companies are currently not major moneymakers, but could become profitable with the rising prices of oil and natural gas.

In 1978 Mokeen was audited by the Department of Energy after complaints had been filed about "overcharging." The audit was conducted by the department's San Antonio enforcement office. It found that Mokeen had "improperly" claimed an exemption from price ceilings on oil and natural gas. Mokeen eventually signed a consent order agreeing to repay purchasers for overcharges.

The third "leg" of the Kennedy fortune involves a large number of holdings in stocks and bonds. This investment is thought to be in the neighborhood of over $100 million.

The portfolio includes New York City bonds and an assortment of blue chip stocks. These are said to include American Express Company, American Telephone and Telegraph, Dow Chemical Company, General Foods, International Business Machines, Standard Oil of California, Texaco, and other major corporations.

These holdings do not include a number of savings accounts and transactions in high-yield bank notes.

Two family foundations comprise the fourth "leg" of the Kennedy fortune. The first is the Joseph P. Kennedy, Jr., Foundation, reported to show a net worth of $20 million in 1978. The foundation, named after Joe Kennedy's first son, made grants of $1.3 million in 1979. The largest of these grants— $490,000—went to support the Special Olympics program for handicapped children. The foundation also donated $395,000 to the Kennedy Center at Georgetown University to underwrite research in bioethics. Grants of $30,000 or more went to Harvard University, the Kennedy Child Study Center in New York, the National Endowment for the Humanities, and the Mailman Center for Child Development in Miami.

The second foundation is the Park Foundation, supported by donations from the Joseph P. Kennedy Foundation. The Park Foundation made grants to 130 institutions in 1979, totaling about $115,000.

All Kennedys in the direct line of descent from Joe Kennedy benefit from the Kennedy fortune. Each son and daughter of Joe Kennedy benefits from the interest on the trust set up for him or her. On his or her death, the trust will be dissolved and the assets will be divided among his or her children. The sum of each trust is thought to be from $12,000,000 to $15,000,000.

On his 1978 Federal income tax return, Senator Edward M. Kennedy of Massachusetts, the youngest of Joe Kennedy's sons, reported earnings of $85,000 from the 1926 trust fund and $419,000 from the 1936 trust.

In addition to that amount, Senator Kennedy holds other inherited assets in a blind trust which was established in 1978 to conform with Government ethics laws. Records show that this trust holds assets worth a maximum of $7.9 million, and is responsible for liabilities worth a maximum of $3 million, giving it a net worth of no more than $4.9 million.

There is no reason to suspect that the income of the other Kennedy siblings of his generation differs much from those figures.

This is a fantastic fortune for one family to hold. It was set up not by the Kennedy children but by the patriarch himself. The management of the trust funds from which they live is accomplished by others. None of the Kennedy siblings has made any of this big money; nor has any of Joe Kennedy's grandchildren. None of them touch the Kennedy fortune itself, but live off its interest and other profits.

The fortune is an integral part of the Kennedy mystique and has been explored in such detail because it is in no way trivial to the Kennedy magic and the Kennedy charisma.

While money is part of the Kennedy charisma, it is definitely not part of the inherent Kennedy personality. *That* is independent of wealth, yet it too takes its form from the patriarch Joe Kennedy and from his personality.

It is a typical Kennedy trait to be sportsminded, athletic, physically aggressive, and competitive. These tendencies were evident in Joe Kennedy and in each of his offspring, almost without exception. To a degree, it is true of the third generation of Kennedy children today.

Joe Kennedy excelled in high school and college sports, because he loved to compete. And he achieved a certain distinction in Harvard because of his scrappiness.

The story goes that he was so enthusiastic when he made the last putout in the 1911 baseball game between Harvard and Yale at first base that he kept the ball and wouldn't give it up to the team captain, as was the custom. The incident exhibited not only his interest in sports but his inability to do things always in the traditional way.

From their youngest days, the Kennedy children—Joe, Jack, Robert, and Ted, and the girls as well—were taught to excel in all sports activities. Touch football became a fetish with the Kennedys—it still is. Sailing also became a keystone of the Kennedy aura. Why? Joe Kennedy knew that the old Boston blue bloods respected sailing and those who could sail. He was getting back at the WASPS once again by beating them at their own sport.

The importance of winning was a hallmark of Joe Kennedy's sense of competitiveness. To play and not win was to Joe ridiculous. No man ever entered a game except to win it.

"If we didn't win we were sent to bed without dinner," Ted Kennedy once told a friend.

Eunice Shriver said that both Joe and his wife Rose were exactly the same kind of people. "Mother was equally competitive about everything. It wasn't that you wanted to destroy anyone; you just wanted to do better than they could. I was twenty-four before I knew I didn't have to win something every day."

Ted Kennedy held that Rose balanced Joe's discipline with love. Others do not agree. "She was the most disciplined person I ever met," Joe Gargan once said about Rose Kennedy. Gargan is Rose's nephew through her sister. "She organized the house terribly well. Everybody knew what he was supposed to do. Our lunches were a horror show. Teddy and I were cross-examined on the news of the day and on our catechism."

In addition to competition and discipline, Joe taught his children to challenge nature in all its manifestations—to swim, to hike, to climb, to shoot the rapids, to ride, to do everything with verve and robustness. They were to compete not only with other men, but with nature itself.

Athleticism has become a Kennedy hallmark.

The Kennedy kids today battle bulls in an arena. They take on the whitewater runs of the world. They ski the most dangerous slopes. They climb the highest mountains. They dive into the deepest waters. They accept every challenge in nature.

"For all of them," a family friend said, "boredom was a very powerful dynamic; they were always moving, all of them, to stave off loneliness, melancholy, introspection, whatever, by playing games, 'chasing broads'—to use their words—skimming books."

"Restlessness charged John Kennedy's presidency," wrote Anne Taylor Fleming. "That and his inherited cold-war view of the world and his own dogged sense of history as heroics. He inherited a war and expanded it, and Robert Kennedy was beside him."

America loves action. It loves its athletes. Football players and baseball players are feted by millions, sell beer, toilet articles, and stocks and bonds on TV, and become household words almost faster than movie stars. America loves anyone who challenges nature and indulges in physical contact sports.

Competitiveness leads to another Kennedy characteristic: an apparent proneness to accidents.

Since the Kennedy kids have it bred in them to play games hard, to win, to strive, and to succeed, they seem to have a built-in probability of mishap.

Not the cautious boy, but the heedless, reckless, and challenging boy—in short, the one Americans consider brave—is the one who will fall out of a tree and break his arm, stumble over a rock and sprain an ankle, dive into water and bang his head, or almost be gored by a wild African antelope.

Because they challenge, the Kennedy kids always seem to be in the news with a new hurt. It almost seems to be a curse of some kind. But is it? Not really.

Yet when each Kennedy kid hurts himself or herself, it's in the newspapers. The American people read about these mishaps with interest. And they make up stories about a curse waiting for the Kennedy kids. Even the kids themselves begin thinking it may be true. Are the Kennedy kids fated to this "curse" of their forebears?

It only seems so. True, Joe Kennedy's immediate off-spring suffered an inordinate number of fatalities that could in no way be considered natural deaths. Two were killed in plane crashes. Two were assassinated. Another was almost killed in a plane crash, but was spared. Serious accidents and actual deaths are very different things. But try to tell that to anyone who becomes fascinated by the Kennedy legend with its overtones of Greek tragedy.

Competitiveness is only one aspect of the masculine combativeness that fascinated Joe Kennedy. In a way, he was simply a product of his times.

The 1920s were years of excitement, social openness, sexual freedom in America and in the world. Joe Kennedy fell into the tradition easily. His forays into Hollywood gave him unlimited freedom to exercise the favorite pastime of the Roaring Twenties—womanizing.

For year he was identified with various big-name motion picture stars like Gloria Swanson. At home his wife suffered all this gossip with a kind of Catholic stoicism—because she knew he would never leave her—and eventually it did all pass over.

During his years as president, John F. Kennedy followed in the general pattern of his father, although strict secrecy was maintained at the time so that his escapades were not public knowledge. Later on they came to light.

Younger brother Ted Kennedy was not so lucky. His disastrous mishap at Chappaquiddick Bridge on Martha's

Vineyard blighted and perhaps ruined forever his hopes for the highest office in the land.

Among the Kennedy kids this penchant for sexual adventure is still an unknown quantity. Nevertheless, the Kennedys' frequent sorties at discos and other watering places of the young produce a strong hint that Old Joe's instincts have been transmitted intact.

There are stories of Joe Kennedy's ruthlessness in financial dealings, too. In 1928 he purchased 200,000 shares of stock in the theater chain of Keith-Albee-Orpheum for $4,200,000 from Edward F. Albee, the president. Albee was a happy man, thinking his fortunes had turned.

Indeed they had, but not in the way he thought.

Kennedy called Albee into his new office for a chat.

"You're out," he told the president—now ex-president.

Albee was stunned. "Just like that?"

"Just like that."

He was ruthless, he worked hard, he believed in the work ethic—but he could play just as hard as he could work.

His penchant for women has been mentioned. His obsession with athletics has been explored. But Joe Kennedy could charm the birds right out of the trees when he wanted to. And when he sat down to enjoy himself, he had a riproaring time.

Work hard, play hard.

He never let his leisure hours interfere with the making of money. Nor did he ever let business interfere with his personal life either. He was an odd combination of the middle-class WASP he hated so and the dissolute old freebooter of an era gone by.

If the stories about Joe Kennedy are true—that he did, indeed, traffic in the purchase, transport, and sale of liquor during the Prohibition years—then his own recklessness and wiliness are in no way exaggerated. That he could manipulate stocks and bonds, just barely skirting the law in many instances, was suspected by many who dealt with him.

Who can then doubt that today the ghost of Joe Kennedy is alive once again and is running with the Kennedy kids who get caught speeding on the highways, are picked up for driving without a license, are charged with possession of marijuana and other drugs, are ordered arrested for nonappearance in court . . . and so on?

Answer: No one.

Nor is it surprising that after their mandatory stint in the backwashes of society, helping the poor, making life a little more comfortable for the destitute, the Kennedy kids throng the discos and night spots, drinking and smoking and carousing to their hearts' content.

Work hard, play hard.

Having a ball is part of the Kennedy mystique—part of the *carpe diem* philosophy that was so affecting in Joe and Jack and Robert and Ted Kennedy.

From his earliest days in Boston, Joe Kennedy was close to practical politics. He would watch his father dispense political savvy from his saloon—sometimes giving people jobs and dispensing power with a few brief sentences.

He learned early on the clout of the political boss—the ability to give out favors to friends, the careful apportioning of food and clothing to those without—in return for future favors.

Joe Kennedy grew up with the same remarkable orientation to people, rather than to facts and figures, that distinguished his father before him. He knew money not for the tracks it left on paper, but for what it would do for him and for others. He *used* money for what it could get him.

When it came time for him to help his offspring on their political fortunes, he had made so many friends among powerful people that he could call in his debts almost at will—debts that had built up not only from money Joe Kennedy had given them, but from favors he had done for them.

The lesson was not lost on the Kennedy sons when Jack was running for office. One of the key last-minute incidents that is said to have swung enough votes to produce a victory for Kennedy over Nixon was the favor Jack and Robert did for Martin Luther King, Jr. who had been imprisoned during the integration struggle in the deep South. They got him out. And won the election.

People.

People were what elected the Kennedys to office.

Nor was this lesson lost on Robert when he became attorney general and worked for many years to integrate the South. It did not die with him in Los Angeles. It lived on in his children. And it lives on today in all the Kennedy kids.

But there are Kennedy traits that aren't so nice. In speaking of Senator Ted Kennedy recently, one source quoted as "a Boston friend," had this to say about Ted Kennedy—and, by extension, Kennedy men in general: "You know what women are to him. He's an MCP."

MCP = Male Chauvinist Pig.

Is it a Kennedy trait to be a Male Chauvinist Pig? (Obviously the question doesn't apply to Kennedy kids who are female—or does it?)

The Kennedy men themselves seem fairly ambivalent on the issue.

The MCP relegates the female members of the family to a role less prominent than the male. Are Eunice, Jean, and Patricia considered as important as John, Robert, and Ted? Are these women, in fact, as important to the men in the family as Jacqueline, Ethel, and Joan who married the Kennedys in question?

It is an interesting point.

None of the women has been relegated to her official "place in the kitchen" which is the basic accusation leveled at the typical MCP—but of course no Kennedy woman, or even a woman married to a Kennedy, is expected to work in the kitchen. She *rules* the kitchen.

Nevertheless, it would appear that the primary function of a Kennedy woman is to bear children. And that is the keystone of the MCP.

The law of primogeniture is also a Kennedy tenet. *Primogeniture* is Latin for "first-born." According to the law of primogeniture, the mantle of authority is handed down to the first-born male, and if then abrogated by death or inability, is handed on to the next-born male. Although Joe Kennedy was American-born, and of Irish background to boot, he believed in primogeniture as a law of inheritance—not only of worldly goods, but responsibility and authority as well.

When Joe, Jr., was killed during World War II, the mantle of authority was passed on to John F. Kennedy, and when John was murdered, the mantle of authority was passed on to Robert F. Kennedy. When Robert was murdered, it was passed on to Edward M. Kennedy.

On the day Jack Kennedy heard of his brother Joe's death, he took the rest of the family sailing. "I remember racing that day afterwards," Eunice Shriver once said. "Jack said, 'Let's go for a sail—that's what Joe would have wanted us to do.' " Then Jack went on to become the first Roman Catholic president of the United States—what Joe, Jr., had told his father he meant to be.

Times have changed from the 1940s when Jack took on the mantle of responsibility, and are as different now as the 1940s differed from the 1920s when Joe started it all. The current crop of Kennedy kids is a product of our times, as much as Joe was of his and Jack was of his.

The first-married of the Kennedy kids share an equality between husband and wife in marriage that would have seemed strange to Rose Kennedy. Kathleen Kennedy, first-born of Robert F. Kennedy's brood, married a red-bearded product of the emancipated 1960s. Joe Kennedy III, second-born, married a specialist in urban affairs who has a career of her own. And so on.

Nevertheless, the legacy of primogeniture continues, with Joe III carrying on as the leader of the Kennedy kids.

There was more to Old Joe Kennedy's ideas about family life than simply inheritance. His was a closely-knit family—he had two sisters and no brothers. Even then, the Kennedy family always stood together. Because Irish immigrants in those days were maligned, ignored, and actually spat upon by outsiders, new arrivals to these shores tended to cling closely together. Most immigrant groups do the same thing. It was an American who said, "Let's all hang together, or we'll all hang separately."

Joe Kennedy brought up his children to believe in each other, to protect each other, to act as if every member of the family was just as important as any other.

Although they might scrap among themselves, the moment any member of the family became threatened from outside, the entire group drew in closely together and turned against the outside threat as one.

This type of reaction to danger is sometimes called clannishness. The Scotch—originally Gaels (Celts) exactly like the Irish—called their family groupings "clans." It was no accident that the Gaelic Kennedys should be clannish like the Gaelic Scots.

The story goes that when both Robert and Ted Kennedy were senators in Washington, a bill came up before the health subcommittee on which they both sat. Robert, bored by the detail involved, and openly bored about senatorial work in general, waded into a discussion, and found himself boxed in and unable to get out.

The Republicans confronted him with demands to elucidate a certain paragraph in the proposal. With his eyes, Robert implored his brother for help. Yet Ted sat there like a lump of stone.

In desperation, Robert scribbled out a note saying: "Goddamn it, why don't you help me out?"

Ted scratched his reply on the bottom of the note and passed it back. "You're not in real trouble yet."

Robert got in deeper and deeper, and finally Ted, who had done his homework—as usual—waded in and bailed him out.

"He didn't want Bobby badly embarrassed," one close associate explained, "but he wanted to sting him a little bit. He was saying, 'You're passing through; I'm the senior senator here.' "

The fact was, Kennedys actually *liked* one another. They liked to be together, to talk together, to play together. They liked to work together, and to have fun together. A tremendous strength and unity grew up from this Kennedy attitude.

Clannishness helped elect John F. Kennedy president. It helped elect Robert F. Kennedy senator. It helped elect Ted Kennedy senator, as well.

And it drew them all together in times of stress—when Jack and Robert were assassinated, when Joe and Kathleen were killed. Through their collective strength, they found their way through those tragic moments more surely and more gracefully.

Now, in the current Kennedy generation, the clannishness continues.

The shaping of the Kennedy family's political instincts began in the family. Nobody ever moves the Kennedys as much as they move each other. They have a genetic preference for each other's company and they have the money and therefore the mobility and time to support that preference. That is the importance of Joe Kennedy's money—not the fact that his offspring can win elections with it.

This inspired unity of the Kennedy clan helps maintain the secrecy and the mystique. That is one reason it is so hard for outsiders to know the real facts about any Kennedy. They tend to keep their skeletons locked up in their private closets. They tend to find a kind of elemental safety in silence.

On a more personal level, the Kennedy mystique embraces a strong and decidedly moral religious faith that is not usual in the United States nor even in the modern age.

Almost without exception, the Kennedy clan is Catholic in religious faith. The men keep the faith while many other men around them drop theirs. The women never doubt their faith at all. From Joe and Rose all the way down the line, most of the Kennedys are devout Catholics and do nothing to fly in the face of any of their religious tenets.

There are some lapses from regularity.

Two of Joe Kennedy's daughters married non-Catholics. One of them was his eldest daughter. She was killed in an air accident and her husband died in World War II. The other was later divorced from her husband—a situation quite the exception to the rule. Most Kennedys take their religion in stride, making no attempt to break away from it or deviate from its rules of order.

One of Joe Kennedy's grandsons married a non-Catholic —another exception to the rule. But then, rules are made to be broken—even by Kennedys.

The generally accepted tradition is for all Kennedys to go to parochial school until a certain age, at which point the boys might go on to a private nondenominational school. The girls continue in Catholic school in some cases until college, at which point they may be educated in a nondenominational college.

There are Kennedys who go all the way through school and college without leaving the religious fold to which they are so accustomed.

Most of the Kennedy kids are unselfconscious about their Catholicism. Photographs appear in magazines showing them wearing St. Christopher medals in plain view. Other pictures show them going to church for Mass. They all carry it off well, particularly so for such a secular age.

There are other Kennedy traits, as we will see. But the ones summarized in the list below seem to be the most obvious, most viable, and most visible ones that help make up the Kennedy magic.

- competitiveness
- athletic prowess
- ruthlessness
- work hard, play hard
- orientation to people
- male chauvinism
- strong family ties
- religious faith

Yet make no mistake about it. Even though these typical Kennedy traits can be found in each Kennedy—even in those who do not carry the magic name—*each* Kennedy is an individual with specific characteristics and attitudes.

Each Kennedy becomes automatically compared to other Kennedys when he or she is viewed by outsiders. Certain Kennedys attain more fame than others; certain attain more infamy than others. In any group of twenty-nine people, there are as many differences as there are similarities between each individual member.

Exactly who are these twenty-nine Kennedy kids we have been talking about? They come from five different family lines.

There are two Kennedys from the line founded by John Fitzgerald Kennedy and Jacqueline Bouvier Kennedy.

Caroline Bouvier Kennedy
John Fitzgerald Kennedy, Jr.

There are eleven Kennedys from the line founded by Robert Francis Kennedy and Ethel Skakel Kennedy.

Kathleen Hartington Kennedy
Joseph Patrick Kennedy III
Robert Francis Kennedy, Jr.
David Anthony Kennedy
Mary Courtney Kennedy
Michael LeMoyne Kennedy
Mary Kerry Kennedy
Christopher George Kennedy
Matthew Maxwell Taylor Kennedy
Douglas Harriman Kennedy
Rory Elizabeth Kennedy

There are three Kennedys from the line founded by Edward M. Kennedy and Joan Bennett Kennedy.

Kara Anne Kennedy
Edward Moore Kennedy, Jr.
Patrick Joseph Kennedy

There are four Kennedys from the line founded by Stephen Smith and Jean Kennedy Smith
Stephen Smith, Jr.
William Smith
Amanda Smith (adopted)
Kym Maria Smith (adopted)

There are four Kennedys from the line founded by Peter Lawford and Patricia Kennedy Lawford.
Christopher Lawford
Sydney Lawford
Victoria Lawford
Robin Lawford

And there are five Kennedys from the line founded by Robert Sargent Shriver, Jr. and Eunice Kennedy Shriver.
Robert Sargent Shriver III
Maria Owings Shriver
Timothy Perry Shriver
Mark Kennedy Shriver
Anthony Paul Kennedy Shriver

In a group of twenty-nine people, there are those you pay attention to, and there are those you don't pay attention to.

Most people pay attention to *any* Kennedy, but there are degrees of interest here, too.

Among the members of this famous generation of Kennedy kids there are those who are *really* famous—and there are those who are only moderately famous. There are even those who are infamous.

Let's look at them a moment and pick out the most renowned. They are the ones we are going to scrutinize more completely than the also-rans.

• No one will be surprised to learn that Caroline B. Kennedy, the daughter of John F. Kennedy and Jacqueline Bouvier Kennedy, is more well-known than any other Kennedy of her generation.

• Nor will anyone doubt that John F. Kennedy, Jr., her brother, is the next-best known of the entire generation of Kennedy kids. They were the two people nearest the center of power during the years when Washington became Camelot.

They were also once again brought to international attention in 1968 when their mother married one of the richest men in the world, the Greek shipping magnate Aristotle Onassis.

With such a legacy, how could Caroline and John fail to draw more attention than anyone else of their generation?

• Following the pattern of primogeniture, it is interesting to note that the next most important figure among the Kennedy kids is the first-born of Robert F. and Ethel Skakel Kennedy—Kathleen Hartington Kennedy. Of the entire generation, she is the oldest. And because she is a product of the union of Robert and Ethel, she seems to possess Ethel's boundless energy and enthusiasm and Robert's sense of competitiveness and service to others.

• Next in line is Joseph Patrick Kennedy III, born a year after Kathleen, and a curious combination of both good and bad Kennedy traits. He has the genius for politics—and he has the seeds of self-destruction as well. Certainly he was on the road to ruin before he straightened out and found himself.

• The same is true of Robert Francis Kennedy, Jr., who was in trouble a great deal of the time during his adolescence. Nevertheless, it was he who became the first book author of the twenty-nine Kennedy kids.

• As for David Anthony Kennedy, the fourth-born of Robert's children, he too is a combination of high-minded ideals and self-destruction. Whether or not he is able to straighten himself out is still a moot question. His troubles are a source of despair to the Kennedy family, as much as they are a source of avid interest to the American people.

The rest of Robert Kennedy's children have not actually failed or succeeded at as many things as their older brothers and sister. Nor have they been received by the public with as much expectation and/or avidity.

• The same is not true of Edward M. Kennedy, Jr., the second child and first son of Edward M. and Joan Bennett Kennedy. The tragedy that afflicted him with a cancerous growth on his leg, necessitating the removal of the leg, subjected him instantly to the national media spotlight. When he courageously rallied after the amputation, he won the hearts of the world.

The children of the Stephen Smiths, the Peter Lawfords, and the Robert Sargent Shrivers are further removed from the centers of power, and consequently, are able to be Kennedys without *seeming* to be Kennedys. The aura is there, but the obvious mystique is a bit obscured.

For some reason, none of them have done the same number of things that the ones closer to the Kennedy power center have. This is true even though the oldest Shriver boy is as old as Robert F. Kennedy, Jr., and the next oldest is two years older than Caroline Kennedy.

The same is true of the Lawford children, the oldest of whom is the same age as David Anthony Kennedy.

Some Kennedy kids draw the lightning; others do not. Consequently, those lightning-drawers are the ones we are going to concentrate on here.

But it shouldn't be forgotten that like their mothers and fathers, each contributes to the Kennedy myth from day to day, and adds to the subliminal, almost spooky quality of the Kennedy mystique. That mystique carries glamour and triumph as well as misery and tragedy.

It shouldn't be forgotten that, like their mothers and fathers, each Kennedy kid who comes along inherits the legacy of the Kennedys. This legacy is not confined to the vast fortune of close to half a billion dollars (the private proceeds of the patriarch's earning years), but also includes the characteristics of the Kennedy genes.

Not one of them has to worry about financial security for life. Each can enjoy frivolity, fame, and fortune in the particular combination each prefers.

And, in the blood line, each inherits his or her own renown. There is a machismo in the men, an athletic prowess, a handsome, windblown, outdoor look. In the women there is a glamour and a graciousness, a regal beauty, an authority, an indomitable feminine mystique.

The clan is enormous when it is all gathered together. To serve the members of this huge family the Hyannis Port compound on Cape Cod was bought by the patriarch early in the century and later split up like so many pieces of pie for his offspring and their families.

There is also a house in Palm Beach, Florida, where the matriarch, Rose Fitzgerald Kennedy, spends half her time. During the proper season it is transformed into a family compound for those who want to visit.

When a Kennedy errs—or when a Kennedy scores a triumph—the shock waves immediately are transmitted to the Kennedy epicenter at Hyannis Port, and almost immediately all the Kennedys are together once again—whether by telephone or by physical contact. What affects one Kennedy affects every Kennedy. That is the rule of the family. Responsibility for other family members is a Kennedy tradition, and it is accepted by each Kennedy as such.

Other characteristics that we have not yet explored— vigor, ambition, self-assurance, conceit, humility, guilt, love, hate—are all evident in a Kennedy. These characteristics tend sometimes to be at war with one another, many times in the same individual. But the charisma and personal charm of a Kennedy makes each action more intensified than it would be in someone else.

There is no middle ground. A Kennedy who suffers a setback suffers not just a wound, or a temporary defeat, but a cataclysmic tragic loss. A Kennedy who achieves a distinction achieves not just an honor, but a triumph. These tragedies and triumphs seem to be part and parcel of the Kennedy persona.

And always death hovers near, brushing each Kennedy with its dark wings. And glittering fame also flirts nearby, lighting each Kennedy for a brief moment with its aura.

A Kennedy is like the girl in the nursery rhyme, with a slight variation in the text:

When she is good, she is very, very good,
And when she is bad, she is—headlines.

CHAPTER 2
Caroline Bouvier Kennedy

No one, outside of European royalty, has had so much general adulation, so much media attention, and so much public exposure as Caroline Bouvier Kennedy. Although she was not the first-born of the third-generation Kennedys, she was the first one who made it big in the world press.

She was "going on three" when her father was elected president of the United States. Overnight she became a "personality"—a status that has existed from that moment and will continue to exist to the last of her days. Although her father and her mother were the center of an irresistible attention on the part of the press, Caroline was never far from the focal point of this onsurge of interest.

The Camelot myth was created by the press, and it was never deliberately questioned or stemmed by the Kennedys. Caroline became the "fairy princess"—quite reminiscent of Alice Roosevelt, President Theodore Roosevelt's daughter, who lived in the White House during her early days and was the fairy princess of that earlier generation. Alice's fame was such that she inspired a popular song of the era that began: "In my sweet Little Alice Blue Gown."

Once the family was installed in the White House, Caroline became a true "presence." Maud Shaw, who was her "nanny" through those early, trying years, said that Caroline exhibited a "sweet character." She inherited her father's sense of fun, his penchant for teasing people and laughing boisterously at jokes.

She would hide Shaw's shoes, or jump out at her from behind a door. Her favorite pastime was to tell some ridiculous riddle, and then burst into laughter when Shaw couldn't answer.

Nevertheless, Shaw recalls, there was a thoughtful, sensitive side to the child that was never too far beneath the surface. If the victim of Caroline's teasing protested, she would immediately stop.

When she was five years old, her mother decided that it would be ridiculous to send Caroline out to school, and so had a schoolroom established in the solarium of the White House on the third floor. To this school came some of Caroline's contemporaries, drawn from the families of the various White House staff members. It was Caroline's first contact with children from the "other world"—except, of course, her Kennedy cousins. But they were "family."

Her brother John, born in 1960, was only two years old at the time. He had none of her inhibitions, but would barge right in on people no matter what the occasion. And he would accept any consequences of his actions, no matter what they were, with either a laugh or a cry of protest.

Caroline was shy with people of her own age. To a degree, she lacked self-confidence. In the solarium school, for example, she became worried that one of the other girls in the class was better than she was at everything. It was her nanny, Shaw, who helped her with her studies and her activities so she could be as good as anyone else.

At first Caroline was afraid to swim. All the other Kennedy cousins swam like fish. Shaw had to take her down to the White House swimming pool to help her gain confidence in the water. Finally Caroline learned to swim. And from that moment, she was never afraid of the water.

The shyness she exhibited with her peers was never visible when she was exhibited by her mother and father to famous visitors from all over the globe. She would treat visiting royalty with absolute self-possession, and curtsy like a perfect lady, if a curtsy was called for.

When the king of Saudi Arabia visited the White House, the situation called for a kiss by the king himself. Caroline reacted to the king's bristling beard, but she suffered her reaction in silence. Later on, she confided: "He's nice—but he kept on kissing me!"

Her mother was determined to raise her daughter in as nearly normal a manner as possible. Jacqueline Kennedy hated the kind of pressure the press exerted on people in positions of power. She hated much of the press, even though she had been a reporter herself when she met John F. Kennedy. Her instinct was to shield her daughter from publicity, fearing that it could spoil her.

Yet there was no way in which Caroline could be shielded from publicity. She was not only at the center of the power structure of the world, but she was one of the most visible of the "beautiful people." She had wealth, she had position, she had charm, and she had breeding. How could she avoid becoming the fairy princess?

Nevertheless, Jacqueline persisted in her attempts to protect her daughter from the prying eyes of the public. During the winter the Kennedy entourage would desert the White House on weekends to spend time at a winter house the president had bought at Glen Ora, near Middleburg, Virginia, in the heart of the horse-breeding country.

There Caroline would ride her pony, Macaroni, alongside Jacqueline, who might be riding Sardar, while holding her baby John in her arms. Wherever they appeared, people gathered. No matter how hard Jacqueline tried, she could not prevent the public from peering.

She ranted and raved at the president to plant trees, or build a fence, or do something to screen off the Glen Ora property from the public.

The same public threatened her privacy during the summer when they would all pack up and fly to Squaw Island, where the Kennedys lived in a rented house. Squaw Island was about a quarter mile off the coast at Hyannis Port.

There Caroline was able to play with a zoo of animals: nine dogs, some hamsters (whose count at different times varied astronomically), a canary, a pair of love birds, a cat, ducks, and so on. Shannon, a cocker spaniel, eventually became the president's favorite dog, and went on to become Caroline's pet after the president's death.

Caroline learned at an early age that she had more material possessions than other children. But she never used her position with arrogance or petulance. She had, according to Shaw, "a gift of gentleness and consideration for other people."

In 1961 when her grandfather, Joseph Patrick Kennedy, had a stroke that left him paralyzed and speechless, Caroline was heartbroken. She would sit by his chair in his Palm Beach mansion with an arm around his shoulder and talk to him.

The Kennedy clan knew that Caroline was Joe's favorite grandchild. He had once said she "was born a little lady and that was what she was going to be."

From John F. Kennedy, Caroline inherited an ability to defuse the tension of an awkward moment with a joke or a smile. She soon learned to be herself with people—firm, but not overpowered by anyone else's prominence or position.

"I don't think Caroline will ever be one to throw her weight about," Shaw wrote, "despite the power and authority her name has bestowed on her."

On August 9, 1963, Patrick Bouvier Kennedy was born. He was the Kennedys' third child. Patrick lived only two-and-a-half days, dying of a respiratory infection. Jacqueline was heartbroken, and so was the president.

Caroline understood the tragedy without being quite aware of what had really happened. On the day of Patrick's burial, John F. Kennedy saw Caroline out in the garden of the summer house on Squaw Island where they were waiting to visit Jacqueline in the hospital.

She was picking black-eyed Susans and blue larkspur to make a bouquet to give to her mother at the hospital.

"Your mother will be proud of you, and so am I," said the president, kissing Caroline.

It was a sad day in the lives of the Kennedy family. A week later Jacqueline was in Athens. Caroline's Aunt Lee Radziwill had convinced the president that the First Lady needed a rest after the loss of her baby boy. Lee's personal friend, Aristotle Onassis, invited Jacqueline to visit him for a cruise on his private yacht, the *Christina,* in the Aegean Sea.

Shortly after Jacqueline's return to Washington, the president started off on a tour of Texas to mend some weak political fences.

And so it happened that on November 22, 1963, John F. Kennedy, the thirty-fifth president of the United States was assassinated in Dallas. Unlike Jacqueline, who was in Dallas, Caroline and John were in Washington in the White House. It fell to their British nanny to tell them what had happened.

"I can't help crying, Caroline," Shaw told her, "because I have some bad news to tell you. Your father has gone to look after Patrick. Patrick was so lonely in heaven. He didn't know anybody there. Now he has the best friend anyone could have."

Unlike her brother John, who was only three, Caroline was deeply affected. Her whole world had been destroyed.

The months following the funeral were a nightmare to Caroline. The sympathy of all those around her was in no way any solace. It simply magnified the enormity of her loss.

Somehow the dismal days passed by. Jacqueline moved out of the White House with Caroline and John and lived at first in a house in Georgetown across the street from the

Averell Harrimans. But soon Jacqueline decided to move to New York, where she purchased a five-bedroom, fifteen-room cooperative apartment at 1040 Fifth Avenue on the corner of 84th Street. Caroline was enrolled at the Convent of the Sacred Heart, a Catholic school nearby. Two of her cousins, Sydney and Victoria Lawford, also attended the school.

In May, 1965, Caroline and John went on a trip with their mother to England to be present at Runnymede, near Windsor Castle, to witness the dedication of a monument built to the memory of President Kennedy. Runnymede, incidentally, was the scene of one of history's greatest events: the signing of the Magna Charta by King John in 1215, granting the people the right to have a hand in self-government.

"I want the children to see as much of London as possible," Jacqueline told the press. And Caroline and John saw the city exactly the way most tourists saw it.

They watched the changing of the guard at Buckingham Palace, visited Hyde Park where amateur politicians and professionals sounded off about the latest social changes, and even cantered on the famous public bridle path called Rotten Row.

The difference in their visit from that of other tourists was the nature of the entourage—two Secret Service men, their nanny, Maud Shaw, a riding instructor, and two Radziwill cousins, children of Jacqueline's sister Lee.

Back in New York, where Caroline was enrolled fulltime at the convent school, she complained to her nanny about the constant probing of her peer group.

"It's the other girls at school," she said. "They keep on telling me how lucky I am to be Caroline Kennedy, and they keep staring at me. Isn't that silly? I'm just the same as anyone else, aren't I?"

But she wasn't the same as anyone else—she was now the fairy princess in perpetuity. She would never be anything less. She was a living proof of Camelot, even though the place was no more and its inhabitants had long since departed.

She wore blue jeans like all the other children. Her

mother gave her ballet lessons, hiring the world-famous Maria Tallchief as her teacher, but she soon gave them up, much to Jacqueline's disappointment. Caroline apparently didn't like the strictures of the art, nor did she particularly like the amount of time she had to devote to practicing.

At this period Caroline developed a certain amount of self-consciousness. Like her mother, she had always been physically modest. Once when she bought a midiskirt, she discovered to her horror that it had a long slit up the side which showed her leg. She made her nanny sew it up.

Her instincts were for loud colors—reds, yellows, greens, blues—but she had no love for big designs or loud patterns.

"I doubt if in later life Caroline will ever be a trend-setter in fashion," an intimate of the family said. "She never did take much to dressing up when she was small."

Pearl Buck, the bestselling author of *The Good Earth,* was fascinated by the Kennedy family, and wrote the book *The Kennedy Women.* Describing Jacqueline Kennedy she said: "I found her withdrawn, as though she were not altogether among us, nor wanted to be: a quality natural to her, I was to discover, and easily understood when one knows her family history." She found Jacqueline charming, well-bred, and delightful—like the members of the Bouvier family from which she had come. But, she pointed out, there were no leaders and very little family tradition among them.

"Her children will absorb from her the good taste, the artistic tendencies, the love of beauty so natural to her," the author went on. "But it is doubtful if they will become leaders in the sense that Ethel Kennedy's children may."

Jacqueline was born first class, and she "never looked back to see who was traveling behind her," Pearl Buck wrote.

And she observed Caroline during her younger years.

"I see how precisely Caroline places her feet together, how she holds herself and with what cool dignity presents herself to the public, in unconscious—or perhaps conscious—imitation of the mother she adores.

"Whatever the future holds for Caroline Kennedy, it cannot fail to present its own extremes of joy and sorrow. Her destiny will carry her high and may bring her low. The sensitivity inherent in her nature will give her joy yet make her suffer to a degree far beyond the ordinary measure. But she is no common child. She is a Kennedy and she inherits, too, the Kennedy courage."

Her nanny, Maud Shaw, once wrote that Caroline always looked a person right in the eye in such a way that it was almost impossible to deceive her—or for her to deceive another. It was necessary, she recalled, to tell Caroline the truth, simply and directly. She would know if you were trying to get around something.

In 1965, Caroline met her nanny's sister, Hettie. Hettie was seven years younger than Shaw, but had gray hair, while Shaw did not. Caroline was trying to make up her mind who was the younger sister.

Neither of the Shaw sisters would tell her.

Caroline thought about it, then turned to her nanny. "You've got more wrinkles than Hettie. I think you are older."

She was, according to Shaw, levelheaded, honest, and sensitive enough to lead a balanced and stable life. Even though surrounded with luxury and living always near a power center of privilege, Caroline was never known by Shaw to have taken advantage of her wealth to hurt anyone.

Nevertheless, there were times when Caroline was like any other young child: petulant, selfish, and obnoxious.

Once when her nanny scolded her for leaving her room sloppy and untidy, she blew up.

"I haven't *time,* Miss Shaw. Can't you see I'm busy?"

"Very well, Caroline," Shaw responded, "but don't be surprised if I'm too busy the next time you ask me to do something for you."

Later on, Caroline repented and apologized. "I've done my room," she said. "I wasn't too busy after all."

Caroline had bad moments with her cousins, too. Sydney

Lawford, the oldest daughter of Aunt Patricia and Uncle Peter, was Caroline's closest friend in the Kennedy family. At one time Caroline expressed a violent jealousy of Sydney.

"I don't like my hair, Miss Shaw!" she complained. "Why can't it be lovely and curly like Sydney Lawford's?"

Shaw shook her head. "You've got beautiful hair. It's like your mummy's, all thick and shiny. You'll be very proud of it when you grow up."

Caroline didn't think so, but she never mentioned it again.

In 1965, Jacqueline let Maud Shaw go, and there was no more nanny in Caroline's life.

The death of the president had left Caroline quiet, withdrawn, and enveloped by sadness. The immediate years after the assassination were crucial in Caroline's growth. In spite of her own busy life, Jacqueline spent a great deal of time with both her children.

She was particularly close to Caroline, playing a more active role in the upbringing of her daughter than the public realized.

In spite of her widely extended social obligations, she would often have dinner with them both in the New York apartment, talking with them, and taking them on trips. Caroline and John both helped their mother christen the aircraft carrier *John F. Kennedy* in May 1967. Reporters covering the event described Caroline as being "ill at ease."

But she was beginning to come out of her introversion. The boisterous Kennedy clan never let any one member keep introverted for long. Uncle Robert, next in line in the family after John, became a kind of surrogate father to Caroline.

Caroline became involved in more and more festive occasions with her cousins. In fact, at the Tenth Annual Pet Show and Costume Party in McLean, Virginia, Caroline and Courtney Kennedy—Robert Kennedy's fifth child and second daughter—dressed up as two of the Three Little Pigs.

Tragically, seventy days later, Uncle Robert was killed by an assassin in Los Angeles. It was the second traumatic event in the life of the growing girl. Now even her surrogate father was dead.

Jacqueline quickly took control of the situation. She arranged for Caroline to go on an extended European trip with her Aunt Lee (Radziwill) and her grandmother, Mrs. Hugh Auchincloss.

Jacqueline's mother, incidentally, had divorced Jacqueline's father, John Bouvier III, some years before and had married Hugh Auchincloss.

Caroline gradually recovered from her uncle's death, and became once again the typical student at the Convent of Sacred Heart. She was finding that she had a good brain. If she concentrated she was able to get high marks at school. It was not a common Kennedy trait.

She liked to work hard until she had solved a problem put before her. But mathematics was not her favorite subject. She did best in English and history. She liked to read at bedtime—biographies of famous men.

But her favorite reading matter was books about horses. She loved all animals, and liked to lead the outdoor life. In the summer she went on long country walks, where she could pick wildflowers and chase butterflies.

In spite of the time she spent at home with Caroline and John, Jacqueline found plenty of time to pursue her own life interests. During those years she found herself more and more in the company of the Greek shipping tycoon, Aristotle Onassis. He had tried to cheer her up on the death of her third child at the request of Jacqueline's sister Lee. As all the world knows, she later married him in one of the most highly publicized weddings ever on record.

The world was stunned, but the "beautiful people" were not. They had been in on the secret for some time. Caroline, however, had not been in on it. She revered her father. She had begun collecting pictures of him, articles about him, books written by and for him, and never failed to ask questions of people who had known him.

She was stunned, upset, desolate. No matter how her mother tried to explain it to her, she would not understand. Why had Jacqueline turned to another man when the memory of her husband was still so fresh in her mind? Was it really right to marry again, particularly when Aristotle Onassis was not a Roman Catholic, but a Greek Orthodox—and a divorced man to boot!

Caroline did not like it at all. Her school work suffered. She began turning inward once again. Jacqueline kept a close eye on her, in spite of her new position as Aristotle Onassis's wife. Onassis made serious efforts to win over Caroline and John, both of whom were reluctant to accept him as their stepfather.

Onassis was no fool. He was a warm, generous, and amusing man. He completely understood how difficult it was for any stepfather to be accepted by the children. He went out of his way to be cordial to them and to their friends, to play with them, and to become a kind of "grand-uncle" to them, since he was obviously too old to be a "father."

Even so, most of his life was spent traveling all over the world to take care of his vast shipping empire and his other business enterprises. Caroline, for her part, had others much closer to her than her new stepfather—for example, her Uncle Ted and close friends of her own father.

It was about this time that Jacqueline suddenly decided that the Convent of the Sacred Heart was perhaps not exactly the right place for her daughter to be studying. Whether or not this decision had anything to do with her marriage to Onassis is open to question. However, she did transfer Caroline to The Brearley School, a prestigious institution with no parochial ties. She told friends that she wanted Caroline to be exposed to a more liberal atmosphere than that involved in a tightly controlled religious school. The climate at Brearley seemed to suit Caroline better than that of the Catholic school she had attended ever since leaving Washington.

Gradually both she and John seemed won over by their stepfather's attempts to ingratiate himself with them. There were frequent trips to Greece—especially to the island of Skorpios, which Onassis owned and on which he had built a huge villa.

But there was yet another step in Caroline's education that would be taken by her mother to set Caroline on the right educational path in her life.

In 1972 she suggested to Caroline that it might be time for her to go to a live-in school away from home where she might be able to achieve a greater degree of freedom and independence.

Caroline agreed. The two of them began looking around for the right place. Jacqueline finally settled on Concord Academy, in the famous old town of Concord, where the Revolutionary battle of Lexington and Concord had been fought and where the "shot heard round the world" was fired. It was about thirty minutes from Boston.

So Caroline was enrolled in the fifty-one-year-old coeducational school as a tenth-grader. She grew to love the town with its quiet shady streets lined with ancient elm trees, its quaint old nineteenth-century square, and the wooden churches with tall spires on their roofs—even though they were Protestant.

She found that Louisa May Alcott's former home was there, and the Old Manse, where Emerson and Hawthorne had lived. Thoreau's Walden Pond was just outside the town.

Caroline roomed at Wheeler House, a clapboard residence hall that was once a private home. She had two roommates, a junior and a senior.

Acclimating herself to the new routine wasn't all that easy for her. One time early in her stay, she kept on talking so much in class that the teacher, after repeatedly asking for silence, finally threatened to throw her out of the class.

Caroline responded with a rather pointed remark; the teacher blew up. When Caroline suddenly realized she had gone too far, she quieted down, and the confrontation subsided.

The headmaster, Russell Mead, soon discovered that Caroline had broken the rules by going off for a ride with some boys from Middlesex, a town nearby.

Mead confronted Caroline on her return. "You aren't supposed to leave the area."

"My mother said I could go," Caroline retorted.

Trying to restrain his anger, Mead reminded Caroline that she had to follow the rules of the school, or she could not stay there.

Caroline continued arguing, saying that she knew it was all right to go because she had her mother's permission.

"Don't let this happen again," Mead warned.

It didn't. The lesson had sunk in, despite Caroline's obstreperous behavior.

In spite of a few lapses, she worked very hard at her studies and did well. She got good grades in hard subjects. For example, she took sophomore English, second-year French, geometry, biology, art, film-making and a humanities course dealing with China.

During exam times she stayed up until three or four in the morning studying, just like everyone else. And she made out well in a school not noted for its laxity in academic pursuits.

One classmate recalled that she was friendly and out-going, laughing most of the time, and kidding around with everyone. But she tended to stay by herself a good deal of the time—a hangover from her early days in New York when she preferred solitude. She needed solitude to study and think.

When she first arrived, she was a little quiet and a little scared like all new students, one of her friends said, but soon she turned into a normal, friendly girl who liked to have fun like anyone else.

One night the occupants of the boys' dorm at Concord raided Wheeler House while the girls were out and tossed all the mattresses downstairs, piling them in a ceiling-high heap in the living room. The girls came back and had to clean up the mess.

When they were plotting revenge, Caroline took a leading role in planning a reprisal raid. Without realizing it, probably, she had taken the famed advice of her father: "Don't get mad, get even."

During her stay at Concord Academy, Caroline began to collect more and more memorabilia relating to her father. In her room at the Manhattan apartment she kept one wall full of John F. Kennedy pictures. She acquired over 300 stamps dedicated to Kennedy from all over the world.

She spent her weekends at home in the big apartment on 84th Street or at the Kennedy compound at Hyannis Port. She would always be back in Concord Sunday evening in time for compulsory vespers. Sometimes she spent time visiting Middlesex, where several of her Kennedy cousins were enrolled.

For recreation, she took up tennis in Central Park, getting lessons two or three times a week from the park's chief pro, Hank Fenton. He dubbed her as "pretty good and learning fast." But horseback riding was her mainstay. Each weekend during the season, she rode and went fox hunting in Peapack, New Jersey, where Jacqueline had bought a country house.

In addition to physical sports, she took up a new hobby—photography. In this endeavor she was coached by Peter Beard, a successful writer/photographer and friend of the family.

She borrowed a 35-millimeter Nikon from him, and went around taking pictures of everything that interested her. She immediately fell under the spell of the hobby. When Jacqueline saw how interested in camera work she was, she bought her a $1,000 Leicaflex, one of the world's best and most famous cameras.

Caroline began doing character studies and photo reporting of action scenes. In New York she began taking pictures of people wherever she went. She once photographed a woman under a dryer in a beauty parlor, with curlers and then after her comb-out.

The woman remarked to a reporter: "She didn't seem at all like the morose girl I'd read about. She had a great deal of self-assurance and wasn't at all hesitant about coming up to me. She was delightfully fresh and natural, with a great deal of—well—*pizzazz* about her."

The woman was referring to a commonly held public misconception about Caroline, nurtured by the press. But there was a very good reason for this "bad press" that Caroline was apt to get—whether deliberate or unintentional.

By 1969, the world was peering more intently than ever, with the help of the media, at the woman who had been First Lady of the Land and who was now Mrs. Rich Greek Shipowner. Jacqueline grew particularly annoyed at the paparazzi, the photographers that made their living taking pictures of famous people.

One of them, Ron Galella, had taken some 4,000 pictures of Jacqueline as First Lady and as widow—none of which was truly, deliberately unflattering. Nevertheless, about the time the newspapers began to print stories denigrating Jacqueline's selection of a second husband, she tired of the publicity.

Jackie felt that models get paid thousands of dollars to appear on magazine covers and in print. They put her pictures on all the newspapers and magazines, and she didn't receive a cent for it. Why should she let them take her picture?

That was the essence of her animus against the paparazzi.

It came to a head in 1969 when Galella tried to take a picture of Jacqueline walking through Central Park with Caroline's brother John. When Jacqueline spied him, she called to her Secret Service guards and ordered them to get the film from Galella.

Three guards—one was John's—grabbed Galella and tried to get the camera. He resisted, but they finally persuaded him to hand over the film. He did so, threatening them with court action.

To forestall that, Jacqueline had her attorneys bring charges against Galella for "harassment." Galella was finally cleared of the charges, but not until a great deal of newspaper space was used up telling the story.

The result of the trial was that Galella was enjoined not to photograph Jacqueline any closer than 150 feet, and not to photograph Caroline or John any closer than 225 feet. If that wasn't ludicrous enough, the order was changed in 1973 to 25 feet for Jacqueline and 30 feet for the children, as if time had, perhaps, made them less photogenic.

Needless to say, the photographic community went on its merry way without regard for the consequences. And it was only normal that the Fourth Estate should begin dumping on Jacqueline and hers as much rubbish as it could print within the bounds of legality.

And so Caroline was portrayed as a morose, hang-dog, sad, unsmiling little moppet.

Which she wasn't at all.

The irony in this situation was that Caroline had herself become a photographer. Jacqueline, of course, didn't like to see her daughter as one of the hated paparazzi, but she didn't protest. Caroline seemed to enjoy the hobby. Perhaps it might become a profession for her.

She made action pictures everywhere. On a visit to Onassis in Greece, she took her camera along and made a series of pictures of people on farms and in Athens. Later on, during a visit to Spain, she took more pictures of the behind-the-scenes action before and during a typical bullfight.

But the press was always waiting to pounce. At an ice cream shop in New York near the apartment, she strolled in one day, in a bit of a hurry. She said she wanted service immediately.

"You'll have to take a number," said the man behind the counter. "Just like everyone else."

"But I'm Caroline Kennedy!" she protested.

"You'll have to wait," the clerk informed her.

She stormed out.

But usually she was completely amenable to standing in line.

In the fall of 1972, Caroline got her first taste of politics. And, like all the Kennedys before her, she started out ringing doorbells on the precinct level. She was working for a young man named John Kerry, who was an antiwar candidate for Congress. He was, of course, a Democrat.

Later on, she joined with groups of her schoolmates and drove up to New Hampshire to campaign for Senator George McGovern, the Democratic candidate who was running against Richard M. Nixon for the presidency.

Caroline made her first public political appearance as a speaker in Boston. She was accompanied by her Uncle Ted and her Aunt Joan. It was a McGovern fundraising affair. As she opened her talk, she received a tumultuous welcome.

She was growing up now, going through the unsettling years of the teens. At fifteen, she was a mature-looking young woman, about five feet six, with a completely different frame and build from her mother. She was well-proportioned, with a slender waist and a small bosom, but with strong and shapely legs. She wore her thick, wavy blond hair parted in the middle and long, halfway down her back.

At thirteen she had been getting fat, but had disciplined herself so that she slimmed down to a more normal proportion. She learned not to splurge on rich foods—except for an occasional pizza or crabmeat crepe.

And she battled the dreaded condition of acne as most of her contemporaries did. She had a heavy sprinkling of freckles on her nose and under her eyes, as did her mother. When she got rid of the orthodontic braces she had worn during her early teens, she began to smile once again. During those years she had rarely let her lips part to show the braces on her teeth.

She was always a favorite of her cousins. Mary Kerry Kennedy, her Uncle Robert's third daughter, always called her a "good sport," explaining that "she plays for fun, not to win."

And her cousin Michael, Uncle Robert's son and Caroline's contemporary, said, "Caroline is a good dancer and she does the bump very well." Maria Shriver, two years older, said: "Caroline has dates, but no one special person. We go in groups."

Her cousins inspired her to a great deal more than dancing and riding. For some years now, several of Robert's children in their middle teens had spent part of their summers working with deprived and homeless people in various parts of the country.

One worked in a city ghetto, another worked in a rural area, and a third on an Indian reservation. Caroline learned what they did with the Indians, the Chicanos, and the people of the Appalachians, and she suddenly decided that perhaps she should take up working with poor people as a kind of continuation of her father's beliefs.

Through the urging of her cousins, she went to the Robert F. Kennedy Memorial in Washington, D.C., an organization set up to carry on the kind of community projects with which her Uncle Robert had been so closely identified.

They put her to work immediately. In the summer of 1973 she spent six weeks in the hill country of Tennessee with a film crew that was making a documentary movie about the lives and work of coal miners. It was funded by the Federation of Communities in Service.

Wearing faded patched jeans and looking every inch the hill farmer, Caroline Kennedy labored with the crew in the mountain country as they photographed every different type of person they could find.

"You would never know she's the daughter of the late

president, and so rich," one woman said. "She goes up and down those mountains just like us other hillbillies."

In mid-June the crew arrived in the tiny town of Clairfield just below the Kentucky border, in the most rugged of the Appalachian area. There was no publicity attending Caroline's arrival. She was indistinguishable from the rest of the crew members.

She helped not only with the camera work, but in the film processing as well. During her stay there, Caroline lived with a family in Clairfield.

She visited a miner who had been paralyzed for fourteen years because of a mine accident.

"Caroline is as pretty as a silver dollar," the miner said. "She's just plain folks."

While there, Caroline went with a group of local boys and girls to a Tex Ritter country-music concert. The late Tex Ritter, the father of John Ritter of television's top-rated series "Three's Company," gave her his autograph. "She was the politest one in the bunch," he said about Caroline.

Her coverage by the Secret Service, who had been guarding her ever since her father's assassination, finally ceased by law in the winter of 1973 when she turned sixteen. Up to that time she had made a game out of trying to outwit them— much in the manner of Franklin D. Roosevelt, she delighted in vanishing from the sight of her guards and then reappearing suddenly to surprise and confound them.

Once she set them up by climbing onto a public bus, and then making a quick exit before the two operatives knew what had happened. They followed the bus for miles and finally clambered in at the end of the line to confront the astounded bus driver with frantic questions. What the bus driver said has not been recorded.

Another time she left the two men sitting outside Wheeler Hall at Concord Academy patiently thinking they were guarding her, while she left through the back door and drove seventeen miles to listen to Uncle Ted make a speech to some political constituents. Luckily, nothing untoward happened to her on the trip.

Nevertheless Caroline's dreams of independence at age sixteen vanished when Jacqueline confounded her by hiring two private eyes to continue the surveillance. Caroline blew her top, but there was nothing she could do about it except accept them in the same way she had accepted the Secret Service guards.

Jacqueline was impressed with the photographs Caroline was taking. She had professionals look at them, and their reaction was good. The pictures seemed to be the work of someone who knew what photography was all about. It occurred to Jacqueline that Caroline could have a showing of her pictures that could perhaps open up the way to a career in photography.

It was easy to persuade one New York amateur photography gallery to set aside a place for her photographs. Once plans for the exhibition became known, however, the press descended on the gallery and began to ask questions and badger the officials for stories to publicize the coming event.

Jacqueline was upset. In her naiveté she had assumed that the showing would be a simple affair, an almost *private* showing, quite like one arranged for any other rich and affluent person—a simple show that no one paid much attention to but that was an ego trip for the person involved.

Her reaction was reminiscent of her astonishment at the furor aroused by William Manchester's publication of *Death of a President,* which Jacqueline apparently thought would be quietly printed with perhaps two or three hundred copies just for friends.

After some spirited exchanges with the gallery proprietors and public relations officials, Jacqueline ordered the showing canceled. Caroline was dismayed, for she had really wanted to see her own show put on. She swallowed her disappointment, however, and never mentioned it again.

In the summer that year, Caroline was invited to help

out in her Uncle Ted's office in the Senate Building in Washington. She worked on a project researching the effects of air transport on pet animals. She also distinguished herself by playing on the staff-and-intern softball team.

She was very definitely not playing her usual "beautiful people" role, but her contemporaries in the office were overawed by her presence. Once when she started to make a telephone call, a secretary leaped up to help her. Caroline eyed her coolly and said: "I can dial."

It wasn't a put-down. It was simply a statement of competence and independence.

The people working with her in the Senate Building were amazed at her. They expected to see a hothouse variety teenager who dressed like a fashion plate and rarely addressed the common rabble. Instead they found a girl who wore recycled denim skirts and drank cold beer from the can. She also ate French fries, drank hot chocolate, and spoke the current teenage jargon, using the words "retarded" and "gross" just like anyone else.

A budding romance began in the fall of 1974 when Caroline was visiting her Aunt Ethel's home in McLean. There her cousin Michael introduced her to his best friend, Juan Cameron. Cameron was going to Middlesex Academy, located near Concord. It was only natural that Juan and Caroline should start going out together.

Juan was surprised at how sensitive she was about herself and her relationship with other people.

"Everyone hates me!" she told him. "They all think I'm a snob."

Juan tried to reassure her that it wasn't true.

"It means an awful lot to Caroline not to be thought arrogant," he told a magazine writer. "Actually, I've never seen any signs that people think she is, and I keep telling her that, but sometimes she doesn't believe me."

But there were others who remembered another incident. Caroline was visiting a Concord ice-cream shop with some of her girl friends from school. They were taking their time finishing their food and paying their bills, and two boys who were waiting for a seat blamed it all on Caroline.

"Who does she think she is?" one of them muttered.

Caroline heard him and suddenly burst into tears and ran out of the shop.

Another time she tried to get service at a bank in a hurry. Because she was late getting where she was going, she tried to elbow her way in at the head of the line. Several patrons who were in the line objected.

She burst out in anger and told them that *she* was *Caroline Kennedy*. But it seemed that the name didn't mean anything to the bank patrons, and they wouldn't let her in ahead of them. She had to wait her turn at her place at the rear of the line.

Naturally, the national press heard about it, and Caroline was in the newspapers again.

To counteract such incidents, there were admiring anecdotes about Caroline's personality, especially what came to be known as her "unpredictability." One such tale had it that she sat staring at her face in a mirror in her dormitory room and suddenly burst out in anger: "My face is too symmetrical."

With that, she quickly shaved off one of her eyebrows.

Another quirk in her personality that seized everyone's attention was her love of practical jokes. This trait went back to her early days in the White House, when she had played tricks on her nanny. Some attributed the quirk to a similar vein of humor in her father.

Once, the story went, she poured bubble bath into the tank of a drinking-water fountain so that everyone drawing a glass of water would get a detergent cocktail. Another time, she added chocolate laxative to the batter for a batch of brownies she and her boyfriend Juan Cameron were baking for a cake sale at the school.

The years at Concord Academy were generally good ones for Caroline. She was steering a careful course through the rocky years of adolescence, and she seemed to have conquered a great deal of the so-called "moroseness" and "inability to smile" that her mother had tried to eradicate from her image.

During those crucial years of growing up, she and her mother had been able to remain on good terms, with only occasional minor squabbles.

"They have never had that love-hate business that so many mothers and daughters get into," one friend of the family reported.

K. LeMoyne Billings, close to the Kennedy family since the days when he was John F. Kennedy's roommate at Choate, was quoted in a magazine article about Caroline and John:

"I've never seen any children so beautifully brought up. That's why I really admire Jacqueline. It's the greatest thing she has ever done—a woman with all her problems, raising two such normal and attractive children. She's a wonderful mother."

The only relationship that never really got off the ground was that between Caroline and her stepfather, Aristotle Onassis. Yet even though it never blossomed into the kind of feeling she had for her own father during the short period when she knew him, or the kind of relationship a child can have with a father in a normal family situation, she did become somewhat more fond of the Greek magnate during the years of his marriage to her mother.

"Onassis made a big effort to be a good stepfather," Billings said. Onassis knew that he was, basically and inescapably, a foreigner to Caroline. He was not American, but Greek. And he was acting as a surrogate not for a dimly remembered, shadowy figure—the kind of misty memory that a child has of a father who has died early—but for a world-famous, charismatic, extremely dynamic person who had always dominated her even for the short period of their time together.

During her school vacations, Caroline spent a great deal of time on Skorpios, the private island off the coast of Greece owned by Onassis, and on his yacht, the *Christina,* named for his daughter, Caroline's stepsister. During those days, Onassis was not always around, but on farflung visits to his immense commercial empire.

Whenever Onassis came to New York he would bring Caroline presents, always determining in advance what her interests were so that the gifts would be appropriate and fill some need or desire. And if any of Caroline's peers were visiting the apartment when he was there, he would turn on the charm, of which he had a surprisingly abundant supply, and make them feel at home.

Like her mother, Caroline tended to plunge passionately into certain hobbies and pursuits, only to lose interest quite suddenly and quickly drop them.

During her teens she quite suddenly developed an interest in learning how to fly an airplane. A flier named Frank Comerford, who had been John F. Kennedy's pilot for short hops made during his campaigns for the House and Senate in the 1950s, now ran a flying school at Hanscom Field a few miles outside of Concord.

Caroline started her lessons, paying $30 an hour, in a Cessna 150 single-engine two-seater airplane, with a woman flight instructor named Laurie Cannon.

After fifteen lessons, she was almost ready to solo when quite abruptly she never appeared at the field again. She said that the pressure of her studies was too much and she could not go on with the lessons.

"She did fine," said her instructor, "with no trouble, just the usual ups and downs."

In her senior year at Concord Academy, Caroline was involved in a six-week off-campus project for one of her classes in film-making. (Seniors at Concord receive academic credit for approved off-campus jobs.) Caroline's project occurred during February and March, 1975, and involved a 26,000-mile television film-making trip through Beirut, Khartoum, Cairo, and other Middle East cities. Caroline's job, as unpaid girl Friday, was to help carry cameras, lights, and other equipment for the camera crew.

The film was a segment for *Weekend,* an NBC news feature. The story concerned an eccentric and slightly mysterious Saudi Arabian entrepreneur named Adnan Khashoggi, a self-proclaimed "budding Onassis" who was trying to make it as a tycoon in the style of Caroline's stepfather.

Caroline took along her Leicaflex and snapped a batch of pictures of the crew at work, of the entrepreneur, and of the scenery.

Living conditions ran the gamut from palatial to ghetto-like. One day the crew would be billeted in a luxurious presidential guest house in Khartoum, and next day in a cramped flat in Jidda, Saudi Arabia.

Reuven Frank, executive producer of the show, explained: "There are few hotels in Jidda, so they found us some rooms in a residential area. The moment we walked in, a huge rat scuttled across the kitchen floor."

It was probably the first rat Caroline had ever seen.

"Caroline took it all in stride," Frank reported. "I told her teacher back in Concord that she deserved an A-plus for her work. You know, she's very much a typical seventeen-year-old."

Her pictures turned out well enough for four of them to be selected for use as publicity releases when the project was scheduled for broadcast.

One crew member thought she was not only a willing worker, but a shrewd and capable one as well. "She's uncanny," he said. "She absolutely zeroed in on everybody. She just picks up on people—on who's real and who's phony."

The crew arrived back in New York after their grueling sojourn in the Mideast to edit the film and prepare it for telecasting. It was part of Caroline's project to stay with the crew and help them get the film into proper shape for broadcast. When it was scheduled in February, Jacqueline flew back from Europe to be with Caroline during the telecast.

All was not going well with Caroline's mother and her stepfather. Their personalities, which had tended to mesh well during the early period of the marriage, seemed to be clashing regularly. There were extended fights, outbursts of temper, and fiery denunciations.

Onassis was discovered to be suffering from myasthenia gravis, a disorder of the muscular system in which the face, lips, tongue, throat, and neck become progressively paralyzed. He was beginning to sense the limits of his mortality; he was depressed and obsessed with thoughts of imminent death.

Although his daughter Christina wanted him to be hospitalized in Athens, Jacqueline insisted that he be flown to Paris, where she took an apartment on the Avenue Foch. He followed her instructions, although he rarely talked to her any more. For weeks he lay in bed, and by the beginning of the year, his condition appeared to have improved.

It was then that Jacqueline went to New York to be with her children. She was there, in fact, when Onassis took a turn for the worse and died. At his bedside were his daughter and his former wife—but not Jacqueline.

Jacqueline, Caroline, and John attended his funeral in Greece.

In June Caroline graduated with honors from Concord Academy. By now most of her classmates had settled on college and were planning to enroll at the institutions of their choice in the fall. Not Caroline. Jacqueline had prevailed upon her in the past few years to think about studying abroad as part of her education. Jacqueline herself had been sent to Paris to study at the Sorbonne.

Caroline had no desire to follow in her mother's footsteps. She liked Paris and considered it a nice place to visit but didn't want to go to college there. She and her mother had for some time considered whether or not she would go to Brown University. For the time being, the decision was postponed.

During this time of indecision, Caroline met a young man

whom she knew from her summer vacation in the Bahamas three years earlier. His name was Mark Shand, and he was a Londoner who, at the time, had just completed an art course at Sotheby's, the famed London art dealers. It was he who gave her a possible direction.

Both Caroline and Jacqueline had been impressed by Shand's knowledge of painting, sculpture, and antiques. Now, in 1975, they both met Shand once again in New York. Shand had become an international art dealer, and a successful one at that.

Jacqueline was doubly impressed. And Caroline thought she might be able to profit from art training of the kind that Shand had mentioned. By the time Caroline graduated, Jacqueline was already putting the wheels in motion to send Caroline to London, where there were many Kennedy friends, dating back to the 1930s when the patriarch, Joe Kennedy, was the United States Ambassador to Britain.

There were the Harlechs, the Frasers, and the Lambtons. The members of this exclusive circle of landed gentry and rich aristocrats were known to the British as "country society," or "Squires from the Shires." The circle was equivalent to the Long Island socialites that lived in mansions and inhabited the country clubs that were Jacqueline's haunts when she was her daughter's age.

It was Shand himself who arranged for Caroline to join the lucky fifty students who were taking the course at Sotheby's in 1975 for the quite reasonable fee of £850 (about $1,735 at the then going rate of exchange). Jacqueline then contacted Lord Harlech and Hugh Fraser.

Until arrangements could be made to get Caroline an apartment of her own, she would stay at the home of Hugh Fraser, a member of Parliament who had recently separated from his wife, Lady Antonia Fraser, an historian. Lady Antonia had been named as "the other woman" in a sensational divorce suit lodged against playwright Harold Pinter by his wife. The Frasers' eldest children would be ideal companions for Caroline.

In the fall Caroline flew to London and joined the Frasers, who threw a party to introduce her to their friends: Adam Carr, whose father was Warden of St. Antony's College, Oxford; Lord Hesketh, a racing enthusiast, and his brother, Bobby Fermor-Hesketh; Nicholas Soames, Sir Winston Churchill's grandson; and others.

It was heady stuff, with all doors opened to her. Shand's brother-in-law, Andrew Parker-Bowles, had dated Princess Anne before the princess had chosen another man for her husband.

At Sotheby's, Caroline settled in and learned what she would be doing during her courses: attending lectures, visiting museums and stately homes with groups of her classmates, watching auctions in progress, and inspecting art treasures on sale. In addition—and this almost floored her—she would be required to read a mass of literature that she thought was staggering in its magnitude.

Caroline began to discover London and London began to discover her. One new-found friend said: "When her hair is properly done, she is really beautiful."

Another was astounded: "She's been everywhere—fabulous!"

When Adam Carr took her to dinner at Morton's, a trendy club, he told her he had been teaching in Morocco.

"Mother had a house in Morocco," Caroline noted. "A gift from King Hassan."

She settled in with the Frasers and the Harlechs, living in Fraser's Campden Hill Square house. At first Hugh Fraser drove her every day to Sotheby's in his Jaguar XJ6, but when she was properly acclimated to the London underground system, he took her to the Holland Park Underground Station, where she got the train.

At 8:30 on the morning of October 23, 1975, Caroline

was getting ready to leave for school in her upstairs room at the Fraser residence. Fraser was speaking on the telephone to a fellow member of Parliament, a call which had delayed their departure for the tube station.

Suddenly the floors and walls shook and a moment later an ear-splitting explosion sounded outside. All the glass in the windows shattered.

Caroline was bowled over backward into her bed. Fraser was knocked off his chair and hit by flying glass.

Fraser's Jaguar sedan, parked just outside the house, had been blown up by a time bomb, and was now reduced to a mass of smoking, twisted metal. A neighbor, Dr. Gordon Hamilton Fairley, a leading cancer specialist, had been walking his poodles past the Fraser car, and had stopped to investigate a suspicious-looking package under the car at the curb. The force of the bomb blast hurled his dismembered corpse into the Fraser garden in front of the house.

"Thank God for the telephone," Fraser said. "If it had not been for the call, we would all have died. There's no doubt it was meant for me. Someone obviously wants to blow me up."

Irish terrorists, thought by Scotland Yard investigators to have been part of the Irish Republican Army, had been threatening the life of Fraser, along with the lives of other members of Parliament. The bomb was believed to have been planted in retaliation for the life sentences handed down the day before in the courts to four IRA terrorists who had blown up an English pub, killing five people.

Fraser supported the death penalty for terrorists convicted of murder. At one time he had been a member of a British military unit that had done undercover work in Ulster.

Caroline was quickly taken to Lord Harlech's house by worried Scotland Yard operatives. Harlech immediately called Jacqueline in New York to explain to her that her daughter was safe. He was afraid she would hear news reports that might not be completely accurate.

Jacqueline got on the phone to her daughter. "You've got to come home immediately," she said.

"I was awfully lucky," Caroline told her. "I didn't even get cut by the glass."

"You've got to come home," Jacqueline insisted.

"No, Mother!"

It was obvious that Jacqueline thought the bomb was intended for Caroline. The tragedies in Dallas and in Los Angeles were still clear in her mind.

"You must come home!"

"I want to stay!" Caroline pleaded. "I'm fine. I'm sure this has nothing to do with me."

"How can you be sure?" Jacqueline persisted.

"I can't be. But it doesn't make sense."

"You come home right away. I'll get your ticket."

"No!"

It took several heated phone calls to cool down the exchanges between them. "Mummy can be so *thick!*" Caroline told a friend after one of them. "I don't want to leave London! What would I do for the rest of the year if I went home now?"

Jacqueline arranged with Christina Onassis, her stepdaughter, for Caroline to move into Christina's London apartment.

In fact, Caroline was *not* calm, but very upset and shaken. She could not get the near miss out of her mind. She thought of the deaths of her father, her Uncle Robert, her Aunt Kathleen, her Uncle Joe. Was that bomb meant for her? Had she escaped by a hair's breadth? Would death be waiting for her in some unknown Samarra?

She was determined to grit it out. She missed only that morning's lessons at school. After moving her things to her step-sister Christina's apartment, she went off to Sotheby's and took up her studies again.

Jacqueline now arranged for Caroline to stay at the home

of her sister Lee's former husband Prince Stanislas Radziwill. At the time, Lee was preparing a huge party to introduce a new book of Andy Warhol's, an avant-garde friend of hers. The party was to take place at Lord Lambton's home and his daughter, Lady Anne, was to be hostess.

It was a swinging affair, with blue bloods mingling with show biz stars, and some weird characters. Warhol reacted to them with the astonished cry: "Freaks—all freaks!"

Photographers were having a field day, catching Caroline with different dancing partners. Caroline posed for them all, even opening the door once to ask: "Have you got all the pictures you want?"

Pictures of Caroline appeared everywhere—including New York. Jacqueline's blood pressure rose. She began fuming. She called it "overexposure." She was on the telephone immediately, warning Caroline to stay away from photographers, away from journalists. Caroline was not surprised. She had been expecting something like that for some time. She knew how her mother felt about the press.

That very night she saw them waiting for her outside Sotheby's because she was still hot news after her narrow escape from death. She walked into a sandwich bar nearby, trying to evade them, but they found her and ran for her. She grabbed up a glass of water and threw it at one of the most persistent of the paparazzi. The incident was amply covered by the pictures that appeared the next morning in the papers.

Later on, she went to a discothèque with a friend and walked out into the street to be caught in a merciless barrage of exploding flashbulbs.

Caroline looked as if she might cry. Her companion saved the situation by quickly finding a cab. The next day, however, the photos were printed with captions suggesting that Caroline was going steady with a certain young man.

She confessed to friends that the constant prying and consequent loss of privacy made her wish she could leave London.

"But you are a public figure," a friend reminded her.

"I don't want to be a public figure!" she complained.

"Why not?"

"Why should I?" she shot back.

The same companion wrote about her in a magazine piece: "She's not a snob, and I doubt she'll ever be one. In many ways, she is just a nice, all-American girl who likes to chew bubble gum and do crossword puzzles. But inevitably, she is also very different from other girls, the result of being somehow 'an important person' since the day she was born. That is a heavy load for such young shoulders, but I believe that Caroline is well on the way to discovering the person she wants to be in her own right. And when she does, she will be that person first and a Kennedy second. I've enjoyed knowing her."

During the months she studied in London, she was in constant touch with her mother, by letter and telephone, and it was during those moments of contact that the two of them had discussed the next important phase of Caroline's education —college.

For some reason, both Caroline and her brother John had always liked Brown University, despite the fact that their father had graduated from Harvard.

After discussing the matter with her mother, Caroline finally decided that she would pay attention after all to her father's background and go to Radcliffe, a women's college which is actually a division of Harvard University. It is also very much in the old Harvard tradition. Three generations of Kennedys—Caroline's grandfather, her father, three uncles, and several cousins—had studied there.

During her last days in London, she filled out the application forms and sent them to Radcliffe, the only college she applied to. And, quite naturally, she was accepted. (How could Radcliffe have turned her down?)

In the fall of 1976 she was back in New York and ready to enter Radcliffe. She had finished her year at Sotheby's with marked success, and she had discovered an unexpected aptitude for art and art treasures, modeled, no doubt, on her mother's interest in such pursuits.

She had evolved a way of studying and knew she would be able to fit in with the college scene. After mastering the enormous reading list she had been given in London, she knew that she would never have trouble in applying herself to collegiate studies.

It was like old-home week at Winthrop House, one of the twelve live-in dormitories at Harvard, when Caroline Kennedy found herself ensconced there. Her own father, her Uncle Robert, her Uncle Ted, and her cousin Kathleen had all lived there before her. In fact, it was known on campus already under the unofficial title of "Kennedy House."

She had successfully argued with her mother about the propriety of having a "coming out party"—the traditional debutante ball given by most American blue bloods for their daughters. The battle had been a long and ardent one between Jacqueline, who insisted that Caroline must be "presented," and Caroline, who insisted that the tradition was obsolete and moribund, if not dead.

Finally Jacqueline had caved in and thrown up her hands. Caroline did not "come out."

She was majoring in fine arts. Her Concord Academy background proved very handy, but more important, her experience at Sotheby's gave her an edge on many of her classmates.

Caroline Kennedy fitted easily into the campus scene. She loved the gloomy old quarters of Winthrop House, especially the high-ceilinged, dingy dining room.

Three of Caroline's cousins were at Harvard: Steven Smith, Jr., David Kennedy, and Robert Kennedy, Jr. In addition, her brother John was only twenty miles away at Phillips Academy in Andover.

At Radcliffe, Caroline found it quite easy to conceal the fact that she came from a family of great wealth. Caroline lived on a careful, yet comfortable budget. Her only outward sign of wealth was the ostentatious BMW sports car that she had bought just before coming to Radcliffe. She rarely used it, however, except to drive to and from New York. In Cambridge, she always preferred to walk or take her bicycle to class.

Her friends and acquaintances understood her reluctance to tool about the college town in the flashy car.

"She doesn't use the car too much around here," one friend of hers said, "and she doesn't let anyone else drive it, but she's always willing to give you a lift if you haven't got a car."

Like her peers, Caroline Kennedy settled easily into the blue-jeans-and-baggy-sweater costume of the 1970s. She was in no way a carbon copy of her mother, who had always dressed to the nines of fashion in expensive, sometimes daring, and always original clothes.

At Anthony's Pier 4, an exclusive restaurant in Boston, her Aunt Eunice Shriver acted once as hostess at a huge and impressive party. The women were wearing long formal dresses, and the men all had on suits and ties.

Caroline breezed in from campus, wearing corduroy Levis, a plaid cotton shirt, and a sweater with the sleeves tied around her shoulders.

She became known around Cambridge not exactly as a cheapskate, but at least as one who did not in any way throw her money around. Waiters and waitresses were distressed to learn that she was a lousy tipper. Nevertheless, they were glad to see her come, because her presence always seemed to bring in extra customers.

Her favorite haunts became immediate legend—and the profits of the places rose proportionately. Tommy's Lunch on Mount Auburn Street, Cambridge, was favored by her presence, and so was the Oxford Ale House on Church Street.

She dated occasionally, but she didn't seem to go steady with any particular man on campus. She could usually be found in a group—clusters of women and clusters of men.

"She never had a steady boyfriend at Harvard," one friend said. "She didn't flirt around. A lot of the guys looked upon her in an almost sisterly fashion. As far as her love life was concerned, she was always a bit of a mystery. Sitting around the pub on a Friday night, her girl friends would frequently remark on the attractive men they saw at the bar. But Caroline never discussed that sort of thing. Other students would gossip about their relationships, even give intimate details. But Caroline would only sit and listen."

That didn't mean that she was a social failure and kept silent when she was out with a group of friends.

"Caroline could be a lot of fun if you took the time to draw her out," an acquaintance said. "She had a good sense of humor and had wonderfully entertaining stories to tell.

"Nevertheless, Caroline could be very detached, almost as if she were afraid of becoming 'involved in a relationship.' "

Caroline soon earned a job on the staff of the *Harvard Crimson*, the prestigious college newspaper. She passed all the preliminary tests. There was a ten-week training period, during which she worked for eight hours twice a week. After four weeks of trial, there was a cutoff period, at which those who were not deemed worthy were dropped.

She passed the first cut, then the second, and at the end of eight weeks she was accepted. After that she performed several stints as night editor. It was her job to select and assign stories, edit and position them in the paper.

After her freshman year finals, she went down to the New York *Daily News* for an interview about a job as "copy person" in the city room. She was interviewed, accepted, and filled out her application form on May 9, 1977. She was then taken on a tour of the editorial department and the composing room, where she signed many autographs.

Ken O'Malley, another applicant for the same kind of job, told reporters that he would be glad to do some of her chores for her during the summer. "The girl is history," said O'Malley.

The New York Times reported that she was paid $156.89 per week for the work.

A writer on the *Daily News* summed up her stay on the paper this way: "She was an unqualified success, even though, because of her celebrity, her assignments were for the most part confined to inside the building. Certain editors seemed to like sending her on coffee runs, however, just so they could say that Caroline Kennedy served them coffee. She did so graciously."

When Elvis Presley died quite suddenly at the end of the summer, Caroline traveled on her own to Graceland, Presley's famous estate just outside Memphis. As a freelance reporter she covered the story, which turned out to be one of the notable funerals of the decade.

Even after the funeral was over, crowds continued to make problems for the police. Caroline stayed around and continued to write, interviewing visitors and business associates of Presley.

The Kennedy name paid off in one way. She was the only reporter invited to visit the mansion at length. She wrote up detailed descriptions of the furnishings and the decor. She also talked to Priscilla Beaulieu Presley, the singer's first wife, whom he had divorced in 1973, and Presley's nine-year-old daughter, Lisa Marie.

When she had finished, she flew up to western Massachusetts where her Uncle Ted was staying, and spent a few days on vacation before she returned to Radcliffe.

The story she wrote, "Graceland," appeared in a special commemorative issue of *Rolling Stone,* September 22, 1977.

She handled the event as a half-news, half-in-depth story. After detailing the death and the turmoil of the crowd, she included quotes from various people with whom she had talked:

"Wanda Magyor, 33, of Latrobe, Pennsylvania, jiggled a baby on her hip as she told of her love for Elvis. 'We'll stay out here all night just to get into the cemetery. We drove all night to get here. I *will* get a flower from the cemetery.' "

The scenes inside the mansion, however, were far more interesting. Caroline wrote about being invited into the house and then led into "a large room filled with gold and white folding chairs. At the far end of the room was the gleaming copper coffin that contained the body of Elvis Presley. His face seemed swollen and his sideburns reached his chin."

She described the southern Gothic-cum-art-deco decor of the Presley mansion:

"Behind the coffin, an arch led to another room where a clear-glass statue of a nude woman stood high off the floor, twirling slowly, adorned by glass beads that looked like water. Potted plastic palms surrounded the coffin and on the wall was a painting of a skyline on black velveteen."

The Scarlett O'Hara-style mansion was "large and ornate," she wrote. "The entrance to the dining room was framed by floor-to-ceiling scarlet drapes tied with gold tassels. There was a massive mahogany dining table in the center of the room, surrounded by huge chairs upholstered in scarlet satin woven with gold thread and tiny rhinestones."

She wrote about Priscilla Presley as follows: "Her auburn hair was pulled away from her face and hung loose in the back. She wore little makeup and appeared calm. . . . The former Mrs. Presley seemed to be putting everyone at ease as she moved around the room greeting old friends."

And, at the conclusion: "Outside the front door were hundreds of wreaths; some spelled 'Elvis' in flowers, others were shaped like crowns, broken hearts, hound dogs, and blue suede shoes."

As can be seen from the excerpts, Caroline had definitely inherited her talent with words from both her mother, who was a newswoman, and her father, who was a journalist for a time and who wrote a Pulitzer Prize-winning, bestselling nonfiction book, *Profiles in Courage.*

Her social conscience seemed to be growing. She began to enjoy her reading, ploughing through volumes on history, political science, and international relations.

In her sophomore year, April 1977, along with 3,500 students, she attended a big protest rally against the Harvard Corporation's ownership of stock in American companies located in South Africa. The group carried candles and torches and marched through the streets chanting:

One, two, three, four,
Throw apartheid out the door,
Five, six, seven, eight,
Don't support the racist state.

She marched until dawn with the rest of them.

But college wasn't all serious protest against political evil. Caroline hadn't really changed all that much from the little girl who had grown up in the White House. She still had her youthful penchant for horseplay and pranks, like her father.

Just before final exams, she and a group of her friends climbed the steep, shaky, off-limits bell tower on top of Harvard's famous old Memorial Hall in a typical collegiate gesture, defying both the establishment and common sense.

It was an old campus tradition to make the climb. While they were there at the apex of the ancient structure, giggling and letting off collegiate steam, the campus police spotted them. Immediately the police officers began shouting at them to get down off the tower, warning them how dangerous it was and how easily they might hurt themselves.

Then, suddenly, one of them saw Caroline and recognized her. What would happen if Caroline Kennedy fell off the tower and killed herself? Considerably abashed, the cops renewed their appeals, but in more loving tones, and the dissident group of tower-climbers finally clambered down, much to the relief of the Cambridge constabulary.

In the winter of 1977–78, when she accompanied her Uncle Ted and numerous cousins and aunts on a trip to China, Caroline's puckish sense of humor had not yet deserted her.

Jan Kalicki, Senator Ted Kennedy's foreign policy adviser, carried a small black suitcase with him. Everyone noted immediately that he refused to let any porter carry it, or any servant touch it.

No one could find out what was in the black bag.

Once when she had the chance, Caroline impishly grabbed it and hid it. When Kalicki discovered its disappearance, his face turned absolutely white. He rushed around, looking frantically for it. When Caroline finally was convinced that he would certainly have a heart attack, she led him to its hiding place and gave it back to him.

Kalicki was not amused.

She never did find out what had been in the bag. Nor would anyone enlighten her.

Almost as if to prove that even Caroline Kennedy could fall into the same kind of trap as other Kennedy cousins, Caroline discovered to her horror that during her China trip a warrant had been issued for her arrest in Suffolk County, Long Island!

She had been stopped on a speeding violation charge in her BMW during the summer of 1977. For whatever reason she might have had, she did not appear in answer to the summons. A warning notice was posted to her, and when she did not then appear, a further notice was sent to her address.

Finally, the warrant was issued on January 12, 1978, and a story appeared next morning in *The New York Times,* which has ambitious stringers working all over the Island.

On the day after the story appeared, three of Jacqueline's attorneys hurriedly appeared in court almost before the ink was dry on the *Times* pages, entering a plea of not guilty.

"Miss Kennedy is traveling in China with Senator Ted Kennedy and her family," one of them told the court with excellent courtroom humility. The warrant for Caroline's arrest was withdrawn.

"For a $25 fine, she brings in $3,000 worth of attorneys," commented the incredulous judge.

The Suffolk County Highway Police officer who clocked

Caroline for speeding remembered her as "very calm and polite."

When the traveling Kennedys returned and discovered what had happened, Jacqueline was furious with her daughter, but by then everything had settled and she was off the hook.

Caroline Kennedy might have been grown up in her own mind, but when she was visiting her grandmother, Rose, at the Palm Beach house in Florida, she became just one more of the matriarch's grandchildren. During one Easter holiday, the servants quit in a dispute over wages, and Rose ordered the grandchildren to do the housework that was piling up.

Like a modern-day Cinderella, Caroline Kennedy spent one morning on her hands and knees, scrubbing a rubber mat and cleaning up bits and pieces of scullery-ware.

Nor did Rose let any of her brood lead a privileged life. When Caroline would arrive, say, with Robin and Victoria Lawford, the three girls would be put into one room to sleep on three folding cots.

This treatment was reserved for a young lady for whom photographers would sit all day in a car parked across the street, waiting for her to walk down to the beach so they could follow and perhaps get a picture of her in a bathing suit!

In the summer of 1978 her cousin Robert Sargent Shriver, Jr., invited her to try out for a job as reporter on the *Los Angeles Herald Examiner,* where he worked as a feature writer. Caroline applied, and was accepted. She was eager to take the job, because she had never lived for any time in Los Angeles, and wanted to see what it was like. She liked newspaper work, too. Her school job on the *Crimson* was working out well.

Unfortunately, news of the job leaked out in the press and the story was picked up everywhere. Reluctantly, she turned down the position when Jacqueline pointed out that she would be followed by reporters and photographers everywhere. *She* would become the story instead of the person or event she was trying to report.

On November 27, 1978 Caroline Kennedy turned twenty-one. For that occasion, Jacqueline threw an elaborate party—a joint birthday party for both Caroline and her brother John, whose birthday was only two days before hers, on November 25—at Le Club, a famous disco on East 55th Street in New York.

Jacqueline had always had a soft spot in her heart for Le Club. For her, its enchantment dated back to the 1960s. When she was lonely and depressed in the years immediately after her husband's assassination, she had made it a habit to drop in at Le Club during the evenings.

Aristotle Onassis loved the place, too, as did Jacqueline's sister Lee. Perhaps it was the Henry V furnishings and the seventeenth-century French hunting-lodge decor of the rooms.

Whatever it was, she held Caroline and John's surprise birthday party for 140 people there on the night of November 27, 1978. Understandably, it was not an easy thing to keep a complete secret. Especially with well-known public figures like K. LeMoyne Billings, Freddie and George Plimpton, columnist Pete Hamill, and Peter Davis present—not to mention Sydney and Robin Lawford, a passel of Robert Kennedy's children, and Kennedys Ethel, Pat, and Jean.

Social note:

Caroline actually wore a dress.

John wore a tie.

The party was written up as a "private" party in the newspapers the following morning.

Now that she was twenty-one, Caroline began dating a more worldly set of men—Peter Beard, her photography teacher, fashion designer Willie Woo, *Rolling Stone* editor Jann S. Wenner, and a reporter on the *Daily News* named Rick Licato.

But there was another man she actually preferred to these well-known names. She had met him through her mother.

Jacqueline had recently gotten a job working at Doubleday Inc., the publishing company, after having held an editing job for some time at Viking Press, a rival company.

It was at Doubleday that Jacqueline ran into a young man who had been a copywriter at the company several years before her. His name was Tom Carney.

In an unsigned profile on Caroline in the March, 1980 issue, *Ladies' Home Journal* gave the public a look at her new boyfriend. Carney was an Irish Catholic and a graduate of Yale. He had spent some of his youth in a Beverly Hills home that was once owned by Humphrey Bogart and Lauren Bacall. The rest of the time he spent growing up with his two brothers and his parents on an isolated ranch in Wyoming.

He was cut to the mold of the Kennedys—able to hold his own both in civilized society and in the wilderness.

His father Otis was a novelist and screenwriter and had recently spent some time working with Marlon Brando on the script of a film concerning the American Indian. The senior Carney now operated a cattle ranch in Wyoming, and lived on a second ranch in Arizona with his wife, Fredrika.

Tom Carney was first and foremost a writer who tried to make his living by his writing—an unenviable feat in these days of low writing wages and high living costs.

Tom Carney's first novel, *Daylight Moon,* did fairly well, but wasn't a world-beater by any means. Advertised as "a bold work of scorching sex and savage suspense," it was published in 1979.

He had written for national magazines such as *Penthouse* and *Esquire.* His career at Yale had gone well up to his senior year, when his grades dropped because he was spending most of his time working on a novel.

Nevertheless, he succeeded in getting a job as a cub reporter on a newspaper in Los Angeles after graduation. He soon tired of that, and went back to Wyoming to his father's ranch. There he spent eight months working as a genuine cattle rancher.

But the writing bug had bitten him, and the smell of beef on the hoof wasn't sweet enough to hold him. He went back to New York, where he got a job at Doubleday as a copywriter. He was also assigned a job to ghostwrite a book on acupuncture.

"It was a total disaster and I didn't even get paid for it," he said.

After the copy job fizzled out at Doubleday, he went to work for a firm moving furniture. Then he sent out direct-mail appeals for money for several charities—"stuffing envelopes," as he recalled.

But he kept up with his writing, doing free-lance articles on subjects like "the shortage of medical cadavers," and "a woman who saw visions of the Virgin Mary."

"I once wrote an article on author Tom McGuane for *Esquire*," he said. The profile was far more revealing than McGuane had wanted.

It was after he had contracted for his first novel—*Daylight Moon*—that he met Jacqueline Onassis at Doubleday one day when he was visiting friends there.

He reported later that he was "somewhat intimidated at his first meeting with Mrs. Onassis." Nevertheless, she liked him and was impressed enough to introduce him to Caroline.

That was in May, 1978. In a matter of months, he and Caroline were dating regularly.

Carney found Caroline "stimulating company from their first meeting," one observer said.

"She may be a lot younger than I am, but as soon as I met her I thought she was interesting," Carney admitted. "I liked her very much right from the start."

In August, Caroline and her mother took him with them on a vacation to the Caribbean island of St. Martin. Later on, Caroline spent a Christmas with him in Barbados.

At thirty, Carney was ten years older than she, but he was enough in the Kennedy mold to attract her. He was Catholic, and he was a goodlooking, muscular man. Outdoor-oriented, and given to wearing jeans, sneakers, and blazers, he favored all the other Kennedys Caroline knew so well.

"I grew up with all the social graces," Carney admitted to a friend, "even if we did spend some time atop a mountain, in isolation."

By "social graces," Carney meant the ability to feel at ease with women. People who knew Carney said he could feel more at ease with women than many other men could.

"I get along well with women," he noted. "I enjoy them, I like them as friends." Carney explained that he learned to relate so well with women from his mother.

Relating to women was one of the traits that obviously fascinated Caroline. Most of the Kennedys didn't *need* someone who could "relate" to them. They were and are gregarious, rambunctious, and thick-skinned; they need no one to hang onto.

In contrast, Caroline was usually quiet, shy, and withdrawn—a follower rather than a leader, in the mold of her mother, of course. Because Carney could apparently break through her reserve, however, he was able to establish a link with her that was not the normal thing in her relationships with other people—particularly with men.

Carney's parents were also taken with Caroline. Tom and Caroline went out to Wyoming and stayed at the Carney ranch. The Carney family found Caroline "delightful, refreshing and remarkably unspoiled."

The experience of meeting and going with Tom Carney changed Caroline's life in subtle and not-too-subtle ways. It became obvious to her friends on campus in Cambridge that something had happened. And gradually the story began leaking out.

She introduced him to her friends in 1979. He came up to stay with her on several of the weekends. But suddenly she disappeared from her usual haunts in the Cambridge area. Her friends were used to spending time with her drinking in the Oxford Ale House, or other low-key Cambridge bars.

"Until she met Carney," one of her classmates said, "she was a regular visitor here. Now she rarely comes. She drank mostly beer and always took her turn in buying a round of drinks."

It was obvious she was missed.

"Nobody has seen much of her recently," a Harvard friend confided. "She's been spending most weekends back in New York where she sees a lot of Tom."

As for Caroline, most of the Radcliffe and Harvard set had her pegged quite well. "Caroline is a pretty straight sort of gal," one of them said. "In a way, she's a bit prudish, sort of straitlaced. She's not the type who would just jump into the sack with a guy.

"I wouldn't be surprised if she married Carney. She's never been attracted to slick, playboy types. Carney fits right in with the image she likes. He's sort of preppy with a good upbringing."

The Caroline Kennedy/Tom Carney liaison was good for all kinds of speculation in the press, of course. As soon as news of Caroline's interest in him leaked out, free-lance writers, reporters, editors, and all kinds of media people began searching them and their friends out and probing them for their thoughts about each other.

In late 1979, the gossip columns were suddenly filled with eager speculation about Caroline Kennedy and Tom Carney.

"Her friends seem to think Caroline Kennedy will be getting herself engaged soon to Tom Carney, the young writer she's been seeing for a couple of years," wrote Suzy Knickerbocker in a syndicated column.

"Everyone likes Tom," Suzy gushed, "who is goodlooking, personable, and best of all, nice. Caroline has good taste in men, if you go by Tom. If this all comes to pass, don't expect a big church wedding. Caroline doesn't like fanfare.

"For the past couple of weeks, Caroline and Tom have been together in Wyoming where his family has a house."

That kind of thing dismayed Carney.

"The whole interest in Caroline and me on the part of the press has been stressful," he said. "I can understand Caroline's reluctance to talk. At the same time I'm uncomfortable about refusing interviews, having been a reporter myself. After all, reporters are nice people, too. It's all rather ironic, really —I'm a bit of a hermit by nature."

The fishbowl atmosphere led Carney to admit: "Caroline and I are happiest in New York. We both like to keep out of the limelight. Here, we can disappear. We've been to discothèques only twice." The trouble with the chic spots, of course, was the photographers.

"This sort of thing can be a terrible burden," Carney noted. "I don't know yet how to deal with it—it's really rather disagreeable."

Yet the relentless probing continued. Finally, in a kind of explosive reaction, Carney told one writer:

"Obviously, I am in love with her." But as for the possibilities of marriage, "I can't answer for that."

Carney was asked a number of times how he felt about marriage to Caroline Kennedy. His response was usually to say that he was certainly ready to marry—after all he *was* thirty years old—but he also considered marriage a move that should not be rushed.

"I don't believe in divorce," he said. "I believe you only do it once. Religion was a very strong force in my life when I was growing up . . . I was an altar boy."

Although he changed somewhat when he matured, he still retained a sense of religion. "I don't attend Mass regularly anymore," he reported. "I stopped doing that when I went to Yale. . . . But I would want to get married in the eyes of the Church and raise my children as Catholics."

Caroline simply wouldn't answer any questions put to her about marriage. She mentioned marriage only to close friends. One of these friends said about her feelings for Carney:

"They're very much in love and one day they will get married. Being in the spotlight may put a strain on their relationship at times but they will work it through. Their relationship is strong, they're very compatible. I consider them very lucky."

As for setting up a household, neither of them considered it much of a chore. Carney was discovered to be living unpretentiously in a three-room Manhattan apartment he had bought three years before at a bargain price. He spent his time there, as he called it, "living like a typical bachelor."

He always ate out. "I don't get close enough to the kitchen even to open a can," he told a friend. And that made him even-up with Caroline. He laughed once when reporters got him onto a discussion of their domestic traits. "Neither of us can cook!" For that reason they would go to movies and eat at small out-of-the-way restaurants.

The romance didn't keep Caroline from plunging into her Uncle Ted's campaign for the presidency, when he announced for the office in late 1979. All third-generation Kennedys old enough to participate actively were quickly assigned to specific localities to work the crowds.

Caroline was allotted Burlington, Vermont. In December she was pictured in the newspapers stumping for her Uncle Ted.

"It's part of a program to get all members of the family involved and over their heads as quickly as possible," she joked with the reporters.

And perhaps with Uncle Ted there ready to step to the fore, Camelot wasn't really dead at all. Just resting.

CHAPTER 3
John Fitzgerald
Kennedy, Jr.

It was one of the most heart-wrenching sights of all time. In the flag-draped casket lay the body of the thirty-fifth president of the United States of America, gunned down by an assassin's bullets in a sun-drenched Dallas street. In front of the casket, dressed in an overcoat, stood a small boy, on his third birthday, looking at the coffin and slowly making a brave salute to his dead father.

No one who ever saw the moment or a photograph of it will ever forget it.

If they had never heard of John Fitzgerald Kennedy, Jr. before that moment, the picture would stay in their memory forever.

But most people had heard of him before that, and had read about him in countless newspaper and magazine stories about life in the White House under President Kennedy.

Most knew that he was a fearless little boy who played cowboys and Indians with his father in the historic rooms of the White House.

He was born at 12:22 A.M. on November 25, 1960, before his father had even moved into the White House, just three weeks after he had been elected president of the United States in a squeaker of an election against Richard M. Nixon.

John's birth inspired a deluge of telephone calls, letters, and telegrams to John Fitzgerald Kennedy and Jacqueline Bouvier Kennedy. Former President Eisenhower wrote a note. Queen Elizabeth cabled.

The world knew when John was christened, and it knew also that he was christened in the very same long, old-fashioned dress in which his father had been christened forty-three years before.

The world watched fondly as he lay in his carriage on the White House lawn, being tickled under the chin by an admiring Iranian empress visiting his father.

The world looked at and goggled at photographs of the young child dancing to the rhythm of his father's clapping hands. The world smiled when it read in a magazine that John once burst into his father's office to tell the president, with great excitement:

"The sky is turning!"

He meant that the revolving lights at the Washington National Airport were sweeping the heavens.

"Why do pictures show me crying?" he asked as he looked at a picture in the newspaper showing him bidding goodbye to his father at the airport.

"Because the president is going away in a plane and a helicopter," he was informed by his father.

A great deal of the stories were exploitive and even inaccurate. For example, John Fitzgerald Kennedy, Jr. became known fondly by the press as "John-John."

In truth, President Kennedy never called his son "John-John," nor even intended to call him "John-John." Yet the press picked it up and made the president's son, John, into its own creation.

One White House intimate once explained how the "John-John" myth began. Both Caroline and her younger brother were constantly on call around the White House.

The president loved them and indeed liked to show them off to visiting royalty and statesmen.

He would go to the windows that looked out into the garden and clap his hands quickly:

"Caroline! John!" he would cry, summoning them inside.

Sometimes when they didn't immediately respond, he would clap his hands two or three times in rapid succession, loudly, so they would hear.

The cries became:

"Caroline!" Clap. "John!" Clap.

Or, if only John was outside:

"John!" Clap. "John!" Clap.

Reporters failed—deliberately or involuntarily—to hear that handclap. They only heard: "John! John!" spoken quickly. And so was invented: John-John.

It remained John-John in the media all during the president's lifetime. After the president's assassination, when John and his sister moved to New York, Jacqueline tried to blot out the memory of "John-John," but it was virtually impossible.

It was equally as hard to blot out the millions of words that had been written about him:

"Anytime the chopper whirled into Hyannis Port last summer, Junior's joyous greeting was 'Daddy-swim.' "

That kind of thing died hard.

So did the lifestyle that both John and Caroline became accustomed to in the White House. Evelyn Lincoln, the president's secretary, used to keep jars of candy for them so that when they came in during the afternoon, they could both have something to munch on.

John took after his father in his love of practical jokes. Even when he was living in the White House, John would sometimes sneak sugar cubes into visitors' cups of coffee. He was not even three years old at the time.

There was a hinged door in the president's desk that Caroline had used to hide behind when too many strangers entered the Oval Room. However, John had a different temperament. He had no fear of people; if anything, he was exactly the opposite of Caroline. He used the door to enter the desk where he would hide. He once popped out during an important governmental meeting.

After a few polite laughs, he was hustled out by the president.

The president loved to play with his children. During October, 1962, when the Cuban Missile Crisis was casting a pall of anxiety over the government and the world, the president sneaked away to be with John and Caroline; there he helped them carve out a Halloween pumpkin. To the president, that was quite as important as the international crisis he was confronting.

He loved to play with John and would be seen frequently walking with the little boy through the corridors of the White House. One time when the helicopter had delivered the family to Camp David on a weekend, Secret Service men were appalled to find both the president and his son missing.

Finally one haggard agent located them both in the chopper, now landed and inoperable on the pad. John was at the controls, which he could barely reach. The president was sitting beside him, smiling. John was flying the chopper to rescue his father in the South Pacific after his PT boat had been shot out from under him during World War II.

But that wonderful life all ended with an assassin's bullets in Dallas on November 22, 1963. From that moment on, John and Caroline were international figures.

By December 6, the Kennedys had departed from the White House forever. When they left John carried along an American flag and a black box that contained his father's Medal of Freedom, earned during World War II in the South Pacific.

The Kennedys eventually settled in a $200,000 fifteen-room cooperative apartment, which overlooked Central Park, with the Metropolitan Museum and the reservoir in plain sight from the front windows. John was put in school at St. David's, a Catholic institution nearby. Jacqueline wanted him to have a good religious background.

Besides that, his cousin Christopher Lawford went there.

His stay there did not last long. Jacqueline soon decided that he had received enough religious training and now needed a more outreaching environment. She was following the lead of Joe Kennedy, Sr. in seeking a secular education after a religious one. He had given all his sons secular educations. She transferred John to Collegiate School, located on West 77th Street, when he started the third grade.

The choice of Collegiate over several other more prestigious and fashionable schools—Buckley or St. Bernard's, for example—is an interesting one. Collegiate was an integrated school, both racially and economically. Jacqueline was determined that her children would *not* grow up isolated from the world. She was determined that they have a *normal* upbringing.

The purpose was a noble one, but obviously impossible under the circumstances. She was one of the most ogled and most famous people in the world, as were her children. How could John or Caroline grow up in the same way as other children?

Her attempts at giving them a normal upbringing succeeded only to a degree. There were overtones that bordered on the comic. A typical morning for John began when a bus from Collegiate came by the Fifth Avenue building to pick up John.

Two Secret Service agents would hop into a car and drive after the bus, watch to see John alight at the school, and then retire to the cellar of the school, where they would play cards and talk until John went home at night.

Then the opposite pattern would be followed.

The Secret Service surveillance was definitely needed. (The children would be guarded until they were sixteen years old.) Numerous kidnapping threats surfaced during those years, driving Jacqueline almost to distraction.

Her equanimity was not soothed any when the two children would indulge in pranks against the Secret Service guards.

When he was six, John got into a running battle with the guards during a wedding of a half-aunt, Janet Jennings Auchincloss, to Lewis Rutherford, in Newport. The Newport estate had ponies on it, and John got a stick and began driving the ponies about in a mock Western movie roundup—except that he was herding them directly toward the reception area where the guests and the food were assembled.

The Secret Service men finally corralled him, and the game stopped. The ponies were easier to handle than John.

As John grew up, the pranks against his guards seemed to die out gradually, and he seemed finally to become reconciled to having his two shadows with him at all times.

His bodyguards weren't always capable of keeping him out of harm's way. One day when John was in the third grade at Collegiate, one of his classmates began calling him John-John.

As has been mentioned, there was nothing that steamed John Fitzgerald Kennedy, Jr., more than being called "John-John." Although half the population of the world knew him subconsciously as John-John, thanks to the enormous influence of the American press, no one in his family had ever called him that.

The classmate, either deliberately or in all innocence, addressed him as John-John and when John's reaction proved to be one of towering rage, the bully continued to use the term in derogation.

Before his Secret Service nannies could intervene, John had jumped on his tormenter and given him a bloody nose.

For some reason Jacqueline had gotten it into her head that her son was not displaying enough masculinity. Perhaps because he had no father, she was afraid he would grow up to be a sissy.

One friend of the Kennedys during the White House

years once remarked on Jacqueline's concern about John. "She commented once about the nanny, Maud Shaw, hovering around John so much. 'I'm afraid he's going to grow up and be a fruit,' she said."

According to Shaw, Jacqueline was responsible for a great deal of her son's early torment. She insisted that he "measure up." In Shaw's words, "She made the little mite go through hell."

Shaw continued, "When we moved to New York from the White House, she got it into her mind that she wanted to toughen up little John. She told the Secret Service agents to give him boxing lessons. John was a frail, highly emotional little boy and he used to cry a lot."

According to Shaw, just after the assassination, Jacqueline had made John sleep in his father's bed—alone. She related how he cried out in the night and woke up the whole household. "I would have to go running in to him."

John was a one-hundred percent Kennedy boy, and had plenty of exercise. He would have had it even if Jacqueline hadn't wanted to "toughen him up." He loved to run around and exert himself physically. He learned to swim at an early age, experiencing none of the problems his sister had with water.

Each summer he sailed with his cousins off the Cape. He could horseback ride at an early age. But horses presented a somewhat strange problem: John had an allergy to horse flesh, and whenever he was near one, his eyes began to water.

But he stuck it out, and continued riding anyway.

He could ski, both on snow and on water, and he became serious about track at school. Soon he was learning to play tennis on the public courts in Central Park, under the tutelage of Hank Fenton, the park coach.

From the beginning his school work was weak. He simply did it with a kind of casual offhanded abandon. It wasn't that he found it hard; on the contrary, he found it quite boring.

A teacher at Collegiate put it this way:

"John is a sharp kid. You have to be to stay in that school. They don't keep a kid if he isn't bright—not even a Kennedy."

John made B's—never C's or D's—but rarely A's.

Even though studying bored him, he did take after his father in one particular: he loved to read. He began early in school to read bestselling novels and adventure stories.

While his sister, Caroline, was considered shy and withdrawn, John was always considered gregarious and active.

"John is not as much like Jackie as his sister, Caroline, who is introverted like her mother," said his maternal grandmother, Mrs. Hugh Auchincloss. "Neither is he as shy as Jackie and Caroline."

Cry a lot or not, his interest in sports caused him to develop a sense of fairness. He found that he could be competitive and aggressive, but at the same time be a good moderator.

Like his father, he had a good sense of humor and a lively mind. His cousin Christopher Lawford, with whom he was very friendly, once told a writer: "He's one of the funniest guys I've ever known. He tells these long, involved old Irish jokes, in an accent. I don't know where he learned them."

Another cousin, Timothy Shriver, summed him up this way: "John's mother has a lot of influence on him, but he is not as intellectually or artistically inclined as she is. He likes more active things."

In other words, he was growing up to be a typical American boy.

And yet not that, really.

People would recognize him on the street and say, "Hello John." His reaction at certain times would be to smile and wave a hand and hurry on. At other times he would pause, cross his eyes, stick his thumbs in his ears, push out his tongue, wiggle his fingers, and say just about every four-letter word known to man.

It all depended on the mood.

"John *is* mischievous," Christopher Lawford said. "But he is serious when he wants to be. And he is on top of things; he's concerned about what is going on in the world. I wasn't at his age."

When he was six, he was a real handful. Once he was in Hawaii on a camping trip. A fire had been built to cook over. John was fooling around and accidentally stumbled backward into the hot coals.

It took a well-known plastic surgeon a half hour to lance the blisters and take the dead skin from his bottom.

In 1968, his Uncle Robert Kennedy was killed and death was once again close to the family. John felt the trauma deeply. He was older now than he had been at the time of his own father's death. The death of a man who had often been a surrogate father to him wounded him deeply.

Jacqueline knew that her son needed a father, probably more than Caroline needed one. She could understand the way a young man might miss masculine attachment as he grew up.

Whether or not this had anything to do with her marriage to Aristotle Onassis is not known. Nevertheless, when Onassis became John's stepfather, John took to him easily. They seemed completely compatible—much more so than Onassis and Caroline.

Caroline had always treaded softly in regard to Onassis. John seemed to thrive on every minute he had with him. Onassis would drop in at the house on Fifth Avenue, and soon he and John would be deep in conversation about flying, traveling, warships, and all kinds of adventures.

John tended to be a brat at times, and it is notable that Onassis could bring him in line with a few well-chosen words. And there would be no rancor exhibited afterwards on John's side. The two were quite understanding of one another.

It was great, too, being able to fly off to Skorpios, the island Onassis owned, and spend time on his big yacht.

John's young life was a vital, eventful one. Not many children his age traveled as extensively as he did during his vacations and weekends. It was not unusual for him to be bundled off to Paris for a weekend, Greece for the summer, England for a visit, or even Russia.

He was constantly talking with heads of state and well-known artists and intellectuals right in his own living room.

A lot of these good things were directly attributable to Jacqueline. No matter how complicated her schedules were, she never slacked up on the amount of time she spent with either her daughter or her son. She would go ice skating with John at Rockefeller Center, bicycle ride and play tennis with him in Central Park. Jacqueline could be counted on to take him to the movies and to concerts, ride with him in horse shows, and attend baseball games with him.

She had great patience with both her children and constantly had programs for their self-improvement. With John these programs were designed not only to build him up physically, but to get him acquainted with the arts.

John was the one in the family who most liked pets. Shannon, a cocker spaniel given to the family by the prime minister of Ireland when John was only a baby, became his favorite pet through the years.

The summer of 1972 produced a traumatic experience for Jacqueline, and for John, too. It had become a tradition for both children and Jacqueline to spend part of the summer cruising about the Aegean Sea with Onassis on his palatial yacht, *Christina.*

Suddenly in July, 1972, a spokesman for the military-backed junta that was ruling Greece announced that eight men had been arrested as terrorists. The terrorists, political leftists modeled on Uruguay's Tupamaros and Turkish extremists, had put together a chilling scenario of robberies and abductions in order to cause the Greek government embarrassment and perhaps even cause its downfall.

Calling themselves members of the New Left, they intended to kidnap government officials, diplomats, and prominent people, and hold them for ransom. One of their principal targets was Thomas Pappas, a wealthy Greek-American; another was the chief of the Greek Armed Forces; a third was the Greek labor minister.

And the fourth was John F. Kennedy, Jr.

Needless to say, this news upset the Kennedy/Onassis family profoundly. There was some discussion about calling the cruise off and hurrying John back to the States. John protested vehemently. Finally Jacqueline agreed to continue.

A court-martial was held and the terrorist plot was brought to light. The defense called the "plot" nothing more than "idle, romantic talk," and said that the only proof that existed was a number of Communist pamphlets found in the house of the gang's leader, Christos Ramadonis, along with some books by Herbert Marcuse.

Five of the eight men were sentenced to differing terms from seven months to thirty months on charges of terrorist activities in Greece. The other three were let off.

Later on that summer John went on a bicycle trip through France with a group of his school friends from Collegiate.

John and Caroline then joined the Robert Sargent Shrivers and three of their children—Maria, Robert and Timothy—on a trip to Russia. John studied up on Russia, so he'd be ready for it.

Timothy Shriver reported: "We went to Moscow and around the whole country. It was sort of an intellectual-type trip, given by the Russian government. We went to plants and factories and learned an incredible amount—what they were interested in, their social system—and everywhere we went John asked good questions."

John's main interest turned out to be the Russian Museum. He hung around there long after everyone else was tired and ready to go.

"He also liked the Russian ballet," Timothy revealed with surprise, "which was kind of freaky, because he usually doesn't like ballet." Then he went on: "But no one could *not* enjoy the Bolshoi."

One of the main things Timothy remembered about John on the trip was his extraordinary appetite.

"He was a garbage can," said Timothy. "He ate everything—ice cream, caviar, anything."

He could be a typical brattish twelve-year-old showoff, too. Dave Powers, a family friend who was a professional writer, remembered once when John came running up to him as soon as Powers had come into the apartment on Fifth Avenue.

"I'll bet you twenty-five cents you can't tell me the ball-player who knocked a home run off Sandy Koufax and also caught a touchdown pass from Y. A. Tittle of the New York Giants!"

Powers admitted he couldn't.

"Alvin Dark!" crowed John.

He demanded the twenty-five cents immediately—and got it.

John was exhibiting a Kennedy trait that could be traced back to his father and to his Uncle Robert as well. On the night Robert Kennedy was murdered in Los Angeles, he had confounded the reporters he was talking with by conducting a political quiz show.

" 'Politics is an honorable adventure,' " he said. "That's a quote, and I'll bet you don't know who said it."

Nobody knew.

"It was Lord Tweedsmuir."

Again nobody knew who Lord Tweedsmuir was.

"Lord Tweedsmuir was also known as John Buchan, and he wrote *The Thirty-Nine Steps*. He was governor general of Canada, too."

The threat of kidnapping and violence seemed to swirl around the Kennedys, no matter where they were and what they were doing. In the spring of 1974, John was in Central Park riding his bicycle over to take his afternoon tennis lesson with Hank Fenton. It was about five o'clock. John entered Central Park at the East Drive entrance at 90th Street just six blocks from the house, and began cycling along the path. Suddenly a youth, who seemed about eighteen, jumped out of the brush and grabbed John's bike, wielding a thick tree branch in his right hand.

"Get off," he told John.

There was no one around. For once the ubiquitous Secret Service guards were nowhere to be seen. Sometimes they left him alone when he went for his tennis lessons. He had complained enough about their presence.

John decided he didn't want a dent in the head from the tree branch, and he climbed off the bike.

"Give me the tennis racket," the mugger said.

John handed it over.

"Now get out of here!" he called to John, and with that, the young man cycled quickly off down the path, leaving John alone.

John immediately found a police patrol car and told them what had happened. The police drove John all through the park, looking for the youth with his bike, but he had gone.

The story broke in the morning papers. There was an immediate uproar. Where, everyone wanted to know, were the Secret Service guards who were protecting John Kennedy at such great public expense?

The Kennedys closed up like clams. The only news anyone could get was from the police blotter of the 23rd Precinct Station on East 102nd Street. Reporters prowled about, trying to sniff out news leads. Because the family had clammed up so completely, the scribes had no information— and news was what they were paid to get.

A television newsman was talking to an elevator operator in the building in which the Kennedys lived. After a few beers in a Bronx bar, the elevator operator began gabbing about the Secret Service guards.

It came out that he thought the Secret Service men were doing a poor job of guarding John and Caroline Kennedy. In fact, he told the television reporter, he knew of an instance of mental illness in someone working at the building who had never even been investigated by the Secret Service!

After some more beers, the operator admitted that *he* himself was the man. Although he loved the Kennedy children and would never hurt them, he had been surprised that a more thorough investigation had not been made of the people working in the building.

Eventually the story was filmed by WNEW-TV, with an interview of the elevator operator by Christopher Jones. The editorial slant of the filmed interview was an attack on the laxity of the Secret Service in looking after the safety of John F. Kennedy, Jr.

The show was criticized by many as an exploitation of the unfortunate elevator operator—and the station was roundly criticized for its "yellow journalism." Channel 5 defended the use of the film as "valid reporting," because it shed some light on the inadequacy of the guarding of the Kennedy children. The station also received a few hundred disapproving phone calls about the show.

The effect of all this was to infuriate Jacqueline, who was determined to keep as far away from the press as possible.

In fact, her reaction was to rush John up to New Hampshire with a group of his school friends to a tennis camp far away from Central Park.

The police continued their search for the bicycle and tennis racket, but were initially unsuccessful. However, they did find certain leads that when followed up gave them access to information about the actual whereabouts of the stolen bicycle. It had been sold and was in the possession of another party. By tracing back along the line of the sale, they located a twenty-year-old drug addict named Robert Lopez, who was married and had a two-month-old child.

Lopez denied having stolen the bicycle and the tennis racket. The police exerted some pressure on him, and finally, towards the end of July, Lopez walked into the 23rd Precinct

*The Shrivers at their home
in Bethesda, Maryland, in 1964.*
Left to right: *Bobby, Timothy, Eunice,
Mark, Maria, and Sargent Shriver*

*Ethel and Bobby Kennedy with some of their children
on an outing to the Bronx Zoo in 1964.
In front* left to right: *Mary, Bobby, Kerry, Michael;
in back* left to right: *Joseph, Kathleen, David, Ethel, Bobby, Jr.*

*Above: on a family visit to
the graves of
Robert F. Kennedy and
former president
John F. Kennedy in 1970,
young Matthew
Maxwell Taylor Kennedy
starts to climb the
fence near his
father's grave, but
then changes his mind.*

*Right: Kathleen,
speaking at a peace
rally in downtown
Cleveland, while
campaigning for
Senator George
McGovern in 1972.*

*R. Sargent Shriver 3rd (Bobby)
returned from Israel, where he worked
for a movie company, just in time
to see his father nominated as Democratic
vice-presidential candidate in August 1972.*

*Rory and Douglas,
the two youngest children
of Ethel and Bobby Kennedy,
playing at their home
in McLean, Virginia, 1973.*

Above: attending the unveiling of a portrait of Robert F. Kennedy at the Justice Department are, left to right: *Ethel, Joan, Rory (seated on brother Joseph's lap), Douglas, and Bobby, Jr.*

Left: David, on the day of his graduation from the Middlesex School in Concord, Massachusetts, June 6, 1974.

*Senator Edward Kennedy and his nephew
Joe at the 150th anniversary celebration
of the founding of Lowell, Massachusetts,
March 1, 1976.*

Station and gave himself up. He admitted that he had stolen John F. Kennedy, Jr.'s bicycle and his tennis racket.

"I mugged John Kennedy," he said, "but I didn't recognize him at all."

He still had the tennis racket, he admitted, but he no longer had the bike. He had sold it to obtain two bags of cocaine.

When the detectives of the investigations unit asked him why he had selected the young Kennedy as a victim, he shrugged and said that he looked like "an easy hit." Also, the path he was cycling in was deserted and an easy place for a mugging.

Lopez was ordered to appear for trial on September 15.

But John Kennedy was not in New York at all during the summer. He was sailing on the *Christina* off the coast of Greece. A frantic telephone call to Jacqueline brought further disturbing news. John would not be available to go to New York during September. The family had already planned to travel to Kenya in August for a six-week tour.

The district attorney's office was annoyed when it learned that their star witness would not be in New York at all until late fall. However, after some discussion on low and high levels, it was decided to go through with the trial anyway.

Nevertheless, it was made plain to Jacqueline that it would not look good for her son to fail to appear to identify his mugger in a trial that would obviously be covered by the press.

Jacqueline knew all about bad press. She huddled with her husband and some of the Kennedy advisers. It was decided that John would go to Africa no matter what happened. She informed the New York district attorney's office.

Jacqueline was taking a calculated risk. The press could cream the Kennedys once again if John failed to testify. Nevertheless, she flew with John and Caroline from Athens to Nairobi, where they stayed on the night of August 9. From there they moved over to a game lodge in Kenya, where they stayed for several weeks. Suddenly, with no advance notice,

John F. Kennedy, Jr. appeared before the grand jury to testify to the robbery on September 12.

The trial itself didn't take place until October 30, when Lopez told his story and was given a light sentence.

That summer was an eventful one for John. During one of the family's stays at the Kennedy compound on Cape Cod, John and his cousin Timothy Shriver got into a scrape close to home.

They took a small boat out into the Atlantic without asking permission from either Jacqueline or Eunice Shriver. It was a typical Kennedy twist of fate that the day degenerated from a warm quiet one to a gusting stormy one!

Small craft warnings were put out, but John and Timothy had no idea of it. The quick savage storm caught them unawares. The two boys had to fight winds, waves, and savage currents to keep from drowning.

Once the boat foundered, capsized, and almost went down.

Nevertheless they managed to get themselves back to the dock with no more damage than a broken tiller.

Jacqueline and Eunice, beside themselves with worry, were so relieved to see their sons that John and Timothy got off with nothing but a mild warning.

In fact, their mothers were quite proud of their seamanship and thought that the escapade had probably been well worth the effort.

John was growing into a typical Kennedy, driven to challenge the elements with feats of strength and derring-do. He was taking after his Uncle Robert in this particular character trait. It was Robert, not John F. Kennedy, who had always defied the forces of nature, challenged to excel by the fact that he was the "runt" of the pack.

John was no runt. But he did somehow feel he had to prove himself physically. He was growing up now, getting stronger and bigger. But he occasionally lapsed into childhood escapades.

He was fourteen years old—midway between youth and maturity—when he talked his eleven-year-old cousin Mark Shriver into climbing onto the roof of Jacqueline's house at the Kennedy compound.

From this strategic spot, the two boys threw eggs down into a group of their cousins playing on the grass.

This really *made* Mark's spring vacation. "I like John," Mark told a magazine writer. "He's nice."

The travel continued. Pictures that year showed John and Caroline skiing in Gstaad, Switzerland. And they spent time elsewhere as well, much of it on the Onassis yacht. John loved the yacht. There was a swimming pool on it, and he liked to be with his stepfather.

Stephen Birmingham related an anecdote about John and a friend who was a tennis freak. John liked Barry Cramer and considered him his best friend at Collegiate. John's tennis was not the quality of Barry's, but the two got along well.

John invited Barry to go on one of his many trips to Greece with the family. Barry brought along his racket. Unfortunately, there were no tennis courts on the island of Skorpios, nor on the yacht. And Barry was not the swimmer that John was.

"The summer was mostly a big bore," said Barry ruefully. "The *Christina* has a pool on it, but it doesn't have a tennis court."

In July, 1975, John and Timothy Shriver spent two weeks down in the Caroline Islands in the South Pacific on part of their vacation time. They were both avid scuba divers, and loved to poke around the bottom of the sea.

From his extensive reading on World War II, John knew that there were lots of sunken Japanese warships near Truk in the Carolines. With Timothy, he dove around in the water there, poking into the hulls of the wrecked ships.

They went as deep as 180 feet. "We saw a lot of the thirty sunken ships that aren't in real deep water," he told a reporter.

In addition to the time spent surfing, swimming, and getting some sun in the South Pacific, they stopped off in Hawaii as guests of Fernano Parra, a Mexican architect, and old Kennedy family friend. At least John didn't fall over backward into a luau fire that trip.

Jacqueline was still not happy with John's progress. Any boy who could throw eggs off a roof at his cousins was definitely not grown up. Besides, John's school grades were still not shaping up. He simply did not care.

Besides, he was tired of the strictures of Collegiate School and wanted a different school atmosphere. Finally Jacqueline decided on Phillips Academy, a prestigious prep school located in Andover, Massachusetts. It was in Kennedy country, and it was a good school.

John's grades might even begin to get better once he matured, she felt. And so in the fall of 1975, John started in at Phillips Academy. It was the first time he was really away from home. He liked the freedom it gave him, even though he was still trailed by his two Secret Service agents.

They blended in with the atmosphere, however, and didn't cause him any trouble.

If John's grades were fair at Collegiate—and he was no scholastic world-beater, certainly—they were not even anywhere near fair at Phillips. From the beginning he was in over his head academically.

Jacqueline agonized over the situation. Her son was still half boy and half man—a kind of split personality—one minute being a complete adult and the next a small child. When his grades came in the first semester she knew she had to do something about it.

One of New York's top psychiatrists was Ted Becker. He specialized in adolescent problems. Jacqueline decided that she would have to try him out with John. After all, most families with children in the upper classes send their children to psychiatrists almost as a matter of form.

Meanwhile a whole new life was opening up to John.

He was becoming a tall, well-built, somewhat handsome young man with a head of the curly, flying hair that was then in style.

Phillips was different from Collegiate. John buckled down to his studies at first, thanks to the treatment he was getting from Becker when he was in New York, and then he began being assigned parts in some of the school plays.

He turned out to have an unexpected talent for histrionics—not the subtle kind, but the broad, old-fashioned kind. "He's a natural at hamming it up," one of his friends at Andover said. "He's good."

There has always been a strong affinity between political activity and drama. The entire political situation is dramatic to the core. And the image of politics is confrontation and persuasion.

Certainly his father had basic dramatic talents, and his mother had far more than she ever realized. What could be more dramatic than for the widow of a slain president to marry the richest man in the world?

Jacqueline was bound to hear about this new interest of John's—and she did. Although she had many friends in show business, she had never considered it a proper profession. The one man who had truly failed to succeed in the Kennedy camp had been an actor: Peter Lawford.

Even though he was a well brought-up Englishman and had everything that should make for a perfect Kennedy, he had never been accepted by them. (The patriarch Joseph P. Kennedy *hated* him.) Finally, he drifted off and the Patricia Lawford clan simply became a one-parent family.

Jacqueline, with her academic background, her love of art, ballet, and theater, *should* have accepted show business as such. She had been squired around for awhile by Frank Sinatra, and other top talents in the industry. But she could simply not see it for anyone of her flesh and blood.

She went through the ceiling when she heard about John's interest in acting, and told him quite simply that it couldn't be.

John had been amenable about most of his mother's ultimatums, but this one didn't seem quite normal. The arguments were bitter and had lasting effects on both of them.

Jacqueline's reaction was to tighten the noose on him just a little more. She returned to her old gambit of putting him out into the "real world" where the "beautiful people" of the screen were million miles away.

John wound up that year on a Peace Corps mission to Guatemala, which had been hit by a severe earthquake. In the demolished town of Rabinal he helped the victims of the quake and spent several harrowing weeks there helping clean up the rubble and start the town to building again.

He took it all in stride. He knew what his mother's "hangups" were. His reaction was to play along with her version of "Hercules' labors" and see where it would end.

It wasn't going to end very soon. The next year, in June, he was signed up in the Outward Bound survival course. The main purpose of the challenging course was to learn survival tactics.

"Besides providing a survival test," according to the director "the three days alone are just as important as a period of contemplation."

Most of the 26-day course involved sailing a 30-foot open boat, which had to be rowed, with a group of other Outward Bound students around Penobscot Bay, off the rugged coast of Maine. Each of them was then dropped off at Hurricane Island, a completely isolated island, with no food, a gallon of water, a couple of matches, and a book about edible wild plants written by Euell Gibbons.

He survived that all right, went back to school in the fall, and plunged into the books once again.

That season he seemed to do a little better. In fact, except for weekends when he came to New York or went on longer trips, he spent a good deal of time studying.

And he acted in plays.

But in spite of his efforts, his grades were so bad he had

to retake a number of courses. Trying to keep up in his studies was tough indeed.

With the death of his stepfather in February, he had no ties to Greece, and the long summers on the *Christina* were at an end. In a way, Jacqueline was not unhappy. She realized that perhaps John's close observation of actors and actresses aboard the yacht during those days might have been responsible for giving him the acting bug.

John had so much trouble in the coming semesters that he was almost flunked out of Phillips. But he managed to hang on, and somehow he got through.

By his senior year, it seemed reasonably certain that with extra help, and with a lot of application, he might actually graduate.

Almost eighteen, he was becoming fully grown. He had developed into a tall, well-built young man, with thick curly brown hair and a thin, well-chiseled, rather sensitive, almost haunted, face. He wore his hair long, like most of the Kennedys. His haircut looked different from those of his cousins, however; it resembled an English schoolboy cut.

His usual costume at school was corduroys or jeans, the same attire his peers wore. He dressed in expensive tee shirts, usually purchased at Serendipity 3, a posh East Side boutique and restaurant in New York.

The big birthday party that Jacqueline threw for eighteen-year-old John and twenty-one-year-old Caroline at Le Club went off with the usual "exuberant reserve" of any Jacqueline Kennedy affair.

Afterward, as the party left the nightspot, the paparazzi immediately rushed to get a shot of John and Caroline. John tried to duck them, but couldn't. One of his companions came to his rescue, and took a swing at a photographer.

John realized there could be trouble, grabbed his friend and pulled him back, only to find himself down on the sidewalk just as all the flashbulbs popped. The picture wound up in a copy of the revived *Life* magazine.

Actually, John later apologized to the photographer, a *Daily News* staffman, for the fracas.

He was eighteen now, and actually a semester late for starting college. Everybody in his family, including his sister, had gone to Harvard, but John simply felt he didn't want to go the same route. After much brainstorming, he finally decided to try Brown University in Providence, Rhode Island.

He was accepted, and later that year, June 1979, graduated from Phillips. But the lure of the movies was still strong. Producer Robert Stigwood, of "Saturday Night Fever" and "Grease" fame, called up John and started talking about the possibility of John's playing the role of his father in a motion picture based on John F. Kennedy's younger years.

John thought it would be a great idea. But Jacqueline would have nothing to do with it. She wanted him to get on with his schooling, get through college—and *then* do what he wanted with his life. As long as it wasn't the movies.

"All Jacqueline wants is for the dear boy to finish his schooling," a cousin of Jacqueline's told a reporter. "Let's be honest. John doesn't find school work too easy and Jacqueline is well aware of the tremendous temptations he would face if anyone ever enticed him to Hollywood. After all he is a Kennedy and that is big box office if someone manages to sign him up."

After the Stigwood offer, there were numerous other offers from independent agents and producers for screen tests.

"If I were to make a prediction about John Kennedy, I would say he will end up in California," said a former dormitory-mate at Phillips.

Shortly after graduation, John went on a seventy-day survival course arranged by the National Outdoor Leadership School. Part of the outdoor training course took him to Kenya, Africa. There he was put out into the wilds to learn survival in the deep African bush.

There were six in the party—three boys and three girls.

They survived all right, but they were lost for two days. A Masai tracker had to come in and rescue them.

That made headlines, of course.

In the fall of the year he enrolled as a freshman at Brown University. "He got no special consideration in the application process and will get no special treatment as a student," Vice President Robert Reichley announced.

Reichley said there would be no extra security procedures, and that John would be living in a dormitory.

On November 8, shortly after John's enrollment, his Uncle Ted declared that he was a candidate for the office of president of the United States. Senator Kennedy's brother-in-law, Stephen Smith, became his campaign manager. Instantly Kennedys of all ages and sizes were recruited in the excitement of the campaign.

In December, John was dispatched to Portland, Maine, where he was ordered to stump the state for Ted Kennedy. He rang doorbells and spoke at rallies, gatherings, and wherever they sent him.

One state legislator shook his head in nostalgia. "All I can remember is the picture of that little kid saluting at his father's funeral."

John spoke about his Uncle Ted. One reporter wrote that many people turned out just as much to catch a glimpse of John F. Kennedy's son as they did to hear him say that Teddy has the potential to "galvanize the nation."

One writer asked John about his school work.

"I'm at Brown University," said John.

"How about taking a leave of absence from school to devote full time to your uncle's campaign?"

John smiled faintly. "It's my first year. I think it's better if I stick it out."

So did his mother. And yet, there was always the lure of the Hollywood scene—even there in the political wilds of Maine.

"He's the best-looking of all the Kennedy kids," a Kennedy cousin said recently.

The patriarch and founder of the Kennedy dynasty spent some very lucrative and adventurous years of his life in Hollywood. His grandson would not be a stranger to the excitement and glamour of the industry. The Kennedy traits—some of which are definitely a part of John's character—would tend to make him a star in his own right even if he didn't act at all.

But first, the books. Once the diploma was out of the way. . . .

CHAPTER 4
Kathleen Hartington Kennedy

Like a true Yankee Doodle Dandy, Kathleen Hartington Kennedy was born on the Fourth of July, 1951, the first of Joseph P. Kennedy's grandchildren. At the time of her birth, her father, Robert F. Kennedy, was working for the Justice Department in Brooklyn, in a division dealing with the internal security of the government.

Kathleen was named after her aunt, the Marchioness of Hartington, who was killed in a 1948 plane crash. She was baptized by Cardinal Cushing, an event said by her father to have "kind of established the Kennedys."

Although rumored to have been Senator Joe McCarthy's goddaughter, her godfather was really Danny Walsh, the Trappist monk who converted Thomas Mann, and who was also Ethel Kennedy's theology teacher.

Shortly after her birth her father left his work with the Justice Department to campaign for his older brother Jack, running for the United States Senate in Boston.

Kathleen had no time to grow up lonely—no son or daughter of Robert F. Kennedy ever did—and from the beginning, she was an active, wide-awake, energetic child. It was hard to be anything else in that always-active family.

Kathleen had qualities of character that she obviously inherited from both her father and her mother. As she grew up she displayed more and more a combination of characteristics of both parents.

Like her father, she tended to be direct and unassuming. She had no subtleties of temperament, no devious traits, no artifice or laid-on sophistication. She went to the heart of things immediately, showing native-born impatience with trivialities.

Like her mother Ethel, she exerted a great deal of energy from the moment she rose in the morning until she went to bed at night. Nor did she waste her energy in nervous dissipation; her vivacity was channeled and directed into whatever activity in which she was involved.

These were positive characteristics.

On the negative side, she had a tendency to be disorderly, a not unusual trait in an individual so energetic and active. Along with this trait, she displayed a lack of interest in her outward appearance.

In fact, one of the first things her father noticed about his first-born was her sloppiness. She was still quite young on the day he wrote her a note after a visit to her rooms.

"Kathleen," he scrawled on a piece of paper. "I think your room looks terrible, and also your bathroom. I don't think you should leave your room looking like this. Love, Daddy."

Her mother found the note and kept it. Later, Ethel had it framed and hung it on Kathleen's wall as a constant reminder.

In spite of her casual attitude toward housekeeping and neatness, she grew up a steady, reasonable, and intelligent child. The Robert F. Kennedy family believed in strict discipline. Kathleen was reared as a child of more than ordinary rectitude in the observation of the common old-fashioned courtesies.

For example, when Ethel Kennedy entered a room where

the children were playing, all of them were required to get to their feet and stand there until she told them they could go on playing.

Kathleen, as the oldest of the children, was the task-master responsible for these displays of courtesy. When the others were out of line—which was seldom—she was required to exert punishment on them. And she did so, in a straight forward and no-nonsense manner.

The Kennedy children were well behaved at the dinner table, too. In many American families at the time, table conversation consisted of mutterings and small talk, with possibly the discussion of a favorite movie or movie star as the highest plane of intellectualism reached in the conversation.

Not so with the Robert F. Kennedy family.

Kathleen's father believed in instilling a love of politics—or at least a knowledge of the working order of politics—in his children as they grew up.

Remembering his own childhood, where breakfast and dinner were devoted to discussions of politics, current events, and general history, under the strict supervision of the family patriarch, he instituted a similar program of discussion of news events during breakfast.

Then, when Ethel Kennedy had her turn at the car pool, Kathleen and her brothers and sisters were required to "play back" what they had learned at breakfast as they drove along to school.

At night, for dinner, there were more discussions of political activity, with the children programmed to express opinions on events that had occurred during the day. In this fashion, Kathleen acquired the ability of learning, judging, and discussing minor events of the day as well as major events of the day.

Mixed in with news events and politics were other less weighty subjects, but each was treated in the same manner. Kathleen and her brothers and sisters were taught early on to listen and understand, to weigh and consider, and to analyze and expound on a gamut of subjects from trivial to momentous.

Being articulate and able to expound orally on subjects at will did not entirely satisfy Robert Kennedy. He demanded that his children learn to write as well as speak. Each Sunday, Kathleen and her siblings were required to research a public figure of some importance and write a report on him or her. The report would then be submitted to the family for perusal, discussion, and evaluation.

Sometimes the children were more merciless with one another than their parents were. Kathleen exerted a great deal of tough-mindedness in her critiques on the work of the others. But she was always fair. Her fairness and basic honesty were qualities that were natural to her, and in turn they brought out the same kinds of qualities in the others.

In addition to speaking and writing, reading chores were set by the head of the household. Each of the children were required to read for at least one hour a day. The books were quality fare, not "Nancy Drew" or the "Bobbsey Twins."

Kathleen fell in love with the Bible during that period of her reading life, especially the style of writing.

She preferred the Old Testament to the New because of the wonderful stories that she found there. The Bible also tied in directly with her religious beliefs. No one had to persuade her that religion was important. She always knew, she said later, that it was "important to believe in something."

Yet all the same, the life Kathleen led, and the life her brothers and sisters led from birth, was not the life of an ordinary American child. How could it be, with the family worth millions of dollars even at the time she was born, and her father rapidly becoming a public figure.

She always realized she was rich and different from other kids. Yet to counterbalance the ease and affluence money gave her, she was taught that there was another side to the picture. Although much was given to her, at the same time, much was expected of her.

"The lesson was actually taught that we were privileged, that we had more than other people," she said. "Of course, it was obvious to us when we looked around, but when we were young we didn't see many people who weren't rich."

Money itself was never discussed in the Kennedy family. In fact, in most extremely rich families, money is not discussed *as money*. It exists, and it is used, but it is not the problem it is in the average American family. It is not an object to be fought for, an object to be grasped and coveted, an object to use to buy wonderful things.

"You didn't think about whether you had a lot or didn't have a lot," Kathleen once said. "It just wasn't one of those things you thought about."

In fact, looking back on it later, Kathleen admitted that she was obviously ambivalent about money. Her Bible readings, however, helped explain something about money. "It made a big difference that I had a Catholic education," she observed. "You're taught that it's easier for a camel to go through the eye of a needle than it is for a rich man to get to heaven. That had an impact on me."

By the time she was nine years old, Kathleen had six brothers and sisters. The family was almost bursting at the seams. But more important, at that time her father became actively involved in politics to a degree he had never imagined he might ever be.

It was 1960, and her father ran her Uncle Jack's campaign for the presidency of the United States. John F. Kennedy was elected president, and almost immediately Uncle Jack selected her father as his attorney general-designate, head of the Justice Department, and a member of his cabinet.

During that crucial year, Kathleen began meeting and talking to people she had read about in the newspapers. These politicians became familiar to her, became actual visitors to the house—people you could touch.

"In those days," she recalled, "I didn't know that the word 'politician' has a bad connotation." Unlike the average

American, she looked on politicians as simply hard-working human beings who were trying to do something right for their country.

In 1955 the Robert F. Kennedys had moved into a rambling, picturesque old white mansion called Hickory Hill, situated on the rolling verdant countryside of McLean, Virginia. The mansion had been the headquarters of General McClellan of the Union Army during the Civil War.

The house, built in 1810, was constructed on a hill surrounded by sloping lawns and finely landscaped grounds. In one corner a tennis court was located, and in the back, a large swimming pool. Nearby was a boathouse used sometimes to screen movies on weekends.

Uncle Jack had leased the place in 1953, but when Kathleen's father moved to Washington to take up duties as counsel for the Senate Anti-Crime Committee, he bought the place and moved the family there. The extensive site was ideal for the rapidly expanding family.

Hickory Hill was simply bursting with activity. There were not only kids everywhere, but animals as well.

Writer Pete Hamill once visited while Robert Kennedy was running the Rackets Investigation Committee. As he entered the grounds, he wrote, "suddenly there was a loud crash and a sliding, scratching noise, and a sound of many feet. We had obviously strolled into ambush country. There were dogs and kids everywhere: sniffing dogs and leaping kids, barking dogs and barking kids, big kids, little kids, kids grabbing Kennedy by the legs and lapels and the necktie. There was mad laughter and raucous squalling, and then two kids (male) had their hands up, and were sparring with each other, while a great black Newfoundland dog named Brumus leaped between them. . . ."

And in the distance, Hamill recalled, stood Ethel Kennedy, stifling her laughter.

At the McLean home during Kathleen's childhood there was an assortment of animals.

Sandy, a sea lion, lived in the swimming pool, except when there were certain guests who didn't care to share their bathing with the playful animal. In addition to Sandy, there were two horses, three ponies, one donkey, four dogs, one kitten, ten ducks, five chickens, two roosters, one goose, five rabbits, four pigeons, several squirrels, a parakeet, a cockatoo, plenty of goldfish, snakes, and so on.

There were human beings, as well. There were the Kennedy children and there were secretaries, maids, cooks, and a gardener.

The years 1960–1963 were exciting, exhilarating years for Kathleen, as they were for most people in the United States. Yet to Kathleen there seemed to be nothing exceptional about her position in the world.

"Having the president for an uncle doesn't necessarily give you a whole lot of respect for the office," she said later, "especially when you combine it with what the presidents after him did."

But it wasn't the president who was so close to her—it was the attorney general. And the attorney general was suddenly in the middle of a brawl he had never really anticipated: the integration of the South.

The integration of the University of Mississippi made big headlines, as did the integration of the University of Alabama. In both cases, Kathleen's father was prominently displayed in the papers and on television.

She was not quite yet twelve years old at this time, and yet the reassessment of America during the 1960s was starting to make a deep impression on her. She had already learned that she had more material things than most other people. Now she learned that her status in society was also much higher than most other people's.

Her concern over social conditions was deeply rooted in her religious beliefs. She became aware of what she later called "the strands that form you. It's really hard to separate them."

Because of her father's early work on the Rackets Committee investigating the presence of organized crime in the unions, and because of his aggressive manner of pushing integration in the teeth of active resistance from the political figures of the South, he had earned the distinction of being "ruthless," and hard-driving. "The word 'ruthless' was used so often," she recalled. "Whenever I hear it, I just kind of smile."

She knew the trait for what it really was. It was simply the inborn and inbred Kennedy trait of stubborn persistence against all odds.

Her father and Uncle Jack were very close in the administration. Some journalists said that Kathleen's father was actually the Number Two man in the government, rather than Lyndon B. Johnson, the duly-elected vice president.

But Kennedys were always close. It was not an unusual thing at all. During the Cuban Missile Crisis, her father became the real Number Two man in the strategic sessions.

And then, when she was only twelve, a cataclysmic event occurred that shook the very foundations of America's democratic structure. President Kennedy, Kathleen's uncle, was assassinated in Dallas, Texas, by a misguided radical who may have been jealous of the president's great charisma.

The death of his brother stunned Kathleen's father. He withdrew from life for a time, then resigned from the Justice Department, and tried to get himself together again. When he did, he established residence in New York and ran for the U.S. Senate. Winning easily, the New York senator moved back to Washington and entered the Senate.

Politicians, journalists, and intellectuals once again flocked to the McLean mansion. Her father saw integration as a most important problem in America.

"Daddy would come home and tell us about the children who did not have half what we had to eat. We learned very quickly what problems there are once you get out of a nice environment."

Kathleen was expanding her horizons, and one thing

that bothered her was the fairly restricted outlook on life represented by her schoolmates. She was going to the Stoneridge Country Day School of the Sacred Heart, in Bethesda, Maryland, and had been going there for years.

"Everybody came from the same social background," she explained. "You always got the Catholic point of view, pro or versus. I kept arguing and sounding off in religion class. Every Monday we had to wear white gloves and polished shoes to hear our week's report. Once I got six D's, including courtesy, neatness, discipline."

In short, Kathleen suddenly rebelled. It was time for high school, and she didn't want to go to a girls' school. She hated the daily routine, the limited way of knowing people.

After considerable study and talks with people, she opted to go to Putney School in Vermont. Putney was described once by her mother as "superprogressive." Ethel explained: "That's as different as you can get from a convent!"

News of Kathleen's rebellion spread through the Kennedy family like wildfire. She was the oldest of the third generation of Kennedys—and she was turning against Catholicism! What was wrong with her?

Not much, really. She had been sheltered, and she had now reached an age of decision. She wanted to come out from under the shelter. About Catholicism she said once, "They give you too many straight answers." She wanted to experience a wider outlook on life.

Ethel and the Kennedy sisters of the older generation were shocked and disappointed. But Kathleen took heart. Her father rather liked the idea. And her grandfather Joe had always wanted his sons to have secular educations in addition to their religious education, although he had never included women in these calculations.

If the Kennedy men could have secular educations, why couldn't Kathleen? After a great deal of argument and frustration, Kathleen got her way and enrolled at Putney.

Putney was an eyeopener for her. She was immediately

enthusiastic about the curriculum as well as the extracurricular activities. There was skiing in the winter, riding in the spring and fall, crafts at all times, and school work as well.

She was associating with the sons and daughters of writers, teachers, radicals, farmers, and blue-collar laborers.

"I didn't know a soul there at first, and I liked that," she said. "Growing up with a Catholic education, you're taught to be very generous, polite, and giving. At Putney nobody made much of an effort. It took a long time to know people, but I found *that* kind of knowing can be more rewarding—though at first all that introversion shocked me. And the fact that all their 'givens' weren't *my* 'givens'!"

Rose Kennedy, completely a Catholic, once discussed religion with her granddaughter. Rose mentioned the stability, the inner peace, and the tranquillity that the true faith gave one. But Kathleen told her grandmother that she wanted to find things out for herself, and not accept life without hard questioning. She thought Catholicism didn't give you that chance.

What hurt Ethel was the fact that while at Putney, Kathleen stopped going to Mass regularly.

Kathleen put it this way: "To try to answer questions with a simple faith—well, I decided not to rely wholly on Catholicism, though it's deeply ingrained in me. I want to think things through for myself—though you don't do anything by yourself, do you?"

When she was fourteen the family traveled out West to the Colorado River for a "white water" raft expedition. The rafts were delayed, and there was nothing for them to do but wait.

"Daddy used the opportunity to take us to visit an Indian reservation," Kathleen recalled. "It was such a shock to be there for reasons of pleasure, and then to see the awful contrast; the way people in the area lived. I assume most wealthy people never see that part of life. That's why they're not moved to do something."

The experience affected Kathleen profoundly. She had *believed* that there were differences in people's "conditions," but until she saw exactly what it was like on that reservation, she had not really *felt* what it was like.

Her happy-go-lucky outlook on life began to assume a more serious maturity. She knew very well how people of her own social status lived. Now she could imagine and see how people of other social statuses had to exist. She decided that she must begin to do something to change it.

Meanwhile, as the Johnson Administration wallowed in the public backlash of discontent engendered by the Vietnam War, Kathleen's father was prompted to challenge Johnson for the party's nomination in the upcoming presidential election.

When Johnson decided not to run, the senator began his campaign. The entire Kennedy clan was once again swept up into the familiar excitement of politics. Kathleen's brothers, sisters, and cousins all joined forces and started to work.

Kathleen's contribution to the campaign was volunteer work on an Indian reservation. She had been so impressed by the poverty and despair on the reservation she had visited two summers before that she had promised herself that she would try to help out those less privileged than she. Through the influence of her father, who was head of a Senate subcommittee on Indian Affairs, she was assigned to teach English to the Navahos on a reservation in Chinle, Arizona.

She was sixteen years old at that time. She recognized at last the "almost impassable barrier between the rich and the invisible poor." Her plans were all made and she was just finishing up another year at Putney when a jolting emotional trauma hit the Kennedy family once again.

In Los Angeles, on the night of his victory in the California primary, Senator Kennedy was assassinated by a Palestinian dissident who thought the senator was too soft on Israel.

Kathleen was devastated, as was the entire family. But she had been brought up by a man obsessed by an almost Greek stoicism about life. Where many sons and daughters might have given way to despair, Kathleen eschewed it.

"It just wouldn't occur to me," she said. "It wasn't the way we were brought up."

Nor did hatred or despair play any part in her reaction. "You never resent people or hate. I just go on from what Daddy has given me, what he's given to everybody.

"Everything that happens changes you. I'm suddenly a thinking human being." But she did not blame politics nor turn from politics. "That's just saying 'forget it' to everything that he ever worked for. He had a ten-times-worse loss when his brother was assassinated; yet he went back and tried. If I didn't keep trying, that would be forgetting what he lived for."

To work off her grief and keep her promise to herself, she arrived at the reservation, and worked with the Navahos all that summer.

"It was embarrassing," she said. "I learned so much more from them than they learned from me."

She found she liked to work with people, and went back to school that fall, trying to get over the traumatic experience of her father's assassination.

By now her goal in life had become more clear to her. She decided that her interests lay in public service. She was finishing high school now, and eventually was accepted at Radcliffe College, where she wanted to study history and literature.

Her work in the summer of 1970 took her to Alaska where she got a job in a day-care center, taking care of children of working women and other mothers who couldn't take care of them. She worked for three months there with the Eskimos who used the center, in the company of a Putney roommate.

Meanwhile, her interest in writing—engendered in those far-off days when her father had made her write a paper each Sunday on an American personality—continued to grow.

She tried to establish a newspaper at the day-care center. During the months she worked there, it flourished, but after she left, it died.

Upon graduation from Putney School, she enrolled at Radcliffe. There was no use not going to Radcliffe—after all, it was the female part of Harvard! Her father, her uncles, and her grandfather had been Harvard students.

She found it not too different from Putney, and she thrived on the atmosphere. Her studies were no problem, and she took up her extra-curricular activities with zest and gusto, true to the Kennedy style.

While at Radcliffe she spent one semester living in Florence, Italy, doing "independent study." In Italy, she lived with a mechanic's family and worked in a potting studio. She learned to speak and write Italian, made pottery at the studio with Italian craftsmen, ate vegetables, and decided to become a vegetarian.

She found that she could feel very "liberated" about the Germans. She had not lived through World War II. The Italians with whom she worked *had* lived through war, and would never get over it. They had seen people killed, members of their own families and good friends. To Kathleen the lesson was obvious: It was next to impossible to put yourself in anybody else's shoes on emotional issues.

One summer while she was at Radcliffe she hitchhiked through Greece alone. "I felt great loneliness," she recalled. "I realized that some people live that way always. There's nobody at the end of the trip to welcome them home."

It was the early 1970s, and the values of the 1960s were still quite viable among college-age people. So was backpacking, dressing in blue jeans, and wearing floppy hats, old clothes, and long hair. Kathleen traveled to Paris with a friend from Radcliffe, with the plan of bicycling through the Loire Valley.

It was in Paris that Kathleen visited her grandmother, Rose Kennedy. Rose used to stay at the Ritz Hotel, one of the swankiest in Paris—in fact, in the world. When Kathleen and her friend Ann got into the city, it was raining and miserable. Kathleen decided it was time to pay Grandma a visit.

The two young women, backpacks covered with torn raincoats soaking up the water, trudged fifteen blocks after taking the subway and getting off at the wrong metro station. At the Ritz the supercilious clerk, eyeing them as he might eye roaches climbing up out of the baseboard, explained that unfortunately Rose Kennedy was not staying at the Ritz that year, but at—his voice dropped to an anguished whisper—the Plaza Athené.

The girls went out into the rain again and sloshed to the Plaza Athené. Once again they attacked the front desk, to the obvious horror of the chief clerk. Raising an eyebrow at the soaked, soiled, disheveled young women, he rang Rose's room and announced the arrival of Kathleen and friend.

Kathleen wrote later:

"She could hardly believe it when these two dirty kids arrived in her hotel room. But she was terrific. She sort of gasped and said well, ah, go over and do this and sit down. She didn't know exactly what to do with us."

She gave the girls some tea and suggested that they might want to use the bathroom to clean up.

"She was terrific, you know," Kathleen reported. "She always wants to help out but she doesn't know exactly how to do it."

Anyway, once they had bathed and washed up, they got on the telephone and finally reached some friends from Radcliffe. The other Radcliffe women knew a good cheap place, and told them about it.

Once Kathleen explained to her grandmother where it was, Rose checked with the concierge. That eminent Frenchman had never *heard* of the place, and as Kathleen reported, was "totally disdainful about it."

Nevertheless, Rose agreed to take Kathleen and her friend

over to the hotel and see them settled in. The three got into a cab and motored over to the Left Bank.

Kathleen: "With her long Dior gown on, [Rose] walked into this halfway-shabby hotel and interviewed the concierge there."

"Will these girls be safe?" she asked the clerk. "Is there a shower?" Rose even tried out her French.

Eventually she decided that the place would be all right, and let Kathleen stay there for the next few days. During those days, she took the two girls all over Paris, to see Notre Dame Cathedral, Les Invalides, and the Louvre.

At the Louvre, Rose was pleasantly surprised to find that Kathleen actually knew the differences among the Doric, Ionic, and Corinthian columns.

What disturbed Kathleen's grandmother during the entire adventure was what had always disturbed her about Kathleen and the generation to which she belonged.

"When my children were growing up," she said plaintively to Kathleen once, "we all liked nice clothes. You don't like that sort of clothes. What can I give you?"

As the girls were leaving, Rose tried again.

"Can I give you a Dior dress? I don't know, Kathleen, what exactly do you *like?*"

The values of the times were changing. Although her grandmother might never really see *why,* Kathleen did. It was partly what Rose and her generation stood for that was now under siege. The affluent—the terribly affluent—were being challenged by masses of people all over the world. The entire structure that had produced the affluent was under attack by intellectuals and nonintellectuals alike.

Kathleen understood it. She knew that the structure under siege had produced too tremendous a difference between the rich and the poor. She was working with the poor. She wanted to dedicate herself to relieving their poverty and disproportionate anxieties about life.

To do that, she had to disprove her own affluence. And she did so by wearing blue jeans and floppy hats and torn raincoats, and never dressing up.

She reached the needy by reaching *around* her insular privilege. Her grandmother could understand that all right, when she thought about it. Kennedys always worked to try to alleviate the frustration and despair of the poor. But Rose could never really feel that it was necessary to give up everything she had just to appear right.

Politics always bubbled below the surface in Kathleen, exactly the same way it did in all Kennedys, no matter what generation. After the mining of Haiphong Bay in the Vietnam War, she began speaking out for an old family friend—George McGovern.

"I felt such mixed emotions—rage, anger, disbelief. I had to do something, not just protest in school. After the Cambodian invasion we all stopped going to class; I marched on Washington."

It was a good catharsis for her. It helped in some ways to let all her anger at the war out on Nixon, who was, after all, a Republican—everything her Uncle Jack and her father had hated and disdained.

"I'm not sure how much good it did me," she later confessed.

When McGovern started campaigning for the presidential nomination in 1972, Kathleen joined up. And McGovern was tickled pink to have the oldest of the third-generation Kennedys in his camp.

Life magazine reported: "They hustled [her] into the campaign's most glamorous job, traveling with the candidate himself. For the next seventy-two hours, [she] exhorted enthusiastic crowds in Massachusetts and Pennsylvania to give McGovern their votes."

"He's a good man," she told them. "He cares so much, as my father did. He'll get us out of Vietnam."

One reporter asked her if her appearance at McGovern's side might not be "trading on the family name of Kennedy."

"Why not? If you want your candidate to win, you do what's most useful," she retorted.

Her mother heard about Kathleen's adventures on the campaign trail and telephoned Kathleen to say: "I hear you're working for McGovern. I'm jealous."

It wasn't all kudos and applause, however. At one gathering in Brooklyn, where she was actually working for Allard Lowenstein, an old friend of her father's, she spoke to a group of high school students.

One of the students asked Kathleen if it was true that McGovern had supported Henry Wallace in 1948.

Kathleen said it was true. She said that it was also true that Henry Wallace "was a Communist and I guess Senator McGovern was a Communist then too, but he isn't any more."

Lowenstein turned white, grabbed at the microphone, and rushed in to cover up the gaffe.

"Anybody who says that [McGovern was a Communist] is speaking out of ignorance, trying to confuse you," he said.

Kathleen realized she had made a serious mistake, and went back to rectify it.

"Personally," she told the students, "I don't think you have to worry if someone's a Communist. Some people have one point of view, and other people have another point of view."

Bill Buckley in his syndicated column called Kathleen "the all-American McGovern girl" after burying her in a recital of the Brooklyn fiasco.

Lowenstein, incidentally, was to figure in a grisly Manhattan murder that was every bit as bizarre as the deaths of Robert and Jack Kennedy.

In March, 1980—oddly enough during the primary campaign of Senator Ted Kennedy for the presidency—Lowenstein was shot to death in his office in Rockefeller Center by an antidraft Vietnam War activist and former student Lowenstein had known while he was dean of men at Stanford University.

Because of Lowenstein's friendship with the Kennedys—he was working actively for Ted Kennedy's campaign in New York State—Kathleen's uncle flew immediately to New York from Chicago where he was trying to build up support in Illinois.

"Once again," Senator Kennedy said, "we've seen violence in our society. As one whose family has been touched by violence, I deplore this senseless act."

Certainly the idea of the Kennedy curse surfaced once again among the Kennedys. Lowenstein had supported Robert F. Kennedy during his last campaign. In fact, one of Lowenstein's sons was named Thomas Kennedy Lowenstein after Norman Thomas and Robert F. Kennedy. The night of Robert Kennedy's murder, Lowenstein was waiting in Los Angeles for a short conference with the candidate which was abrogated by the senator's assassination.

Kathleen's tutor at Radcliffe in 1972 was a Harvard graduate student named David Lee Townsend, a young man four years older than she. Born in Baltimore, Maryland, he had been educated first at Loyola College, and then had taken a Ph.D. at Harvard. He had written his thesis on American visionary poetry.

Kathleen and David had a great deal in common. Both were interested in American literature, and both were interested in history and languages. Kathleen had learned Italian on her one-semester stay in Italy, and David knew Greek and French.

A red-bearded young man, six feet four inches tall, he was quite attractive to Kathleen. A friend who knew them both once described David as "kind."

In addition, he was a Catholic like Kathleen. "It's nice," decided Kathleen, "because it gives you more in common."

She had broken once with Kennedy tradition when she had opted for Putney Academy over a Catholic high school. She decided not to break with it again.

But what drew them together even more was their interest in the America of the 1960s—even though it was now 1972. They were both ecology-minded, dressed casually, and were interested in living simply.

David had interested Kathleen in reading about the flourishing, hopeful, forward-looking America of the nineteenth century. Both of them were fascinated with Mark Twain's America. From their reading of *Life on the Mississippi* they conceived a marvelous plan—to take a raft down the river just like Huck Finn!

Kathleen had gone down the Colorado River in a raft with her family some years before. David was outdoors-oriented, too. The two of them made up their minds and talked three friends into doing a raft trip with them.

For some time, Kathleen had enjoyed the friendship of Janna Malamud, daughter of writer Bernard Malamud. Janna was enthusiastic. David mentioned the scheme to Gary Carson, a graduate student at Harvard, and a tutor like David. He too agreed to crew. The fifth member of the party was a friend of Kathleen's named Briget Murnaghan.

"Nobody at Radcliffe does anything with their hands," Kathleen said in explanation of her desire to float the river. "I wanted to get away from all that talk, talk, talk. I loved sailing that raft. I even liked the river mud. School isn't a vital part of my life; there's too much to do outside."

The raft trip down the Mississippi was supposed to begin in the early days of June. Although sailing down the Mississippi was thought to be great fun by Kathleen and her contemporaries, Kathleen's mother wanted to check out the safety factors and try to find out if it could even be done.

She telephoned Senator James O. Eastland, of Mississippi, whom she had known for years. When Eastland heard about what Kathleen was planning to do, he almost climbed the nearest wall. He warned Ethel that it was bad out on the river, that there were "dangerous currents." Besides that, he said, there were "river rats."

But Kathleen wouldn't be dissuaded by her mother. She and her four companions traveled out to Cape Girardeau, Missouri, and there began building the raft, using Neelys Landing, twelve miles north of Cape Girardeau, as their dry dock.

There they had the much-needed help of Bill Seiden-sticker, a practical-minded friend of David Townsend. He knew the river and understood how to attack it. The five hopefuls lived in the Seidensticker basement during construc-tion throes.

The craft wasn't actually a raft. A raft is free-floating; this one had an outboard engine attached so it could maneuver the eddies and channels more easily. To keep the raft afloat, twelve empty 55-gallon oil drums were secured to the bottom.

The group thought they could build the raft in three days; in actual fact it took them ten. They made two false starts, and finally finished on the third try. Seidensticker was a life-saver; without him they never would have finished it.

It resembled a houseboat more than a raft. It was flat, with a cabin structure built on top, like some kind of shack in the woods. Kathleen called it the "house that Jack built."

They christened it the *Snopes,* after the sly, tasteless, and disreputable family in Roknapatawpha County, chron-icled by William Faulkner.

Kathleen had to return home to be hostess at a fund-raising party for McGovern, and she was away when the raft was launched. When she returned, the *Snopes* had gone.

Seidensticker drove her to Columbus, Kentucky, about sixty miles down the river, where the *Snopes* was tied up for the night. She went on board and immediately heard hair-raising tales of woe. The raft had almost sunk, appropriately enough at a spot called Dogtooth Bend.

At Hickman, Kentucky, about fifteen miles downriver,

they pulled over the next day to refuel, and found that the outboard wouldn't start up again. They had mounted it six inches too deep in the water.

While trying to get it remounted, they were boarded by a Kentucky river patrol that wanted to make sure they were using the right kind of life preservers.

The river patrol leader, who turned out to be a county sheriff, asked them to show their boat license. None of them had ever heard they needed a boat license, and it took a day of their time to procure a suitable one from the sheriff. Then they were off again.

At Osceola, Arkansas, about seventy-five miles further on, they tried to go into a cove at night to tie up, but ran aground on a sand bar. Then the mosquitoes began to eat them alive, and they had to slosh on what David called "woodsman's fly dope" to ward them off.

That night a sixty-mile-an-hour gale blew up, complete with pounding rain. The raft's cabin had screens, but no windows. The five members held up a plastic sheet to try to keep the water out of the cabin.

Eventually the storm blew over, but they were all soaking wet.

At Memphis, Tennessee, they drove inland down to Oxford, Mississippi, the scene of Robert F. Kennedy's triumph during the years when he was attorney general. Oxford had been integrated, but with great opposition. The populace knew the Kennedy name, and greeted them by claiming that Kathleen's father was responsible for much "misunderstanding and destruction." They held Kathleen guilty as well.

Nevertheless, the travelers were able to meet William Faulkner's niece, and then returned to the river.

Another storm blew up, this one also lasting two days. When calm prevailed, they found the motor wouldn't start up. They had no lights because the lantern had broken in the storm and there were no batteries for the flashlights. They huddled in the dark, feeling miserable.

It was a memorable day: the Fourth of July, Kathleen's twentieth birthday!

When the storm passed, they sailed on after getting the outboard going, only to find themselves stranded on the left bank of the Mississippi River somewhere near Clarksdale, Mississippi.

At this point the outboard once again refused to start. David hung an American flag upside down in the time-honored tradition of the sea. But nobody would stop—in fact, no one even saw them.

They had brought aboard a light boat in case of emergency, but the oars had been washed over during the rainstorm. Nevertheless, Kathleen and Gary Carson set out in the light boat, letting it drift down in the heavy current.

Finally two fishermen helped them ashore, although the two men were quite suspicious of them. When they told their story, Kathleen let southerner Gary do the talking. The anglers finally drove them to the nearest store, which was about twenty miles from shore.

There they made contact with a boat engine repairman, who drove them out to the river and examined the outboard. There was as much water in the gasoline as there was gasoline; nothing was wrong with the outboard that proper fuel wouldn't start.

They made Greenville, Mississippi, that night, after traveling sixty miles in one day. Just as they were landing, David slipped and fell into the river, striking his head on the side of the raft on his way down.

Kathleen and Gary took him to the nearest hospital. Two hours later, he was still sitting in the emergency room waiting for help. Finally Kathleen did something she never believed in doing: she pulled rank by using her name and impressing it upon the hospital crew as to exactly which Kennedy she was.

In minutes, David was being attended to. The doctor took X-rays and found David had a hairline skull fracture. David was ordered to rest for a day.

Eventually the *Snopes* arrived at New Orleans. It was July 6. Just as they got there, the motor died for good. On July 8, Kathleen left for Miami, where she was scheduled to attend the Democratic Convention.

The rest of the group remained behind, trying to sell the raft "as is" for $150 and a ride to Jackson, Mississippi, but they had no takers. Eventually they were able to unload it for $35, dead outboard and all.

Nevertheless, in spite of their troubles, Kathleen thought the twenty-one days were, to borrow a nautical phrase, the high-water mark of her college career.

David Townsend thought it was time well spent, himself. In spite of all their landlubber's mistakes—setting the outboard too deep, losing the oars to the light boat, losing their lights, mixing water with their fuel supply—they had survived and lived as close to nature as you can in the river milieu.

On schedule, Kathleen checked into Miami's Doral Hotel dressed in blue jeans and carrying a cardboard box trussed with a rope as her luggage. It was not actually in the Kennedy style as approved by Rose Kennedy and Kathleen's assorted aunts, but it was in a thoroughly approved Kathleen Kennedy fashion.

The convention was mildly exciting, with McGovern nominated, as expected, for the presidency, and Senator Thomas F. Eagleton named vice-presidential candidate.

Nevertheless, startling things began happening in the Democratic campaign *after* the convention. Within several days of the announcement of the nominated candidates, a strange and disturbing story began surfacing regarding Eagleton's past. He had been under a psychiatrist's care, but had alerted no one to the fact.

An enormous flap ensued in the Democratic camp and Eagleton was dumped. In his place, McGovern chose Robert Sargent Shriver as vice-presidential candidate, and he accepted the nomination on August 8.

Now Kathleen had an uncle running for vice president!

Nevertheless, all her labors came to naught in November, when McGovern and Uncle Sargent were swamped by the Nixon juggernaut.

Kathleen was back in school at the time of the election, buckling down to her studies once again—and buckling down to a more personal thread of her life as well.

The following September, 1973, she and David Townsend were engaged to be married. The wedding was scheduled for November 17 at Holy Trinity Church in Washington.

She asked her surrogate father, Uncle Ted, the last of the Kennedy brothers, to give her away at the altar. He promised to do so, and plans went ahead for the wedding.

Ironically, the date set for the ceremonies was the same Saturday that Kathleen's cousin, Ted Jr., Senator Kennedy's eldest son, was in Washington's Georgetown University Hospital undergoing amputative surgery of his right leg.

It was touch and go whether or not Uncle Ted could get to the church in time to give the bride away. Kathleen smiled through it all. It was simply another challenge that the Kennedy persona must meet.

The wedding went off on schedule. The only Kennedy not there was Jacqueline Onassis, but she was really a Kennedy by marriage.

About 160 guests were present. Among the big names were John Glenn, the first astronaut, Frank Mankiewicz, Robert F. Kennedy's press secretary, Senator George McGovern and Mrs. McGovern, and Art Buchwald, the Washington columnist.

It was a mixture of formal and informal. Some of the men wore cutaway jackets, and the women formal dresses. Caroline, Courtney, and (Mary) Kerry Kennedy were maids of honor, with Aunt Jean Kennedy Smith the matron of honor. Six Kennedy brothers were ushers.

But where was the man who was going to give the bride away?

Sure enough, Uncle Ted arrived just before eleven o'clock, smiling through his tension, announcing that the surgery had gone well and that he was ready to give the bride away.

Andy Williams, long-time friend of the Kennedy family, sang *Ave Maria* and *Panis angelicus.* The gold rings that were exchanged by the bride and groom had been handcrafted by the groom himself.

Thus were Kathleen Kennedy and David Lee Townsend joined in holy matrimony.

The reception was held at Hickory Hill, the Ethel Kennedy estate. The wedding cake was baked in the replica of a raft, in memory of the unforgettable trip down the Mississippi which Kathleen and the groom had taken more than a year before.

As Kathleen and David rolled off in the rumble seat of a 1932 Packard, Uncle Ted went back to the hospital to be at the side of his son when he came out of the anesthesia.

The happy couple were off to an "undisclosed destination," after which they returned to an apartment in Cambridge. There they set up their household while Kathleen finished her senior year at Radcliffe.

David got a job teaching in Santa Fe, New Mexico, and after Kathleen's graduation, they moved there. Kathleen secured a job working for the Human Rights Commission in Santa Fe.

The newlyweds settled down in a rambling, barnlike house among some piñon trees in the countryside near Santa Fe. Their house was situated ten minutes from the nearest shopping center, and at least fifteen miles from their nearest neighbor.

Kathleen's work with the Indians had taught her how to acclimate herself to the rugged outdoors. In addition to those months spent on the reservations, she had also grown up during the 1960s, when American youths had taken up the "back-to-nature" movement with a vengeance.

The rambling house had a room almost entirely enclosed with glass, which the Townsends used to afford them "passive" solar heat. Kathleen's interior decorating involved placing pieces of driftwood about, along with desert vegetation and rocks. Heat was supplied by a potbellied stove—and this four years before the OPEC countries forced Americans to begin to conserve oil by using wood as fuel!

She and David had numerous books lining the walls, including works of Greek philosophy, Kant, Hegel, Spinoza, and French literature, along with science and math.

Settling down wasn't easy for Kathleen. "I just wasn't taught to be good around the house," she confessed. "I've had to learn." Her husband, however, was always capable domestically. He had been brought up in an atmosphere entirely different from Kathleen's.

Kathleen soon decided to fulfill another ambition she had been nurturing since her graduation from Radcliffe: to attend law school and get a law degree. She enrolled as a law student at the University of New Mexico near Albuquerque, and then got a part-time job working on a Santa Fe newspaper during the summer. In the summer of 1977 she was working as a law clerk in Santa Fe.

She had taken up law because she remembered how her father had once said that his legal experience had helped him a great deal when it came to his work in integrating the South. The law, to Kathleen, meant "doing something for the poor." It was, she knew, a challenge that was not easily met.

During the first few months of 1977 Kathleen found that she was pregnant. She and her husband saw no reason to interrupt their rugged lifestyle simply because they were to become parents. With the typical determination of her generation, she decided to respect her pregnancy by taking care of herself mentally and physically in order to experience a natural and healthy birth.

She exercised ritually, swimming an hour a day during her first months of pregnancy. During those months and up to the day she delivered, she walked long miles in the countryside. On the day the baby was born, she walked five miles in the woods around the house with her husband.

If the rest of the Kennedy family felt Kathleen was acting too "modern" or "selfish," no one actually did anything about it. Instead of attending a hospital as all the Kennedys of the older generation had, Kathleen chose to deliver her baby in the house at Santa Fe by natural childbirth. At the birth, both a doctor and a midwife were present to take care of any problems that might arise. None did.

On November 8, 1977, after twenty-two hours of labor, Meaghan Kennedy Townsend was born. It was an event of great significance in the Kennedy family: the first Kennedy to be born in the generation.

"Having a baby at home seemed a very sane thing to do," Kathleen said. "When you give birth at home, you know it's really your child."

Her second child, Maeve Fahey Kennedy Townsend, was born almost two years later on November 1, 1979, in New Haven, Connecticut, at the home of David's parents. Maeve also was delivered by natural childbirth.

Kathleen's life has settled down into a pleasant routine that enables her to be a mother, a wife, and also a career person with her studies in law, participation in local political causes, and work on law review articles.

She goes to school three days a week, and spends the rest of her time studying, keeping house, and looking for political causes to work at.

A writer who interviewed her describes her as a combination of her father and mother, with brown hair and brown eyes, a self-contained, direct person who wears no makeup, no other jewelry than a thin gold wedding band, and who favors slacks or a skirt and flat walking shoes.

"I want to live so that each day is crucial," Kathleen told the writer, "each day really important, so I will have lived each moment the best way I can, even if tomorrow isn't there."

Clearly she is a child of the 1960s, a product of the movement that stirred in the country during that decade and turned many Americans from their contemplation of the materialistic to a struggle to change the things that were inimical to humanity in their country.

"When I read," Kathleen says, "I read the classics." She points out that she's not *au courant,* as her grandmother would say.

Yet she is a product of the generation her father and her uncle strove to educate to the need for public service—a person who has a sense of her self and of the selves of millions of others and not simply of her own self-importance.

CHAPTER 5
Joseph Patrick Kennedy III

The first male grandson of Joseph P. Kennedy was born September 24, 1952, to Robert and Ethel Kennedy—and was named, appropriately enough, Joseph Patrick Kennedy.

He was named not for one man, but for two.

The first Joseph Patrick Kennedy was the patriarch of the Kennedy clan.

The second Joseph Patrick Kennedy had been killed when the World War II plane in which he was flying blew up in midair over the English Channel, killing him and everyone on board.

John F. Kennedy had always known that if his elder brother had not been killed, Joseph Patrick Kennedy II would have had first crack at the Kennedy political career.

As the first-born male Kennedy of the third generation, Joseph P. Kennedy III was in line to carry on the Kennedy tradition of political activity, public service, and special dedication to humanity.

Like his sister Kathleen, Joe was subjected to the extreme rigors of life that are normal to every young Kennedy. Early on, he was indoctrinated into the Kennedy syndrome of playing hard to win and exerting the maximum of physical effort in everything he did.

He learned to articulate as well as all Kennedys, took to argument happily, and exerted himself in the acceptable manner. He was just eleven years old when his Uncle Jack was murdered in Dallas. It affected him deeply, as it affected his brothers and sisters and cousins. More than that, he was old enough to see firsthand what it did to his own father.

Joe Kennedy's attitude toward life was one of freewheeling independence. He loved to brawl and indulge in physical feats with his brothers, sisters, cousins, and friends. He loved to lead his companions in daring physical tests of courage and panache. He was a big boy, and his activities built him into a strong young man.

Joe understood something that his sister Kathleen had never really perceived. Although she realized that the Kennedy family was privileged, Joe had a more practical concept of what privilege meant. It meant he could do pretty much what he wanted to do outside the family—if he toed the mark *within the family*.

He adhered to the ritual of the Kennedy household: discussion of current events, papers on statesmen and public figures, strict church attendance. But outside the house he knew he had more clout than his peers, and he began to use it whenever he could. He knew from the first that he was different because he was a Kennedy.

At school he got by with as little work as he could. He started out at Our Lady of Victory School, then transferred to Georgetown Prep, after which he switched to Milton Academy in Milton, Massachusetts. He felt that there was little need to excel in the academic world. He knew what made people famous—it was their ability to wield power. Joe knew teachers didn't wield much power. If he became a good student, what was there ahead for him except to teach?

To Joe, teaching was for women. As were most of the Kennedys, Joe was instinctively a male chauvinist.

As a result of his sage perceptions, Joe Kennedy never really applied himself to his school work through those youthful years. He got by—but barely.

His father tried to convince him that studying was all-important, but got nowhere with his oldest boy. When Ethel tried to prod him on to more scholastic effort, Joe rebelled. He and his mother had arguments that left them both smoldering.

Not that Joe didn't always go by the rules of the house. When his mother came into the room, he stood. When he had a paper due, he delivered it. And when he was supposed to speak, he did so.

But there was an underlying element of conflict between him and his mother.

Ethel Kennedy, however, had other children besides Joe to worry about. She could only cajole and bluster. Her concern left a small mark on Joe, but it did not turn him around in the right direction as far as his academic studies were concerned.

A boy brought up to understand the effectiveness of athletic ability, the clout of good looks, the power of money, was not going to change overnight to become a great scholar, or even a mediocre one.

It was four-thirty on the morning of June 6, 1968. Joe was asleep in his room at Milton Academy. Suddenly the light came on, and Joe woke up to find someone in the room with him. It was Richard Clasby, Uncle Ted's classmate at Harvard, and married to a Kennedy cousin.

"What is it?" Joe asked, but from the look on Clasby's face, he knew something terrible had happened. What had happened was that Joe's father had been shot by someone out in Los Angeles.

"I sat there in his little room and told him what had happened," Clasby related. "Joe didn't cry. But the expression on his face was one of terrible hurt. I'll never forget it."

They sat talking quietly the rest of the night. Then Clasby drove Joe down to the Cape where the family was gathering.

"Do you think he has a chance?" Joe kept asking. His father was not yet dead. "Do you think he can make it?"

Clasby couldn't answer.

They remained at the Cape for several hours, and then his mother telephoned from Los Angeles. Joe flew to Washington, where K. LeMoyne Billings, another family friend, flew west with him to see his unconscious father a few hours before he died.

Like his brothers and sisters, Joe was utterly shattered by this appalling turn of events. He had argued with his father, he had been afraid of him, he had yelled at him when his punishments seemed disproportionate—but he loved his father.

Now Robert F. Kennedy was dead.

There was only one adult Kennedy left—his Uncle Ted.

There were, of course, three Kennedy sisters of the same generation as his father, but they didn't count in Joe's male-oriented outlook. Nor were they actually Kennedys any longer; they were, instead, a Shriver, a Lawford, and a Smith.

And so it was that Joe and his Uncle Ted automatically were elected to bear the burden of Robert Kennedy's death. Joe helped take charge of the funeral arrangements. His mother ably bore the brunt of the unending publicity.

It was on the funeral train itself that Joe came into his own as a national figure. His father's body had been flown in from Los Angeles, had lain in state at St. Patrick's Cathedral in New York, and then had been placed aboard a funeral train bound from New York to Washington.

Joe took over for his mother. He spent most of the time while the train was moving toward Washington walking up and down the corridors and greeting everyone who was there—newsmen and television reporters as well—with the words:

"Hi, I'm Joe Kennedy. Thanks a lot for coming."

He knew what to do, and he did it well. He shook everyone's hand, even though for the first time in his life he was truly grief-stricken.

Now Joe really felt the weight of the family name. When his father had been there—tough, resilient, and vigorous—the pressure of public attention had been focused on him. His mother had taken some of the limelight as well, but only to a minor degree. Now there was a vacuum in the Robert Kennedy family. Both Joe and his mother felt it.

It should have sobered him up and produced a startling turnaround—a transfiguration similar to that of Prince Hal to King Henry V in Shakespeare's *Henry IV*. But it didn't.

Instead, when Joe returned to school he found himself in more and more trouble with his studies.

"It was too much for anybody to take," an observer at Milton Academy said. "His uncle had been murdered and had become a legend in America. Now his father, on his way to the presidency, had been cut down. Certainly this was enough to make any young man unable to concentrate on studying."

But one of his schoolmates felt differently about Joe. "It was a great excuse for him. He never was any good at studying. His father's assassination was the perfect shield for him to hide behind. And he used it."

One of Joe's teachers refused to accept the excuse that Joe had "more important" things on his mind.

"He wouldn't apply himself," the teacher said. "He didn't think he had to. He thought he was somehow exempt from having to work hard for good grades like everybody else."

Joe was heading into a familiar Kennedy cul-de-sac: rich, spoiled playboy.

The rift between him and his mother widened. She had many more details to take care of—running the family, and just being a Kennedy widow. She didn't have time to concentrate all her efforts on her oldest boy. And the younger ones were around the house, clamoring to be trained and taught.

The last of the Robert Kennedy children, Rory, was born six months after her father's murder. There were eleven children now. True, Uncle Ted tried to be surrogate father, but he was a busy man.

Joe felt himself somehow alienated from the family. No longer was he anchored to his kin by the strong ties with his father. He was growing fast, too, springing up into a lanky six-foot, muscular, good-looking, tawny-haired youth. He was tough, brash, and basically a swinger as were most of the male Kennedys.

He loved sports, and was especially adept at sailing. He spent summer after summer on the water, crewing transatlantic sailing races of all classes.

Because he was next to Ted Kennedy in the Kennedy line, the press woke up to Joe and began following him everywhere. He had gone on vacations before, but when he went now, he found reporters, photographers, and television crews hanging around him and peering into his life. At first it was fun, but then it got to be a bore, especially as the press he was getting turned sour.

He was in Seville, Spain, one month after his father's murder. The family had decided that the children should try to get away from the pressures of Washington and the tragedy of Robert Kennedy's murder.

When Joe, with his Uncle Ted, was visiting a field where baby bulls were tested, photographers coaxed him into trying a pass with a cape at a bull. Joe did so, waving the cloak the way he had seen people in the movies do it. He was scratched up and bloodied before it was over.

The picture was printed all around the world. It looked as if Joe was carrying on the flame of the death-defying, derring-do Kennedys and was stepping into his father's shoes.

They were very big shoes, however. Once the first enormous surge of interest in him had subsided, he found himself back at school, trapped in the academic grind with the same old problems cropping up once more.

Now, it was different. Now when he failed a course in school, the fact made the papers—not the headlines, certainly, but the "personality" columns. The press loved to poke fun at the rich, the powerful, and the famous. Joe began to get a very heavy dose of bad press in those few years.

"[There are] those of us who have had to learn quickly that publicity is a two-edged sword," he said later as he looked back at those rather mixed-up years of his life.

One summer Joe took out for the Northwest, where he spent some weeks learning how to be a guide for climbers of Mount Rainier, the peak that everyone who visits Seattle can see out the window. It is 14,408 feet high.

It was muscular, physically exhausting work, and he liked it. His mother even flew out to be with him, climbing four miles to Camp Muir at the two-mile level.

The physical effort of climbing was good therapy and he came home feeling better. It was 1970, and Uncle Ted's first Senate term was over. He was running for reelection to the Senate. The Kennedy family huddled, and it was decided that Joe should help out as an advance-man, even though he was only eighteen years old.

Joe asked for a leave of absence from Milton Academy, where he was entering his senior year. But since his grades were not good at all, the school refused to let him take the time off. He dropped out.

He did well, working for his uncle, going through all the prescribed motions he was expected to. He helped with the nitty-gritty details and acted as a kind of top-level go-for.

But if he was expected to take the bit in his teeth and run with it, as quite probably many of his Kennedy peers and elders expected him to do, he disappointed one and all by his rather remote attitude toward the business.

In November, after the successful election of his uncle, he enrolled for his senior year at Manter Hall, a day school on Mt. Auburn Street in Cambridge, and the following June he graduated.

"He's no mathematician," Headmaster Robert G. Hall said of Joe.

But he did earn a 90 in economics, 92 in modern European history and 81 in English.

On the strength of that, he applied to Stanford University in Palo Alto, California, but they turned him down. In fact, he never did apply to Harvard, where the patriarch and his father and uncles had gone. He applied to the University of California at Berkeley and was accepted.

To prepare for his work at Berkeley, he attended seminars at the Massachusetts Institute of Technology in Cambridge. He felt they would help him get into the swing of college study.

The Kennedy wanderlust took him to Africa in 1971, where he found himself working with an ABC-TV "American Sportsman" television crew making a documentary on animals in Kenya. The crew was following an expedition sponsored by the East African Wildlife Society. The purpose of the expedition was similar to a Wild West cowboy roundup: to gather and lead wild African antelopes from the wilds to a newly created national park.

The roan antelope is a huge, nasty animal, particularly the African version. It is orange-brown with ugly scimitar-shaped horns, weighing from 400 to 700 pounds. The roundup of these animals was a dusty, dirty, hairy affair. The antelope herd leader took a sudden dislike to Joe when the noise of a helicopter overhead frightened it.

Suddenly, it turned on him, lowered its head, and went after Joe's mount. The horse tried to dodge aside, but took the assault in the chest. Joe was almost shaken loose. Had he been thrown to the ground, he would have been trampled to death.

He hung on for dear life, and the horse kept on its feet too. Finally, the group was able to get the antelopes into the proper corral.

Early in 1972, Joe accompanied his Uncle Ted on a visit to Bangladesh, where the senator was acting as chairman of a Senate subcommittee on refugee problems.

They saw long lines of unemployed, shutdown jute mills, hospitals that were full of war-wounded and short of medicines. They viewed burned-out houses, ravaged land, and exhumed victims of a massacre in Kushtia.

It was an eye-opening visit for Joe.

At the end of the visit in Bangladesh, Joe made a week-long tour of India by motorcycle. After that was finished, he boarded a Lufthansa 747 jumbo jet in New Delhi for the first leg of his trip home.

Suddenly, as the ship took off, Joe found himself in the middle of a skyjacking. Twenty minutes after take-off, five Palestinian Arabs, jittery and unnerved, went running through the plane waving pistols and hand grenades.

The jet was ordered to Aden in South Yemen. The Arabs had seized the West German air carrier as a protest of West Germany's financial and material support for Israel.

"Put your hands on top of your head!" yelled one of the hijackers at Joe.

When Joe didn't move quickly enough, he whacked him on the shoulder with a pistol.

Joe put his hands on top of his head.

The plane was finally ransomed off for $5 million as it sat on the field at Yemen and the 168 passengers were released after at least twenty-four hours of terror.

When reporters asked Joe how he felt about the skyjacking, he said: "I've been scared before, but never for so long. It was just too much!"

Once again back in the States, Joe decided to spend some time working for the Robert F. Kennedy Memorial Organization, helping the dedicated young people who were carrying on his father's work. The program awards fellowships to activists, assigning them to work all across the country in poverty, civil rights, and other community projects.

Joe became a special consultant, whose job it was to visit each of the thirty fellows wherever they were working. For this, he received a small salary.

His first port of call was in San Diego County, where his host and guide Dennis McGee, an Indian and a graduate of San Diego State, was working with 4,000 undernourished California Mission Indians.

Joe visited seventeen reservations in the county, walking up and down sun-baked streets, talking to the people, and seeing firsthand the grinding poverty.

"In the evenings," McGee recalled, "we'd have rap sessions until far into the night. Joe would ask probing questions, just like his dad used to do, to take back as much information as he could about conditions here."

Next came a trip to Jackson, Mississippi, where Aaron Turner was working with delinquent black children. Then Watts. He walked through reservations in Arizona, visited camps of migrant farm laborers, spent weeks in the streets of big-city ghettos.

In the fall he enrolled in Berkeley, but he was already deeply involved in working for George McGovern. Like his sister, he went on the road for him, worked with friends, and made a few personal appearances for the presidential candidate and his uncle, Sargent Shriver.

What he said did not set the political world on fire. Most people could believe he was a Kennedy when they saw him: he was freckled, tousle-headed, blue-eyed, tall, athletic, cocky, and *noticeable*.

Yet when he opened his mouth, the Kennedy impression quickly faded. He might be a ringer, for his father or uncles, but he did not speak with the typical "Cape Cawd" accent of his father or his uncles. He spoke with a typical nonregional accent. He had grown up in Washington, of course, and he was used to traveling with all kinds of people and in all kinds of places. He was not of any particular region. He was of the world.

Yet he did well enough to decide that politics was fun. He decided that if he got another chance, he would come back into the political water.

He never gave Berkeley a chance, really. He attended a few classes, read a few books, but it was no use. Even though McGovern and Shriver had lost the election, Joe found that he thrived on the kind of give-and-take and hustle that was involved in a campaign. He liked to work with people more than with ideas and words. He liked the stand-up confrontations and the behind-the-scenes manipulations that went on.

Joe Kennedy was an outside man, not an inside man. Books and lectures made him yawn. He was getting nowhere in the Halls of Ivy. His teachers could see that easily enough. His grades showed it. He had one more exchange with his mother, and then, fed up with almost everything academic, familiar, and parental, he dropped out of Berkeley in February 1973, and paid a visit to an old family friend, Joseph L. Alioto, who, coincidentally, was then mayor of San Francisco, just across the Bay from Berkeley.

Alioto, knowing the magic of the Kennedy name, suggested he come to work for the city as a social worker in its extensive health program. Joe agreed. Technically, he would be working for Dr. Francis Curry, the public health director of San Francisco. Joe would get $748 a month.

The section in which he was put to work dealt primarily with federally-funded programs set up to control tuberculosis and venereal disease in predominantly black areas. His job description was that of "coordinator of federally funded health programs."

But all was not well in the famed city of cable cars and fog. Like any other city of comparable size, politics was always in full swing. One city supervisor especially didn't take to Joe Kennedy—or *any* Kennedy for that matter. He publically made an issue of Joe's job.

"I'm wondering as to why this particular person was hired," city supervisor John L. Molineri observed to the press. "There may be other people who are better qualified."

Mayor Alioto had his own press conference. He said that he was "impressed by the young man."

Molineri wouldn't allow the mayor to have the last say. He got support from friends and they went to work. Joe wasn't allowed to forget for one moment he was a Kennedy.

Within two days, he had received at least sixty hostile telephone calls about his job, people obviously having been aroused by the hassle developing in the higher echelons of the city.

Then Joe held a press conference, too. He talked about himself. And then he zeroed in on Washington in a typical, roundabout political manner. "You realize the mistrust of higher officials and what government is doing among these people," he told them. "They see countless programs being cut by the administration and feel helpless."

The administration Joe referred to was, of course, the Nixon administration in Washington, a Republican one. Joe was simply following tried and true political rules when he attacked at the top.

But the sixty phone calls and the trouble always simmering just under the surface unnerved Joe. He played the game for four weeks, and then quite suddenly he threw in the towel.

He went in to talk to Curry.

"I can do more good if I am not a city employee," Joe told him.

After some discussion, Curry shrugged and admitted he was probably right. He accepted his resignation with regret. Curry told the press:

"He worked real hard, going from early morning to late at night. I think he did some good and some definite pluses will come out of this."

Joe had vaguely hinted to Curry that he might come back to do some volunteer work, but he never did.

"I remember him," a person close to him in the office of public health said. "He was pretty snooty about the job. But the fault wasn't all on his side. He knew he was being used, and he didn't like it after a while. He thought they'd put him to work on important things. But they just stuck him in the corner to show him off when they needed the glamour. I don't blame him for getting out."

And, of course, there was more bad press. Joe went into seclusion. He was at a crossroads in life, and he had the sense to know it even though he couldn't seem to do anything about it.

The choices were obvious: he could get back to school and finish up his college career by getting a degree; or he could get into politics, which was probably the easiest course, and play on the Kennedy name.

The latter choice bothered him. He didn't want to use the Kennedy name in that fashion. He wanted to prove himself, not his background. He was annoyed with himself for his inability to buckle down with the books and get good grades like everyone else in his family.

He was at an emotional impasse. His anger was inner-directed, his energy was outer-directed, but the two forces canceled one another out. He found himself unable to make any positive decisions regarding his future.

Several days later, on March 24, he was driving through the darkened streets of Berkeley when a car swerved into his car. Joe tried to swing out of the way, but was propelled into a parked car.

The car that had hit him was driven by a sixteen-year-old who was not hurt. Joe was not so lucky. Suffering from chest, skull, and neck injuries, he was placed in the Intensive Care Unit of Herrick Memorial Hospital, for observation.

He did suffer a slight brain concussion, but X-rays showed he had no broken bones.

It was a strange and bizarre ending to an adventure that had started out so well for him at the University.

In the hospital, those two days after the accident, Joe had enough time to look at his life and wonder where he was going. He was horrified at the image of himself that he saw projected in the newspapers and magazines. Was he really just a spoiled playboy who had too much money and no ambition or talent?

Was he actually acting out a psychodrama in which he had become the victim of his own ineptitude, the victim of his own desire to destroy himself? A psychologist could easily have analyzed his past actions as exactly that.

The upshot of this critical emotional confrontation was to flee the West Coast scene. He pulled up stakes completely, and went back home to Massachusetts. He knew he was drifting. But there was nothing he could lash his line to. He envied his sister Kathleen, who at the time was following the legacy of their father and was working for the underprivileged. Joe couldn't seem to get a handle on himself.

He decided to try school again, for the third time. He was able to get his credits transferred from Berkeley to the University of Massachusetts in Dorchester, and was all set to start the semester in September, when another Kennedy tragedy struck.

Ironically, it struck not twenty-five miles from where another Kennedy tragedy had only recently struck at Chappaquiddick Bridge.

Joe was spending a few days on Nantucket Island with his brother David, staying with a family friend in Siasconsett, the only other town besides Nantucket on the island. They had come over from the Cape on Sunday, August 12.

On Monday, they met some girls they knew from Centerville, a town near Hyannis Port, and a group of them went swimming at the beach at Siasconsett. Later that afternoon they decided to drive over to Nantucket, and Joe borrowed the Toyota owned by his host, Peter Van Dyke Emerson.

There were seven of them in the car as they rode off toward Nantucket across the island on the Polpis Road at about 2:30 in the afternoon. Besides Joe and David there were Pamela and Kim Kelley, two sisters from Centerville; Patricia Powers, from Spring Lake, New Jersey; Mary Schlaff, from Grosse Pointe, Michigan; and Francesca de Onis, from Centerville, a friend of the family whose father was a *New York Times* foreign correspondent.

It was crowded in the car, which someone described later as having a capacity of four people. Still another witness said, "People were hanging all over. Some were standing up."

Although the details are still not clear, the Toyota was approaching an intersection about three miles outside of town on the narrow two-lane road when Joe overtook a sightseeing bus. As reconstructed by *Newsweek,* the following took place:

There was little room to pass the bus, and Joe detoured to the left into a crescent-shaped bypass that rejoins the main road within a few hundred yards. When Joe emerged from the crescent bypass, he was on the narrow main road ahead of the bus.

The intersection was dead ahead. Suddenly a car approached the main road from the intersecting road at Joe's left. In order to avoid hitting the car, Joe accelerated the car and shot across the crossroad, narrowly missing the other car.

He swerved onto the shoulder of the narrow road, but there wasn't enough room for Joe to maneuver, and the car turned over, spilling the occupants out of the car.

At the time Joe swerved to avoid the oncoming car, the Toyota was going about fifteen miles an hour, Francesca de Onis testified at a later trial.

The driver of the other vehicle said that he had been driving at from 35 to 40 miles an hour when he saw the Toyota "coming toward me in my lane." He said he braked his car and swerved left just as the driver of the Toyota swerved to the right and accelerated.

"I thought we were going to make it when the car got back on the pavement—and then it flipped," de Onis said in court. "I was horrified."

If Joe had not speeded up, it was brought out in court, the oncoming car would have "cut them in half."

Whatever the details, the Toyota went out of control, spun over, and crashed into a tree after ploughing through the underbrush alongside the road. The car was demolished. All seven occupants were thrown clear of it before it crashed.

When the dust cleared, the police arrived. Then ambulances followed. Everyone had some kind of injury, with the possible exception of Joe.

David had sustained a back injury, and it was not known how bad it was.

Mary Schlaff had a broken pelvis and a broken right leg.

Pamela Kelley had a badly injured back.

Kim Kelley had a small fracture in her right leg.

Patricia Powers had neck, back, and waist injuries.

Francesca de Onis had bruises.

Joe was immediately issued a citation for "operating a vehicle negligently, so that the lives and safety of the public might be endangered."

Ambulances carried the victims first to All-Nantucket Cottage Hospital for preliminary examination. Then they were flown by helicopter to Cape Cod Hospital at Hyannis.

There David was found, happily, to have no fracture of the spine. He was sedated and put to bed.

Mary Schlaff was hospitalized with a broken pelvis and leg.

Pamela Kelley was in the most pain. Her spine was fractured, and the lower part of her body paralyzed.

The others were treated and released.

Immediately the Kennedy family moved in and had consultants in orthopedic surgery and neurosurgery flown in from the Leahy Clinic in Boston. The next day, Pamela Kelley underwent surgery for three hours.

At a hearing held on August 20 in the Nantucket District Court, Joe was found guilty of negligence. Present with him were his mother and Uncle Ted. Joe pleaded not guilty in a court that was crowded to the doors.

Judge George Anastas of the District Court had been a college classmate of Joe's namesake, his father's older brother who had died in World War II.

"Do you believe that a jail sentence is a deterrent to high-way accidents?" the judge asked Joe.

"No, Your Honor, I do not," Joe replied. "I think that a seriously hurt person is more a deterrent to a defendant in a highway accident case."

The prosecutor did not recommend a jail sentence on the charge. It was a disdemeanor carrying a maximum jail term of up to two years or a $200 fine or both.

Joe was fined $100.

"You had a great father and have a great mother," the judge told Joe. "Use your illustrious name as an asset in-stead of coming into court like this."

Joe's brother David eventually recovered completely, but he was in pain for some time and was given medication to alleviate it. This medication led to complications in his life later on. But the sprained back was completely cured.

The two injured girls fared worse than David. One of them, Mary Schlaff, who had been injured in the pelvis and right leg, was still walking with a pronounced limp at least a year later.

But it was Pamela Kelley who suffered the worst in-juries. She remained paralyzed from the waist down and will be confined to a wheelchair for the rest of her life. The insurance settlement made by the Kennedys' policy paid $1 million to Pamela Kelley.

It was about her that Joe brooded the most. But there was nothing he could now do about it. That moment of deci-sion was long past.

The days following the accident were the worst of Joe's life. He reached the depths of despair. He underwent torments of guilt. Now it was not just himself he was hurting in his de-structive flight from whatever demons tortured his psyche.

He had permanently maimed two young women and he had almost killed his brother David.

Somehow, during long periods of introspection that took place during that time, he managed to come to terms with himself. He recognized the dark forces that were at work within himself, even if he did not fully understand them. Was it the grief and hurt he had experienced at the murders of his uncle and father? Was it the fears of a man afraid to meet the challenge of his own destiny?

Whatever it was, Joe made up his mind to fight it, just as his father had taught him to do in meeting any challenge head-on.

"The fact is," Joe was quoted in a *Newsweek* article some years after that, "I am who I am, and I'm never going to change that."

But he did change.

The decade of the permissive 1960s was over. The 1970s were off and rolling. Joe began cutting his curly hair shorter. He began wearing fancy ties with heraldic designs on them rather than tee shirts with open collars. He began paying more attention to the people about him than he had before.

Somewhere along the line he made up his mind to begin paying back the world for all the good things it had heaped up on him. He took his cue from his sister Kathleen.

The first sign of a positive return to a lifestyle of his own was a serious attempt to buckle down to books at the University of Massachusetts to work for a degree. He gave up his night life for a time, and even confined his carousing to a very few hours of the week.

He worked *hard* at his studies.

His grades, while not what an intellectual would think adequate, were better than those he had attained at Berkeley. During the following summer he took a job helping out at the Boys Club in Dorchester, where the college is located.

In addition to the job at the Boys Club, where he devised ways to get summer programs funded by governmental groups, he worked in South Boston for a wealthy philanthropist in a program that was pure delight for Joe. He taught young blacks how to sail a sailboat! It was a sport Joe had always loved and was an expert at.

"The sailing program may not sound like much," Joe told a newspaper reporter, "but it meant a lot to a bunch of kids, and it kept them off the streets in the summer."

Joe began to sense the exultation his sister Kathleen had already experienced during her summers with the Indians.

Working hard, Joe made it through the University, and with all his accumulated credits from other colleges, he finally graduated in the summer of 1975 with a degree in legal services. A family conclave was held, at which the clan discussed Joe's future. He was offered a job in Chicago with one of the Kennedy family's main enterprises.

In 1945 Joseph Patrick Kennedy had made the investment that eventually became the bulwark of the Kennedy family fortune: the purchase of the Merchandise Mart in Chicago. The building with its nineteen stories was an enormous structure, with 4,200,000 square feet of office space in it. Originally constructed by Marshall Field at a cost of $32 million, the building opened for business in 1930. By 1954, with at least one-third of its floor space leased by the U.S. government at very low rent, the building was floundering in debt.

But Joe, Sr., had contacts in Washington who tipped him off that the government would soon be vacating its Mart offices at the expiration of their leases. That meant that at least 1,300,000 square feet bringing in less than $1 a square foot would be empty for new and more profitable leases.

The building was valued at $21 million in 1945, $11 million less than it cost to build it—a fact hard to believe in today's inflationary spiral. But Joe didn't even pay $21 million for it; he got it for $13 million.

Nor did much of that come out of his own pocket. He borrowed $12.5 million on a mortgage, and put up $1 million for broker commissions and legal expenses. Then, four years later, he refinanced the mortgage for $17 million. Even at that point, he had recovered four times his original investment, and was equity owner of the Mart.

With Joe Kennedy III's uncle, Steven Smith, the head of

Park Agency the family could promise Joe a good job there, working in the executive offices and helping manage the enormous building, which today yields $25 million in revenues yearly.

But Joe decided not to take the job. He had been bitten by the political bug and had made up his mind to keep his hand in. He told a magazine writer that he didn't consider himself "locked in on politics," but he did say that it had "a flavor I really haven't seen anywhere else."

Whether he *saw* the flavor or *tasted* it, he was sure of what he wanted, and the waiting around, the marking time, the backing and filling were over.

The fall after he graduated with his legal services degree, he went to work as a juvenile court probation officer in Boston. He was continuing on the track he had followed during his summers in college. Visiting the slums of Boston, he discovered that he had a tremendous empathy for the pains and the problems of the poor.

"What was so unbelievable at first," he said, "was that it was the same problems coming up over and over again in each case. Family problems."

And these problems were what landed the poor into the hands of the law, time after time. Joe settled quickly into the work, eating it up as he advanced from case to case.

He carried a name that the poor recognized and respected. That was part of the battle. But the main reason for success was in Joe's own soul. He knew he had found something to strive for, something that challenged him and drew him on, something that he could take pride in.

He was deep into the work when his Uncle Ted called him in one day.

"I'm running for reelection next year, Joe," Uncle Ted told him. "I want you to help me."

Joe said he would help.

"I want you to manage my campaign." Uncle Ted leaned back and looked at his nephew.

"Wow," Joe said softly to himself. "Sure."

"It won't be easy," said Uncle Ted. He then went on to explain that the Boston school busing dispute had made Ted Kennedy vulnerable in the Boston precincts. In the traditional Irish-American strongholds such as Charlestown and South Boston, he might even lose.

Joe took the job.

A cliff-hanger of a campaign never developed, but Joe plunged right in and learned the ropes. He learned everything the hard way—how to work with the people and the processes that make politics work. This, according to one magazine comment, is "a greening that is essential—and with the Kennedys traditional—if [Joe] is eventually to pursue a political career of his own."

It was inevitable that the public would be curious about the oldest male of the third Kennedy generation. When he visited the Statehouse in Boston, he was accorded the deference due a Bay State dynast. On certain occasions, he stood in for his uncle at headlined events like the opening of Russian ballet defectors Valery and Galina Panov. His appearances frequently occurred at his uncle's side, drawing squeals and requests for autographs from men, women, and children.

During the campaign one development produced a self-deprecating amusement from the candidate: there were more press requests for interviews with Joe, the candidate's manager, than with Ted Kennedy himself.

That led to the frequent use of Joe as a replacement for the candidate, allowing Ted Kennedy to be, in effect, two places at once.

Joe's obvious charisma led *Newsweek* to devote almost a page to him during the summer campaign.

"Though he can talk enthusiastically about petition drives, voter identification, and the selection of area coordinators, even 23-year-old [Joe Kennedy] would not claim that his managerial talents are crucial to Senator Kennedy's political future," the magazine said.

And it brought the public up to date on the third-generation Kennedy torchbearer.

"In appearance he is unmistakably a Kennedy, with the strong jaw, the toothy smile and a barrel chest that seem to make him a composite of all the Kennedy brothers. People who know him say that [Joe] is less moody than either his father or Uncle Ted and more like President Kennedy in temperament."

The magazine hinted at a possibility that Joe might actually be thinking about running for the Massachusetts seventh congressional district seat vacated in 1976 by the death of Torbert MacDonald, his Uncle Jack's roommate at Harvard. But of course that was only a trial balloon of sorts; the magazine itself admitted that Joe was still "two years shy of meeting the constitutional age requirement for congressmen."

One colleague who worked with him during the campaign summed it up this way:

"Joe grew up a lot in 1975 and 1976. He was in fact, as well as in name, the campaign manager. He also reached the point where he could and did establish a new relationship with Ted Kennedy. He talked back to him. He argued strategy with him. This was no longer a boy dealing with a sort of surrogate father. This was a politician dealing with a politician. I think Joe became to Teddy what Teddy had been to Jack and, after Jack died, to Bobby."

Another observer of the campaign said: "Young Joe is bright and his troubles have tempered him. It's only logical that they push him forward now."

And there was no question in anybody's mind that Joe improved in his politicking. "He got so he could work a crowd better than his uncle," one co-worker said. "And I think that when he started giving interviews, particularly one on CBS with Morton Dean, he was really surprised at how good he was. Somehow, when he said it, it sounded good. He's much better than Bobby (his brother) at joshing people. He's got the pure Kennedy charm."

Nevertheless, there were some criticisms of his work. One friend conceded that Joe wasn't "issue-oriented," but was good at schedules, finances, and advertising—the nuts and bolts of campaigning—rather than the theoretical stuff.

"He turned out a lot brighter than I thought," one worker said. "I think almost everyone would agree to that."

By some he was considered "too damned aloof." Joe did not condescend to join the staff for late-night eating and drinking after a rigorous day.

"He didn't 'rap' enough with the rank and file," one rank-and-filer complained.

Upon being reproached for that, Joe responded by explaining that he spent a great deal of his time late at night attending meetings for the next day's work.

During his last years in college, Joe had developed a tendency to lose his temper, quite like his father. But, like most Kennedys, he was quick to forgive. That did not mean that he was quick to forgive deep wounds—like his Uncle Jack, on the bigger issues, Joe had a memory like an elephant.

Like other Kennedys, his Catholicism remained deeply inculcated in him. In Boston, he instructed his speech writers to include the phrase "with God's help" in every closing paragraph of his speeches.

He was as much his mother's son as his father's son. One night when he was going over a speech he was to give the following day, he decided that he needed a good opening joke to catch the attention of the crowd. He decided that the thing to do was to call Woody Allen and get one from him.

It was close to midnight, but Joe got on the telephone and placed a call to the famed comedian. He got his joke.

Needless to say, Uncle Ted won the campaign and was reelected to the U.S. Senate.

Working the campaign earned Joe a new confidence that he had never really felt before. He learned how to ask for advice, and to use it. On the other hand, he let his own instincts determine what path to take.

For example, during the campaign, a good many of the political consultants suggested that he rely heavily on paid television time. The best campaign to run, the sages said, was a totally media-oriented blitz.

Joe was suspicious of this advice, even though it came from people like long-time aides of Uncle Ted and his uncle Steve Smith. He went against their advice and decided not to rely on an electronic media campaign.

He used television and print, but he also demanded that some money be set aside to organize volunteer groups. With good political instincts, he sensed the need for a personal rapport between the candidate and the voters.

He sailed against the wind and won the race. There was a great deal of pressure to depend on television, and he was criticized strongly for going against the best advice available. But it worked anyway. He did a good job.

"We won the primary through organization," one aide said, "and Joe is the guy who organized it."

Joe impressed one close Kennedy friend of many years who worked with him in the campaign. "The last few years, he's changed. He's more serious, more interested in the problems of the country, taking a more active interest in political and public life. He reads the newspapers now, whereas a few years ago I do not think he did."

"He showed a lot of insight," another co-worker said. "He could look at a situation and make a gut judgment that usually turned out to be right."

Gut judgments that turn out right have always been a Kennedy trademark.

Campaign workers who were with him day and night were never able to determine where he lived. Nor were his working colleagues ever able to identify his nonworking companions. Joe was something alien to them. Most politicians and political workers—especially the Kennedys—always share their private lives and public lives.

Joe's had become compartmentalized.

One of them said, "Whatever Joe does—and I frankly don't know if he does anything—he does in a group so small and so close that he doesn't have to worry about someone running to the *Boston Globe* or *The National Enquirer*. I think that's the real reason Joe never joined the campaign staff for late-night partying. He was close to many of them, but not that close. He couldn't be sure someone would not be counting the number of beers, noting the time he got home, etc. I say this without knowing that he does anything more serious than watch Johnny Carson at night. I don't know and he doesn't want me to know."

After Joe's successful completion of his college education and his reentry into politics as his Uncle Ted's campaign manager, his relationship with his mother improved greatly. He would telephone her once or twice a week and exchange gossip and family confidences.

He had always been close to his nearest brother, Robert F. Kennedy, Jr.—"Bobby Junior." The sibling rivalry that existed between John F. Kennedy and Robert F. Kennedy did not really exist between Joe and Bobby, Jr.

Frequently during his campaign days he visited or saw his brother either at Harvard, where Bobby was in school, or at his own apartment. David and Michael were also students at Harvard at the same time, and the four of them saw quite a lot of each other. Cousins Shriver, Smith, and Lawford, all of whom frequented the Boston area, were also present more than once.

The other brothers and sisters were not around Boston but in Washington (Kathleen), California (Courtney), Vermont (Kerry), and McLean, Virginia (Christopher, Max, Douglas, and Rory).

Even after the campaign, Joe kept up his work with the indigent. Whereas his earlier vacations or long weekends had tended to take him to exotic spots of the world, Joe's recreation now tended in a slightly different direction.

Joe took a job in Washington with the Community Services Administration. In April 1977, he made a 2,000 mile flight north to Frobisher Bay during a four-day holiday. The trip was made in the company of Wayne Owens, an excongressman from Utah who was then president of a large Mormon mission that included some Arctic Circle Eskimo villages. There, Joe lived with the Eskimos in exactly the same fashion as his sister Kathleen had. He joined them in eating raw meat, hunting, and doing the day-to-day things Eskimos do.

This kind of activity pleased his mother.

"Joe has a natural sympathy for, and an easy way with, people," she said, "so it's not surprising to me that he feels drawn to public service."

Yet the need for secrecy in his private life continued to pull at Joe, keeping him from becoming a typical media personality like his father and uncles.

He continued to indulge in physical sports the way he always had. Sailing would take up most of his time. On shore, touch football was his favorite, as it had been for years with all Kennedys. Or he might take off and go climb a mountain somewhere. He always kept himself in shape jogging daily.

He had never paid much attention to his clothes, and had once appeared at an unexpected campaign stop without a necktie. In order to save the occasion, he rushed out to buy one on the spot—one that was "horrible," according to his colleagues.

"When he gets some extra money," said a college friend, "he's more likely to invest in new sports gear than in clothes."

There was always a great deal of speculation about Joe's private life. Did he have a girl friend? Was he going with anyone steadily?

"Like most unmarried young men of twenty-four," one newspaper article gushed, "Joe has a girlfriend, whose privacy he also is determined to maintain. He admits she is 'special' and he zealously tries to keep her name out of print."

In 1978, Joe resigned his job with the Community Services Administration and moved to Boston where he suddenly purchased a modest home in Brighton, a working-class section of Boston, for about $30,000. Rumors were immediately flying. For what reason would Joe Kennedy III buy a home in a working-class section of Boston unless he meant to make a run for the congressional district covered by the area? When was Joe III going to declare?

Soon the rumors died down. Joe did not make any announcement, nor did he make any attempt to run for office. He did not even gather about him any group of possible political allies.

But later in the year the gossips found a great deal more to talk about. He announced that he was engaged to Sheila Brewster Rauch. She was a Philadelphia Main Line girl who was well known among the elite in the City of Brotherly Love, and a debutante too.

Joe had met her at Harvard, where she had studied urban planning, receiving both baccalaureate and masters degrees there. She seemed eminently suitable as a Kennedy wife of the current younger-generation Kennedys. After all, Joe was twenty-seven. He was getting on in years and would have to marry soon enough.

But there were two odd facts about Rauch that started the gossips' tongues wagging almost instantly.

First of all, Sheila Rauch was thirty years old—older than Joe by almost three years! No male Kennedy had ever married anyone older than himself. It simply wasn't heard of.

Second of all, and most shocking, Rauch was an Episcopalian, not a Catholic! Further investigation revealed that Rauch had reportedly agreed to raise any children as Catholics, thus satisfying what might easily be Rose Kennedy's stipulations on the marriage.

Gossip or no gossip, the two were married in February 1979, with the usual media coverage, but then as soon as it was over Joe and his bride sank out of sight again. Since his automobile accidents in 1973, Joe had grown increasingly obsessive about his privacy.

His thoughts and actions were now concentrated on the construction of the John F. Kennedy Library, situated at the former site of the Boston city dump. Designed by I. M. Pei, the facility would be a $15 million structure, just adjacent to the University of Massachusetts in Dorchester.

As the building continued to rise and neared completion, Joe was put in charge of coordinating the activities set for the inauguration sometime in 1979.

Since he was actually eligible to run for Congress in 1977, many of his co-workers in the 1976 campaign were looking around for hints that he might be staking out the area for political conquest.

It never materialized.

Joe's involvement in his marriage, the purchase of his house, and the Kennedy Library took up most of his time. His wife had gone to work in Boston, where she served as an urban affairs specialist for the city.

In October 1979, the Library was finally opened and dedicated. President Jimmy Carter and Senator Edward M. Kennedy were there, along with Joe. It was thought that Joe would take the back seat and let the other men carry the day.

But when he rose to speak, he confounded the experts and came out with the most political speech of the day, much more pointed than that used by the two men who would be rivals for the Democratic presidential nomination in 1980.

Asserting that our nation had "a long way to go, both ethically and politically," Joe pointed out that the profits of big oil and coal and "the concentration of wealth and power" were in the wrong hands, and should be "the people's business."

He went on: "Now we are told by the chairman of the Federal Reserve that we have to reduce our standard of living. But what about the standard of living of the people on the boards of the oil companies? Who's stopping them?"

During his speech there was, in one reporter's words, "an uneasy shifting of chairs in the audience."

Joe went on to recall his own father's struggle against "vested interests" on behalf of the downtrodden—migrant workers, blacks, Chicanos, Indians, Eskimos, the poor of Appalachia, and the ordinary working people, who, as he said, "too often get a raw deal from those thinking of themselves as their betters, their leaders."

When it was all over, and the dust had settled, some of the knowledgeable were offended, but most of them felt that Joe had upstaged the two main protagonists of the day, his uncle and the president.

Pierre Salinger, press secretary of President Kennedy, was now working for the media. He called it "a rousing speech, a speech of the 1980s—definitely the wave of the future."

And if it was a wave of the future, the future was already here—and had been here even the night before the festivities at the Kennedy Library. It was then that what journalist William H. Honan called "the largest collection of Kennedys and Kennedyites ever assembled under one roof" met to talk about the future presidency of Ted Kennedy.

The "Kennedy network" included two dozen of the Kennedy children—"shepherded," as Honan wrote, "by Joseph P. Kennedy III, at twenty-seven the eldest son of Robert."

Not all of Uncle Ted's associates admired the younger generation of Kennedys. Many thought them too brash, too conceited, too obsessed with their own prestige. And most of the elders suspected that the young might be just a bit too wet behind the ears to know what really was happening, especially in a tricky game like politics.

Several of them who had watched Joe III's band of youngsters in action during the senatorial reelection campaign of Ted Kennedy in 1976 had noticed the arrogance and pride of the new generation.

One said wryly: "They were totally absorbed with Joe, and if they had some foggy idea that maybe one of his uncles had once been president of the United States, and that some of the older people in the campaign might know what they were doing, they never showed it."

Nevertheless, now was the time to get in the boat and all lend a hand at the oars. Immediately the Kennedy network met, and sections were mapped out for each of the experts— including sections for every member of the younger generation.

Joe drew Iowa, where a state caucus was being held instead of an ordinary primary. Nevertheless, the caucus was being deliberately blurred by the media to make it appear to the public as if it were an honest-to-God primary. In fact, it was being touted as a bellwether for the coming political campaign.

Iowa was Joe's first national political responsibility. He was to act as Uncle Ted's surrogate and chief operative. The Kennedy showing in the caucuses was said to be "crucial," and at the time the group met, the polls were pointing toward a dead heat between the president and Kennedy.

From the first, Joe worked his tail off. His assignment was to get out among the people in Iowa, shake hands, and talk to them. A caucus is not a primary, yet the political mechanics are pretty much the same. Whereas in a primary everybody belonging to a party is allowed to vote for the candidate, a caucus is a selection of delegates from the public-at-large, selected to vote on the candidate.

From the beginning of the Iowa campaign, Joe ran into trouble. As reported by a national magazine, a typical exchange between Joe and a white-haired woman went like this:

"Hi, I'm Joe Kennedy. Are you going to help my Uncle Ted?"

The woman looked at him consideringly. "The Kennedys have sacrificed an awful lot for this country. Maybe it's best that Ted shouldn't do this."

Joe had an answer for that. "It's his decision," he responded immediately. "Now will you help him out?"

And the woman crossed herself.

"Well, you say a prayer for him then," Joe advised her.

The old problem of the Kennedy curse was back again, Joe found, not only in the conversation with this woman, but with others. Although Iowa is a typical midwestern state, it has its generous proportion of Catholics, all of whom were sensitive to the Kennedy legacy and hopeful for Uncle Ted's success.

Nevertheless, it was hard to rally them around the Kennedy banner.

Joe's days were close to drudgery, although he never complained. He hit at least six to ten back rooms and coffee klatches a day for ten straight weeks. If he hadn't been young and virile and energetic, he wouldn't have been able to weather it.

In what *People* magazine reporters Connie Singer and Gail Jennes called his "morning devotional with the Boston teams' results on the sports pages, in his sacrosanct afternoon workout at a local gym and in his request of one hostess for a second glass of milk and an aspirin in the late evening of a long, speechifying day," Joe became more immersed in politics than he ever had been before.

"I like meeting people," he told reporters, "but I don't live for campaigns." His reaction to the drag on his energies and talents was more negative than positive.

His wife came out from Boston to work with him during the campaign. She proved to be a good Kennedy trouper. Her job was to help recruit campaign volunteers on the college campuses and to stump with Joe all across the state.

"She did a great job," Joe reported.

In fact, her acumen continually surprised him.

"I have to ask her to explain half the positions. She's smarter and harder working than I am."

The campaign issues were fairly clear-cut in the Iowa caucuses. The Russians move into Afghanistan led the administration immediately to suspend Soviet grain sales.

Joe's reaction was instant. He told the farmers in that farm-belt state that the president was trying to "run the American farmer up the flagpole." He begged them to attend the sparsely attended caucuses and go all the way over to Senator Kennedy's side of the room to join him in the coming important battle for the presidency.

In addition, he played on their inherent fears. "There are some not-so-nice forces loose in this country," he reminded them time and time again in their living rooms.

He told them that liberalism was not yet dead, even if many politicians were counting it out. He told them that he felt strongly about the causes which Uncle Ted had espoused.

"There is an attitude in my family that the rules should be fair for everyone and that they aren't. There's nothing wrong with working to change that."

It came out that some of the Iowans wondered if he himself might not be planning to run for office someday.

"In my Uncle Ted's 1976 reelection campaign," he told one questioner, "there were rumors that I might run for the state treasurer's job in Massachusetts. One Harvard professor—and I never went to Harvard, you remember—laughed it off as 'preposterous and insulting.'"

Joe smiled ruefully. "Instead of that, I took a job for the federal government in Washington."

Some Iowans questioned his wife about Joe's political ambitions.

"If he really wants to run for office, okay," she answered. "If he thinks someone else wants him to, not so okay."

All in all, the Kennedy campaign for the Iowa delegation was a total and unmitigated disaster. Coming into the race an odds-on favorite, Ted Kennedy wound up whipped by the president of the United States—who was facing double-digit inflation, a stalemate in the Iranian hostage crisis, and Russian troops in Afghanistan—by an incredible proportion of almost two to one.

But a Kennedy never says "die"—or "dead," either.

For some time now Joe had been working on an unannounced plan to help out constituents in the Northeast who depended on fuel oil to keep warm during the winter. A combination of OPEC price rises, ineptly administered gasoline allocations, and the relentless press of inflation had caused most New Englanders to take it on the chin, not only from gasoline prices but fuel oil prices as well.

In 1979, Joe and a group of associates formed the Citizens Energy Corporation, and worked out a deal between Venezuela and Algeria through which the government of Venezuela would sell the state of Massachusetts crude oil at the official price set by OPEC, rather than at the higher prices being charged on the spot market.

The crude oil would be provided by Petroven, Venezuela's state-owned oil company, and shipped to Puerto Rico for refining by the Commonwealth Oil Refining Company. Commonwealth would then retain the gasoline and residual fuel oil produced, and turn over the heating oil to the Kennedy company at prices below market level. Profits realized by the Kennedy company would then be used to further reduce the price charged for the oil to the state of Massachusetts.

Announcement of the cheap oil for New England was made at a press conference in Boston shortly after Senator Ted Kennedy's loss in Iowa.

"Families now face a choice between heating and eating, and that is a completely unacceptable choice for our government to provide," Joe said. "Many people are carrying a disproportionate share of our country's energy burden. Our program is only the first step to lessen that burden."

And he went on to explain: "We're taking all the profits normally made on sales and funneling them back to lower fuel costs."

When reporters suggested that Joe was making the announcement to boost his uncle's sagging campaign for the Democratic presidential primary in Massachusetts, which would occur on March 4, as well as a primary in New Hampshire on February 28, and party caucuses in Maine on February 10, Joe smiled.

"I would have been only too happy to have announced this months ago."

One reporter asked if Joe had any intention of running for office himself.

"If you think this helps me, well, that's up to you," he said. "I did it because I thought there was a gap where I could do something."

Then Joe was off for Maine, where he was working for Uncle Ted.

It was, in its way, a typical move by a third-generation Kennedy—a triumph for one who had experienced his own grim tragedies.

CHAPTER 6
Robert Francis
Kennedy, Jr.

A third child was born to Robert and Ethel Kennedy on January 17, 1954, and was named after his father. Both the dead aunt and the dead uncle had been honored. Now it was time to honor the living.

As the third and youngest child for almost a year and a half, Robert, Jr., found life in the Kennedy household a thing to be revered and enjoyed. While Kathleen tried to keep tabs on her two younger brothers in a serious and loving way, Joe and Bobby loved nothing better than to run off somewhere and cross up Big Sister.

But Bobby was his own man, even at that early age. What distinguished him from his older brother and sister was his obsession with living things. From the time he could walk, he began dragging home all kinds of animals and birds.

It was he who almost single-handedly transformed Hickory Hill into a home not exclusively for people but for all living things. Whether they crept, crawled, galloped, fluttered, or simply lay there, they were first of all Bobby's charges.

As he grew up, he brought in alligators, owls, snakes, iguanas, swans, and other animals—the acquisition of each spurring interested outsiders to suggest more outrageous pets for the already formidable list.

Tales about Bobby's pets abound in the Kennedy legend. Brumus, the enormous black Newfoundland dog, was allowed to roam the entire confines of the estate pretty much at will. In fact, Brumus had staked out his claim to the inside of the house as well as the outside.

When distinguished visitors were on their best behavior at dinnertime, Brumus would appear in the Kennedy dining room, pushing his formidable snout past some astonished guest to grab a T-bone steak on the guest's plate.

One night Art Buchwald was visiting the Kennedys and Brumus sensed a choice morsel in the embodiment of the columnist's leg. Buchwald couldn't let go of that incident any more than Brumus could let go of the humorist's leg.

Next day his column had a mock item in it saying that he had retained a Washington lawyer to bring suit against the Kennedys. He alleged that Brumus had caused him "traumatic shock." But he said his therapeutic needs would be well cared for if he could stay at a Martha's Vineyard acreage at only about $2,000 a month rent—all paid for by the Kennedys, of course.

Another guest was not so amused as Buchwald about Brumus. Ralph de Toledano, who penned many Kennedy-hating books, once wrote:

"Brumus . . . is treated better than important guests. During meals, he is given the run of the dining room. With no admonition from Bobby [Sr.] Brumus will demand food of the guests and, if this is ignored, will simply help himself, reaching onto a plate with his paw for whatever it is that attracts his whim and appetite."

One visitor told de Toledano: "That damned dog was all over me, and Bobby [Sr.] seemed to think that my objections were pretty stuffy if not downright unmannerly. Brumus got most of my meal and left paw marks all over my clothes."

But not all Bobby's animals were amusing, as Brumus

could be. One of the less friendly was a coati mundi, a South American animal closely related to the American raccoon, called "coati" from the Tupian words *coa,* "belt", and *tim,* "nose", because the animal sleeps with its nose close to its belly (belt).

This bushy-tailed animal makes a fine pet. But it does have a wild background and nasty habits that are deeply ingrained in its nature.

One night Ethel Kennedy was showing some visitors around Bobby's basement zoo at Hickory Hill. The coati suddenly turned on her, leaping at her, and digging its sharp claws into her left leg.

Ethel was so startled she recoiled, fell back, and went down to the floor.

"Get him off me, get him off me!" she screamed. "He's biting me!"

The more Ethel fought him off, the harder he clung to her leg. When she turned over to try to shake him off, he released her leg, and climbed up onto her back, biting her and gripping her flesh with his claws.

Writer Dick Schaap, one of the visitors, picked her up off the floor and lifted her to the top of a nearby cabinet. Once she was in the air, the coati's grip relaxed. Schaap kicked at the animal and with the help of the other guests drove the snarling beast into another room.

Finally, Ethel regained her composure, helped by the group of visitors who tried to keep her from hysteria. Her face regained color and she smiled faintly.

Later on she wrote Schaap a letter in which she thanked him for rescuing her from a mad coati mundi, and concluded with "warm wishes and scars."

"She was shook up, no question about it," Schaap said later, "but her recovery was masterful. In a few minutes the sudden, terrifying incident was nearly forgotten."

But Bobby heard about it. What happened to the coati is not recorded.

A sixty-pound sea lion named Sandy lived at various times in the Kennedy swimming pool, a fact that caused merriment on Capitol Hill and chagrin in the Kennedy family. Sandy kept parties from being dull by arriving in the middle of festivities and chasing female guests, for whom he had some kind of secret obsession.

Once he escaped and, using his flippers, got all the way to a shopping center a mile away before he was spotted and nabbed. He was finally removed to the Washington zoo, much to Bobby's unhappiness.

A shipment of iguanas once arrived at the Washington airport for Bobby. When Ethel drove over to pick them up their crate broke, and before anyone knew it, the area was knee-deep in flying iguanas. They were finally recaptured, returned to the crate, and then delivered to the happy animal-lover.

Being the kind of parents they were, Robert and Ethel simply encouraged their young child in this serious interest in animals. As third in line, Bobby was able to live a fairly free and unrestricted life—that is, he was not considered the "leader," as Kathleen was because of her age, nor was he considered the "baby," except for the first eighteen months of his life.

He grew in his own direction and at his own rate of speed. The Kennedy clan was expanding by leaps and bounds. Bobby was almost the same age as Robert Shriver, his cousin on his Aunt Eunice's side. The two boys became almost inseparable as they grew up in the plush suburbs of Virginia.

When they were six years old they were as close to the power center of the world as any boys their age:

- Uncle John was president of the United States.
- Bobby Kennedy's father was attorney general of the United States.
- Bobby Shriver's father was head of the Peace Corps.

But Bobby's main pursuit in his young life was the animals he loved so passionately. In her book *Times to Remember*, Rose Kennedy prints a letter she received from Bobby, Jr., at the time:

"I will be at the Cape in a week. How are you feeling? I have a giant turtle. I will see you soon. Bobby."

Like all the Kennedys who were growing up around him, including the Kennedy, Lawford, Smith, and Shriver cousins, he thrived on sports like running, playing football, swimming, sailing, climbing, and skiing.

He didn't really have the same trouble as his older brother did with his studies. For some reason he took readily to books and read almost as voraciously as his father.

Besides that, his written themes on "personalities" in the public eye were quite readable.

Like all the Kennedy kids, his life was divided between Virginia and the Cape, where the family assembled during summer months and sometimes in the winter as well. Wherever he went, the animals followed. He was like a young Dr. Dolittle.

Then, abruptly, Bobby decided to pack up his things and remove himself to boarding school.

"One evening," Ethel recounted, "he announced he wanted to go away to school and get away from this confusing family. So he went. We got him back on weekends, though."

Bobby went to Georgetown Prep, a five-day boarding school located in Washington.

A visitor to the house, Faith Laursen, the wife of a Long Island newspaper publisher, described Bobby's room:

"On the walls and even the ceiling of his smallish room, Bobby had pasted huge, poster-size pictures of his family, his mother, his uncle the president, and other members of the family."

The assassination of President John F. Kennedy hit him

as hard as it hit every one of his cousins. He saw what it did to his father, and was grief-stricken as well.

When his father began to pull out of the depression caused by his brother's assassination, and ran for the Senate seat in New York, Bobby followed the election with almost a professional's interest, although he was only eleven years old.

In his teens he was transferred to Millbrook School, a swank, upper-class prep school in the American blue-blood tradition. His grades were not all that bad compared to those of his brothers and cousins.

Because of his excellent connections with Capitol Hill, Bobby was able to get a job during the summer at the Washington zoo. His ability to deal with animals improved under the guidance of zoo officials. Animals were becoming more than a hobby with him, although he did not really think of them as leading to a serious career.

In 1967, his father and mother visited Africa on a political tour that Senator Kennedy had thought might enhance the possibility of his campaign for the presidency, even though no one spoke about it in those terms at the time.

Tanzania has a famous national park called the Serengeti at which there are thousands of animals living in their natural habitats.

John Owen, director of Tanzanian national parks, invited them to send Bobby to the Serengeti the following year. Bobby would be fifteen then—not quite old enough to come on his own. It was decided that he would be accompanied by K. LeMoyne Billings, a close family friend.

The excursion was planned for July 1968. In June, the murder of Bobby's father plunged the family into despair once again. Bobby's mother decided that in spite of the death, Bobby should go on to Africa on schedule, just as his brother Joe had gone to Spain for his projected vacation with his Uncle Ted, in spite of his father's death.

The selection of Billings as Bobby's mentor had its amusing aspects. Billings was never as sympatico with animals as Bobby was. Nor had he ever really been able to join in whole-heartedly with the typical Kennedy open-handed ribbing, pummeling, and hilarity.

"I endured him," Billings reported about the trip.

"I had to take care of him," Bobby retorted. "He's afraid of animals, you know."

Billings had a camera, and so did Bobby. The two of them shot hundreds of pictures during the six-week trip. It was Bobby's hope that he could sell the pictures and build a new museum and tourist center in the Serengeti National Park as a memorial to his father.

The antics of the animals fascinated Bobby. When they left Serengeti and got to Nairobi National Park, Bobby found that the baboons were so used to having people around that they would climb up on the car and go for a ride.

"They also bite," Bobby reported later, "so you'd better have your windows rolled up if you're driving through the way we were. Baboons are real showoffs, discreet showoffs." They always seemed to be posing, which gave Bobby something good to shoot at with the camera.

"They have a 'dog' baboon who controls the herd by showing his teeth and stamping both hands," Bobby explained. "In this park, one old dog hasn't *got* any teeth and he's missing one hand, so he bangs that one hand and never shows his teeth or yawns because the others will kill him to get the lead if they know how weak he is.

"Their territory is theirs, and they don't take anything from anyone. The baboons loved the Pixie Stix I had brought along—you know, those long straws full of colored, flavored granules. I had brought them to Africa for the children, but only the baboons were receptive."

Billings didn't think it was anywhere near as amusing as Bobby did, but Bobby was ever fascinated. He soon learned how to catch birds by using a variation on an ancient Boy Scout method of snaring night animals.

"I put a stake under my suitcase, with a string attached to my window, and rocks on top, then hid in our cabin waiting for a bird to wander into my trap. When he went for the bread, I'd pull the string to bring out the stake—and having done all that, then I'd go out and set the bird free."

Some animals, Bobby found, were much smarter than others. The smartest ones proved to be the most dangerous. They always seemed to know instinctively what the two Americans were up to, and they would always be immediately on the defensive.

One of the smartest was the water buffalo—whose looks obviously belied his intelligence.

Bobby thought that of all the animals he had seen in the jungles, the water buffalo was the most dangerous of African animals.

"They're always surrounded by tick birds," he said, "birds that eat the ticks off animals and warn them when real danger is approaching."

Another huge and dangerous animal that interested Bobby was the elephant, an animal that perennially has interested all naturalists.

He usually climbed into a tree nearby so he could focus down on the elephants with his camera. He never knew whether or not the elephants would sense that he was there and pull the tree down to get him, or pull him down out of the tree with their trunks.

Usually the elephants were more interested in eating the leaves off the tree and didn't go after the young man or his camera.

Intelligence in the animals varied a great deal.

"Giraffes aren't exactly the smartest of animals," Bobby reported. "I photographed one in Samburu. It kept running around on the road in front of us. It didn't get out of the way because it apparently hasn't figured out that you won't follow it if it jumps off to the side of the road."

Not only the giraffes proved a bit unpredictable. There was the episode of the vervet monkeys. The monkeys had free run of the house the two visitors were living in. They'd go into the kitchen and beg food from Bobby and Billings rather than catch their own outside.

Bobby put a fruit cocktail on the porch to see if the monkeys would come up after it. They did. One of the vervets was so vicious that it attacked the two men to get the food.

"We were trapped in the house as long as it was on the porch," Bobby related. "So I put Lem's fruit *inside,* held the door open, and when it ran in we ran out."

The two of them were safe, but the monkey had control of the house.

The vervet was angry at having been tricked and stayed inside until it had dirtied the entire cabin, including the beds, and eaten everything in sight, including the toothpaste.

Billings slowly became resigned to this kind of thing.

The two had an adventure trying to steal some honey from a hive, with Bobby being stung twice, and the bees finally overcoming the two of them. But they did get away with the honey—for what it was worth.

"The honey was the worst thing I ever tasted," admitted Bobby.

Billings would not comment.

And there was the gourmet feast they had of wildebeest steak. A wildebeest, besides being a favorite word for a crossword puzzle addict, is actually a gnu, which is a second most favorite crossword puzzle word. Bobby and Billings shot the wildebeest, and had it prepared for dinner. Everything was in the works for a grand meal.

The wildebeest tasted unutterably foul.

"Wildebeest steak is supposed to be a great delicacy, but Lem and I got sick of wildebeest—the first time we ate it," Bobby said.

In Nairobi National Park the roaring of the lions kept

Bobby awake at night. Next morning they found big scratches etched into the surface of the front door of the house where they were staying.

One morning they were driving through the park and came upon a group of lions: three females, one male, and eight cubs. Bobby threw out a football he had lugged all the way to Africa. The ball bounced toward the lions, and they all ran away.

"Then one of the females came right back and picked it up in her mouth," Bobby reported.

It was hard to hold in her teeth. Then she finally got a grip on it and started crunching. The ball exploded in a "pop." The deflated pigskin bored her and she walked away from it.

But the rest of the lions came closer and got to work on it. Bobby brought it back to Millbrook as a souvenir.

"It was Bobby Shriver's ball anyway," he laughed as he showed it around.

A side trip to Cairo included a meal with Egypt's Minister of Justice Abdul Younis and sightseeing in the museums and ancient ruins along the Nile.

On his arrival home, Bobby found that he had been given a baby lion named Mtoto Mbaya (in Swahili "Bad Boy") by television star Jack Paar. The lion later went into Millbrook School's excellent zoo.

Once school was over in the summer, Bobby took the lion back home to McLean. "Mommy will be delighted," he told the drivers as they loaded the growling beast into an animal truck for transport.

Two summers later trouble overtook Bobby.

Just outside the Kennedy compound on Cape Cod there was a two-car garage that had become a kind of "center" for kids. The garage's interior was spray-painted with bright psychedelic colors, having originally served toddlers as a place to play during the day.

At night the place soon became rumored to be a scene for "pot luck"—with real marijuana as the pot.

To check out the possible illegal smoking of marijuana at the garage, an undercover narc got a job as a cabdriver, let his hair grow long, and played the role of a leftover hippie from the previous decade.

He gained the confidence of the local teenagers, and became one of them as they caroused and smoked in the garage. Suddenly he vanished, as if he had never existed.

Shortly thereafter, on July 10, 1970, Hyannis Port was involved in its first pot raid ever. Caught in the raid, along with about forty teenagers from all over the town and area, were Bobby Kennedy, Jr. and Robert Sargent Shriver III.

The illegal smoking of grass was a minor sort of crime to many. The teenaged son of a physician said, "There's really nothing for a young guy to do around here at night *except* smoke pot." The press, however, didn't take it that way.

When the names of Kennedy and Shriver appeared on the court docket, there was a big journalistic flap and once again the Kennedy name was on everybody's lips. Bobby and his cousin appeared in court in August. His mother and Uncle Teddy also appeared for a closed-door hearing at the Barnstable County Court House.

After a twenty-five-minute hearing, Bobby and his cousin pleaded "not true" to the charges. Judge Henry L. Murphy continued the cases "without finding." In juvenile cases, that was standard procedure. What it meant was a period of probation. If the boys stayed clean, there would be no further legal proceedings against them "unless they get into trouble again." The probation period was thirteen months.

"There's a big drug scene here," one surfer said. "But I always thought Bobby Kennedy was the one person in Hyannis who was immune from getting busted."

Not so, obviously.

Bobby stayed out of trouble for twelve months, but

couldn't quite get through the required thirteen months. On August 23 he was arrested once again in Hyannis Port, this time for "loitering."

What happened was not quite clear. The story goes that he was standing around in front of a store, eating ice cream. Because of his court appearance the preceding year, and because every cop in the area was watching him, he was apparently annoyed when a police officer suddenly told him to "move on."

Whatever provoked him, he managed to spit ice cream in the cop's face. That did it. He was arrested for "loitering." And he was in the courtroom once again.

This time he showed up not with the neatly cropped hair he had worn the year before when his mother and uncle accompanied him, but wearing patched blue jeans, a work shirt, and sandals. His hair was shoulder length, in the style of the time, and "disheveled."

He was fined $50 for the charge of loitering, but didn't have the money. The judge gave him a week to come up with the fine. He was freed.

He was able to produce the money almost immediately, and paid the fine.

Things were quiet for a month, and then he and his cousin appeared before the judge once again as the thirteen months' probation was lifted from them.

Needless to say, the combination of his pot bust and appearance in court for loitering caused a great deal of concern in Kennedy family circles. It was really the first time up to that point that any of them had been involved in the law courts.

At a family enclave Bobby was severely reprimanded by his mother, uncle, and the rest of the clan as well. So was his cousin. All they could do was promise they would be more careful in the future.

For the first time it was brought home to Bobby that being a Kennedy was not an easy thing. Dozens of his companions around Hyannis and McLean could do whatever they wanted to. Because he was a Kennedy, however, he found that it was harder to keep out of trouble. What would earn only a cautionary glance from the law for a lesser-known citizen would earn a trip to court for a Kennedy, especially a teenaged one! It wasn't fair, but it was the way it was. After all, as his Uncle Jack had said: "Who ever said life was fair?"

He vowed to himself that he would stay out of trouble. He knew that as a Kennedy he was automatically on the spot, and that many people were just waiting to point the finger at him and sneer.

He graduated from Millbrook School in 1972, and applied to Harvard for undergraduate work. Since his grades weren't bad, he was accepted immediately. He eased into college life as any freshman would who had nothing to fear from the academic world.

His first year in college passed without incident. Things were going well for him outside college, too, and then, suddenly, on March 4, 1973, he was stopped for speeding in New Hampshire, near the Waterville Valley ski area. A state trooper clocked him doing 65 miles an hour in a 35 mile-an-hour zone.

He was told to appear in Plymouth District Court on March 16, but he never showed up. Then, a week later, he telephoned the court house, apologized for not making his scheduled appearance, pleaded guilty by phone, and mailed in $20 to pay the fine.

If he had not defaulted, the story would never have hit the papers, but it did, and now he was in the public eye again, on speeding charges. The Kennedy clan was not happy.

Bobby came into the public view again the next summer. He was in Peru observing the child-rearing practices of a mountain Indian cult as part of a course at Harvard. Summer is skiing time in the Andes, and since he was close by, he flew over to Portillo, the resort town near the best Chilean ski trails.

There he met Blake Fleetwood, a free-lance travel writer, who was doing the ski trails himself to write a story for *The*

New York Times. Bobby joined up with Fleetwood and several other North Americans—one a ski patrolman from Utah and another a college student at the University of Alabama.

They plotted out a cross-country route that would take them twenty miles over the mountains dividing Chile and Argentina at Uspallata Pass and go by the "Christ of the Andes." This famous landmark is a statue forged from melted-down cannon barrels in celebration of the 1903 treaty settling a long-standing border dispute between Argentina and Chile. The statue is placed on the border between the two countries.

It was now late July. Salvador Allende was still clinging desperately to his tottering regime in Chile, before the generals took over and moved the junta in. Things were jittery on the borders.

The group, with Bobby in the lead, was walking along the 13,000-foot-high trail and was just about to cross over into Argentina. Suddenly a Chilean alpine trooper armed with a machine gun appeared in front of them and made gestures to turn back.

Bobby thought little of it, nor did his companions. He continued on, intending to discuss the situation when they reached the trooper. The trooper removed the machine gun from his shoulder and ripped off a series of shots at them.

Bobby was fifteen feet ahead of everyone else. He dropped to the snow immediately. Bullets ricocheted off rocks nearby. Bobby remembered the antelope in Africa that had nearly done him in, and hoped it all wasn't going to end here in the cold and snow.

Then the trooper held the weapon in the air, and waved them impatiently back again.

After a short conference among themselves, the group began moving slowly back down the mountain.

"How many shots did he fire?" Fleetwood asked Bobby at one point.

"I really don't know," Bobby answered. "I wasn't looking."

Back in Portillo the newspapers took up the incident, and before he knew what had happened, Bobby learned that the folks at home were reading that he had been wounded, badly hurt, was dying, or dead.

He spent the rest of the time at Portillo skiing close to the resort, swimming, and diving underwater, and there were no more brushes with death. But that one had been a close one.

Even though as a college student Bobby was unable to spend as much time with his beloved animals as he had been able to when he was in prep school, animals were still one of the great attractions of his life.

When Roger Ailes, a television producer, asked him in 1974 to act as consultant on wild animals with a camera crew in Kenya, Bobby leaped at the chance. Not only did he love animals, but he was excited about television, knowing what it had done for his father and uncles in their political careers.

Nothing could be truer about the Ailes-Kennedy liaison than what Charles Dudley Warner had said a hundred years ago: "Politics makes strange bedfellows." Ailes had been Richard M. Nixon's television guide and image-maker during and after the 1968 presidential campaign. He had also produced "The Mike Douglas Show."

Ailes had an idea for a twenty-six-part television series that would see Africa through the point of view of an American boy. "We want to test the ability of an American urban youth in wildlife situations on his own in an African society," Ailes said in an interview about the project.

The group left for Africa on June 12, 1974, and spent the next months filming animals in exotic locales of Kenya. Bobby, with his special savvy on animals, proved an invaluable aid.

ABC-TV bought the series, and it was premiered at 6:30 EST on September 7, 1975, one year and three months after it was started.

Called "The Last Frontier," it was broadcast in a Sunday evening slot as a "television special."

Bobby Kennedy was the on-camera host for the series, and was used as the voice-over narrator during many of the animal sequences. In publicity and news releases about the show he was described as a "dedicated conservationist."

During 1975, activity once again surfaced regarding the assassinations of John F. Kennedy and Robert F. Kennedy. The "plot" that supposedly did away with Jack Kennedy had been revived before and simply would not die.

Now the county government of Los Angeles began a probe into the city police handling of the Robert F. Kennedy assassination. A number of people came forward to suggest that there was a "second gun" involved in that murder.

Another curious aspect of the case was the reported destruction of ceiling panels at the site of the killing. According to "second gun" theorists, this was an attempt by the police to cover up the fact that there were two people and two guns involved in the killing rather than just one of each.

The proof, it was said, lay in bullets and/or bullet holes in the ceiling, and the ceiling tiles were allegedly removed *to cover this fact up.*

The Los Angeles City Council in August 1975 voted ten to one to reopen the case in order to probe the investigative handling of the killing. A talk show got Bobby on camera and asked him what he thought of the "second gun" theory.

"All it takes is one crazy guy for such an assassination," Bobby declared deliberately.

The talk show host asked him if he thought the case should be reopened.

"I think I can speak for my family," said Bobby slowly. "I just don't see any reason for it."

The probe fizzled out.

Bobby was majoring in American history and literature at Harvard, and for his senior year he was required to write an honors thesis. He decided to do a paper on recent historical and political developments in the South. He knew his father had made a great impact on the integration movement when he was attorney general. Bobby wanted to pursue the idea.

In order to zero in on the subject matter and limit his theme to some specific person or group, he planned a motor trip through the South to seek out more information. Peter Kaplan, his roommate at Harvard, had decided to do his thesis on a political subject similar to Bobby's. Kaplan went along with him, as did Bobby's favorite Gordon setter, Hogan.

When they got to Alabama, both Bobby and Kaplan decided to stay there rather than travel farther on into what was the real Deep South.

They rented a house in Montgomery where they could stay while pursuing their research in the state's capital.

Alabama presented them with a glittering example of old-fashioned repression and reaction—Governor George C. Wallace. At the time of their arrival, Wallace, even though crippled and in a wheelchair, was deep in preparations for his 1976 fight for the presidential candidacy.

Bobby had been thinking a great deal about his paper, and decided that he would concentrate on Governor George C. Wallace. By pointing out the obstructionist tactics Wallace had used, Bobby could bring into focus the drama of the big changes that were taking place in Alabama.

He called up the governor for an interview, and, not surprisingly, considering who he was, he was granted an audience. The governor spent a great deal of time with him.

"I found Governor Wallace very pleasant personally," Bobby reported later. "He has several admirable qualities. He is seriously concerned about states' rights, not racism."

In addition, the two men discussed Bobby's father, and Bobby reported later that the governor "spoke highly" of him.

Reporters around the capital questioned Bobby about his impressions of the South and the political trends he was studying.

"They are indicative of those elsewhere," Bobby countered, "but here they are a lot more obvious."

As Bobby nosed about the capital and familiarized himself with the workings of politics there, he was a bit startled to discover that although Governor Wallace was indeed head of the state, the person with real power was someone else.

His name was Frank Minis Johnson, Jr., and he had been appointed a federal judge by President Dwight D. Eisenhower in 1955. Bobby began to suspect that he might feature Judge Johnson in the book as much as Wallace.

"I found out that basically it was Frank M. Johnson who was running the state of Alabama," Bobby reported later. "I realized after doing preliminary research that Johnson was the real subject and the more influential and exciting personality."

Interestingly enough, Johnson and Wallace had started out in life as fast friends, but had grown so far apart that the governor customarily referred to Johnson as "an integratin', scallywaggin', carpetbaggin', bald-faced, lying federal judge."

Johnson was an apt subject for Bobby's thesis: he was an enemy of Wallace; he was responsible for crushing the Ku Klux Klan in Alabama; he helped invalidate the ignominious poll tax which had been a thorn in the side of blacks for decades; and he succeeded in desegregating schools and recreational facilities at will.

Kaplan decided to quit Montgomery and return to Harvard in January, but Bobby opted to stay in Alabama for almost a year. He had a subject now, and he wanted to research his paper as carefully as he could.

Johnson was every bit as congenial as Wallace. Bobby was able to observe him for a month or more both in court and at leisure. Johnson went fishing with Bobby a number of times. What made him dear to the heart of Bobby Kennedy was the fact that Johnson had a framed letter from Attorney General Robert F. Kennedy in his chambers.

Continuing with his research, Bobby realized that the whole tone of the thesis was beginning to alter in point of view.

"I changed the focus of the thesis—which was broadly

on integration in Alabama. I tried to give a balanced picture of the governor." In addition, he tried to catch the personality of Johnson.

From the beginning, Johnson fascinated Bobby. At the time the two men met, Johnson was fifty-eight years old. He was a lean, six-foot-one outdoorsman weighing about 185 pounds. Unlike many people on the bench, Johnson loved to play golf, fish, and even hunt.

He also had the typical Kennedy love of horseplay and action. During his youth Johnson had always been the bane of his father's existence. His father, also a judge, simply put up with his son's antics the best way he could. At fifteen years of age, young Johnson turned motor-happy. He built a Model-A roadster and fueled it by stealing gasoline from government cars in Montgomery. He and a close friend broke all the speeding laws of the county.

By the time he had totally destroyed his father's brand new Chevy in a crash when he was in high school, he had been deemed incorrigible. His father sent him away to the Gulf Coast Military Academy in Mississippi. There, Johnson suddenly distinguished himself as a football player of note. Through his football prowess he got a scholarship to Birmingham Southern College, but the year he got there the school dropped football and he was out in the cold.

After a short stint at a business school, Johnson finally enrolled at the University of Alabama. It was there that his life became intertwined with George Wallace's. They were both in the same law class. Wallace was bright, shrewd, opportunistic, and survived by the simple expedient of making other people do his dirty work and reaping the benefits himself.

He and Johnson were friends, even though their obvious opposite characters should have made them incompatible. Johnson, unlike Wallace, was a painstakingly serious student, worked hard at learning the law, and prepared his briefs for class with meticulous care to detail.

In contrast, Wallace never cracked a book before going to class. Yet he managed to do very well with a native shrewdness and a talent for keeping one step ahead of everyone else by sheer mental acrobatics.

Bobby didn't seem to notice it, but Wallace's activities were remarkably similar to Bobby's grandfather's. In fact, they almost paralleled the patriarch's academic activities in high school and college.

Acquaintances of both Johnson and Wallace believed that without Johnson's help Wallace never would have finished law school. Johnson would run off copies of his briefs for Wallace and another friend before class.

Interestingly enough, at the time he was in college, Wallace was politically a liberal, progressively minded person, displaying what was at that time a typical antiestablishment point of view. Because he had come up the hard way, he did not have money or background enough to be in the fraternity bloc, which more or less ruled the campus at Montgomery.

During his freshman year, Wallace managed to get himself elected student-body president, largely through the efforts of Johnson and his friends. Wallace was also elected president of the Cotillion Club, and that helped put him through college. He didn't have a cent, and he was paid $100 a month to be the Club's president.

Again, the parallel between Wallace's early days and Joe Kennedy's early days is evident. He, too, was liberal, antiestablishment, and an "outsider." However, Wallace broke with the liberal tradition shortly after graduation, and from then on he drew further and further away from the democratic liberal position he had begun with.

Ironically enough, Johnson was a Republican, yet he veered more and more toward the liberal tradition as he grew older, the exact opposite of Wallace's direction.

These revelations were what caused Bobby to rethink his thesis and focus on the achievements of Johnson.

It took him a year to research the paper. During that

time he stayed in Montgomery, coming home for weekends and during the summer months. Nevertheless, he finished the paper in time and handed it in for his senior thesis.

At Harvard a thesis is not graded A, B, or C. Instead it receives a three- or four-page critique.

"On the basis of that," Bobby said later, "I got a cum plus." "Cum plus," in Harvard jargon, means an A with honors.

So far, politics had played only a nonactive role in Bobby's life. That is, he was beginning to interest himself in the process through study and observation, but he had not yet knocked on any doors the way a ward heeler must.

He was midway through his last semester at Harvard when an opportunity arose for Bobby to take an active role in the political arena.

Through his roommate Peter Kaplan at Harvard, Bobby had met a New Jersey student named Peter Shapiro who was an editor of the *Harvard Crimson*. Shapiro was an interesting young man two years old than Bobby. He was devoted to the study of politics, as well as to journalism.

Although he was an excellent journalist, political aspirations were uppermost in Shapiro's mind during his college days. He believed that politics was a "positive way to change society," and he thought that society needed a change for the better.

This put him in rapport with the Kennedy mystique, and it gave him a good reason to gravitate toward Bobby, who bore the family name in an unassuming and dignified manner.

Bobby liked Shapiro because of his ability to turn dreams and fantasies into action. Shapiro had once hitchhiked from London to Calcutta on $120. To Bobby, this was indeed a man who could get things done, no matter what the odds.

In April 1975, he suddenly got in touch with Bobby, who had just returned from Alabama, and asked him if he would like to "help out" in his campaign for assemblyman in the

Democratic primary in New Jersey. Bobby's roommate Peter Kaplan, who lived in South Orange, was going to help campaign.

Bobby talked it over with Kaplan and told Shapiro he would help out. Bobby also asked Shapiro if his cousin Christopher Lawford could help out. He and Chris were fast friends.

When Shapiro assured him he needed all the help he could get, Bobby called up Chris Lawford and put the proposition to him. Chris thought it would be fun and agreed to help. And so the two joined Shapiro and Kaplan in Newark, where they held a council about what to do.

Shapiro was trying to unseat Assemblyman Rocco Neri, the undersheriff of Essex County, in the 28th District. There were two seats there, and the two highest campaigners would be awarded the slot for the fall election.

The area included Irvington, a community in South Orange where Kaplan lived, composed of blue-collar people living in apartments and two-family houses in the tradition of Archie Bunker, along with sections where poor blacks and Hispanics lived. It was such a mixed bag it might prove a problem for Shapiro to surmount.

Bobby reached back into Kennedy history and came up with the typical Kennedy response: get out and ring doorbells. The Kennedy machine had always depended on a lot of hand-shaking and walking around.

In addition, there was strategy to be considered. Because a lot of elderly people lived in the district, one of the main concerns was the problems of the aging. For the blue-collar voters, there was crime, tax reform, and unemployment. For the blacks and Hispanics, there was unemployment. For the wealthy, crime was also a major concern.

Work started in April. Other people brought into the campaigning included: Paul Bogard, who had campaigned in Newark and Florida for various politicians, and Mary Timm, who had worked on McGovern's Indiana campaign and Brendan Byrne's successful campaign for the New Jersey governorship. Shapiro had worked on Byrne's campaign too.

It was Bobby's job to participate in the walking tours, particularly at the peak of the campaign. *The New York Times* jauntily reported Bobby's costume as "suede cowboy boots and pinstriped suit."

The Kennedy kids worked hard, not only participating in the vigorous door-to-door campaign, but in assembling it and getting out the workers to help.

The last-minute campaigning at the peak of the effort seemed to strike just the right note. When the votes were counted, Shapiro had won an upset victory. He had beaten the machine of Harry Lerner and had come in second in the three-way race, unseating Rocco Neri, who came in third.

"The two Kennedy cousins gave the campaign a shot in the arm," Shapiro said after he had won.

No one working in the campaign considered the Kennedy involvement decisive, according to one analysis of the campaign. "The kid did his work himself," one Essex Democrat said, referring to Shapiro.

But Bobby and Christopher had participated in a winning political event. It whetted Bobby's appetite for possibly more.

But other things were cooking for Bobby, although he did not know it at the time. He graduated from Harvard that June and made plans to enter law school. He had no idea where to go, but he soon opted for the University of Virginia, where his father had gone before him.

At the same time he liked working with the poor, and he liked being in the public eye. He was coming around to the same outlook on politics as that espoused by his older sister Kathleen and his older brother Joe.

He had also been toying with the idea of going to England and entering the London School of Economics, where his Uncle Jack Kennedy had studied for a brief time just before

World War II. But he did not actually make up his mind right away.

He spent the summer after graduation working without pay in the office of Robert Morgenthau, the district attorney of Manhattan. And he began dating New York girls, taking them out to local discos and restaurants.

One newspaper columnist saw him squiring about an attractive young Englishwoman who turned out to be Rebecca Fraser. She was the daughter of Hugh Fraser, a member of the House of Parliament in London, with whom Bobby's cousin Caroline had stayed when she was studying at Sotheby's a year earlier.

Bobby was now an eminently visible, typically ebullient, strikingly handsome Kennedy man. He was beginning to make a name for himself, on his own, in New York. And people couldn't help but notice that he had traits similar to those of his father.

Phyllis Grann, an editor-in-chief at G. P. Putnam's Sons, a New York publishing house, had noticed his name in the gossip columns, where he was being linked with various personalities, including Rebecca Fraser.

But it wasn't until she ran into Jean Kennedy Smith at a cocktail party that she began to get the glimmerings of an idea about Bobby. Aunt Jean mentioned the fact that Bobby had done a thesis for his senior year at Harvard. When she began talking about Johnson, there wasn't much interest in Grann's mind, but when she mentioned Wallace, the editor's ears began to prick up.

Put Wallace and Bobby Kennedy together, stir slightly, and . . .

The upshot of the conversation was that Grann became interested in the possible publication of Bobby's thesis, if he worked on it and expanded it to book length.

Commercially, the book would have been better if it had featured Wallace, but inasmuch as Bobby had switched it over to Johnson once he had begun research, there was no way to

Ethel, her children
and some friends gathered at
Arlington Cemetery on June 6, 1978
to commemorate the tenth anniversary of the
assassination of Senator Robert F. Kennedy.

*Pat Lawford with her daughters,
Robin* left *and Sydney* right,
*at a fund-raising party for the Friends
of the Special Olympics held in New York City
at Bloomingdale's department store, November 1978.*

*In his freshman year at Wesleyan,
Teddy, Jr., acted as a tour guide
for his parents and brother, Patrick* left background,
*when they visited the Middletown, Connecticut,
campus in the fall of 1979.*

*Top left: Caroline center, with her cousins Christopher Lawford
and Maria Shriver, arriving for a dinner party at the
John F. Kennedy Library in Boston on the night before
the official dedication ceremony, October 1979.
Lower left: Joseph and his bride, the former Sheila Brewster Rauch,
leaving St. John the Baptist Catholic Church
in Gladwyne, Pennsylvania, following their wedding
on February 3, 1979.
Above: Jackie, Caroline, and John, at the dedication ceremony
of the John F. Kennedy Library
in Boston, October 20, 1979.*

UPI

*Above: Senator Edward M. Kennedy officially announced
his candidacy for President of the United States
at Faneuil Hall in Boston, November 7, 1979.
Looking on* left to right: *Joan, Kara,
Patrick, and Teddy, Jr.
Opposite below: Patrick, wearing a hat presented to him
when he accompanied his father on a one-day
presidential campaign tour of New Hampshire and
Massachusetts in November 1979.
Opposite above: two generations of Kennedys gathered at
New York's Hotel Pierre in December 1979,
for a fund-raising dinner for Ted's campaign.*
Left to right: *Steve Smith, Sr., Pat Lawford,
Jacqueline Kennedy Onassis, Jean Smith, the Senator,
Kerry Kennedy and Steve Smith, Jr.*

*Bobby, Jr., standing in front of a picture
of his uncle, told a news conference
in Columbia, South Carolina,
on January 23, 1980, that Edward Kennedy
was in the Democratic presidential race
"for the duration." January 1980.*

turn it into a Wallace book without a great deal of rewriting. Nevertheless the publishing company knew that the Kennedy name had a magic of its own on a book jacket.

They decided to go ahead with the project. Bobby and Grann met for talks and finally a contract was signed. The author was instructed to put more of himself into the book, and build up the story of Johnson's life more, enlivening it with anecdotes from the past as well as from the present.

The young Harvard graduate got to work and was deeply immersed in expanding and building up the material—nobody calls it "padding" in the book business; it's always "fleshing out the material with in-depth perceptions"—when an astounding and typical Kennedy piece of luck took place.

In the summer of 1977, while Bobby was laboring assiduously at his grandmother's Palm Beach home polishing up the manuscript, President Jimmy Carter in Washington was casting about for a director of the Federal Bureau of Investigation. Since the death of J. Edgar Hoover, who had been its only head since its inception in the early 1930s, there had been no consistent head. In 1975, Carter had met with Judge Frank Johnson and asked him if he would take over the job—if Carter was elected. Johnson demurred. He didn't want to leave Montgomery for the unfamiliar territory of Washington, D.C., which had been the downfall of too many of his southern friends.

Carter had continued to cast about for a good F.B.I. head but hadn't found any. In August 1977 he once again proffered the offer to Johnson. By now, Johnson, apparently tired of the grind in Montgomery, decided that perhaps a change wouldn't be all that bad. He accepted.

News of the Johnson appointment immediately flashed through all media outlets. Bobby Kennedy heard about it one morning after he had crawled out of bed just before noon. He was deep into the rewriting of the thesis and found his best working time between midnight and dawn.

He was ecstatic. What a fantastic coincidence—to be

working on a book about a relatively unknown southern judge and to have that very man turn out to be the future head of the Federal Bureau of Investigation! It was almost too good to be true.

At Putnam's elation was the order of the day. Grann and the sales force met to determine how many copies of the Johnson book should be published to satiate the obvious hunger for the book that would be generated by the installation of the new director.

The luck of the Kennedys was obvious to *The New York Times* as well. Down flew Herbert Mitgang to Palm Beach to do a one-on-one interview with Bobby.

"Call it coincidence, or call it prescience or perhaps call it a little bit of both," wrote Mitgang, "but the first book likely to appear about Carter's surprise nominee for director of the Federal Bureau of Investigation, United States District Judge Frank M. Johnson, Jr., will be written by none other than Robert F. Kennedy, Jr.!"

"I think he'll be a super director of the F.B.I.," Bobby was quoted as describing Johnson. "He follows the laws, he's an honest guy, and he's a terrific administrator. I think he'll change the image of the Bureau and its activities so that it'll be feared by criminals and not by the average citizen."

Mitgang also extracted from Bobby the fact that he intended to study at the London School of Economics and Political Science in the fall of 1977.

The appointment of Johnson as head of the Federal Bureau of Investigation gave Bobby a shot in the arm, and he plowed through his rewrite and got the manuscript to New York.

During the required medical checkup, an aneurism in Johnson's aorta was discovered by the doctors conducting the study. He underwent surgery by Dr. Michael de Bakey in Houston, but a few weeks later he collapsed with a hernia.

Because of his weakness as a result of the earlier operation, surgeons could not immediately enter to repair the hernia, and he was forced to wait until his condition improved. Johnson felt it was only fair to the country, and especially to the staff of the F.B.I., that he withdraw his acceptance and resign the appointment. He might have to wait months before he could undergo the operation successfully. Meanwhile, morale at the Bureau would deteriorate even lower than it was at the time.

And that was the end of the excitement over Bobby's possible bestseller—third in the family after his father's *The Enemy Within* and his Uncle Jack's *Profiles in Courage* years before.

Nevertheless, work went ahead rapidly at Putnam's, and the publicity department alerted Bobby to the fact that he would be put on tour everywhere to sell the book over television.

Lady Luck had almost smiled on Bobby, but in the end, she had turned her back on him. It was par for the course for a Kennedy, Bobby decided, and accepted the reversal stoically.

As he waited for the book to appear, he took off for a visit to Alabama where in the spring of 1978 he had an unnerving experience that reminded him once again how close to trouble the life of a Kennedy always was.

He was visiting Mobile, Alabama, with several friends, staying at a private home in Point Clear, a small settlement on Mobile Bay across from the city.

He was off by himself, swimming in the bay, when he took a dive off a small pier that jutted out into the water. The water was far less deep than he had thought. He landed on his head and wrenched his back.

Nevertheless, he was able to get out of the water and walk back to the house, where he told his companions what had happened. Then he began feeling back and neck pains. His friends immediately drove him to Mobile Infirmary, where he was admitted and observed for several days.

He was in "good condition," but it took several days before hospital authorities would let him go with a clean bill of health.

Judge Frank M. Johnson, Jr.: A Biography came out in 1978, as scheduled. On the jacket flap Arthur Schlesinger, Jr., no mean historian himself, wrote:

"[Robert F. Kennedy, Jr.] has given us a vivid portrait, drawn with literary grace and in historical detail, of a southern individualist who changed the life of Alabama."

The review in the *Library Journal* said in part:

"Kennedy mixes history, folklore, law, and politics to produce a picture of Johnson as a strong Federal judge who was forced by state resistance to U.S. law and the Constitution to make far-reaching decisions on voting rights, desegregation, mental health, and prison reform. The book is an important contribution to understanding not only Alabama politics, but the South in general. With the exception of some questionable style and occasional repetition, highly recommended."

Not all the reviews were so good-natured.

The two newspapers that mattered the most to him because of his background and because he had lived in Boston and New York were *The Boston Globe* and *The New York Times*.

"They gave it lousy reviews," he said. "But a lot of that was political where I and my family name are concerned. All the publicity also gave people higher expectations of the book than what it set out to do."

Howell Raines reviewed it for *The New York Times Book Review*. He started out his critique in an upbeat fashion, describing one of the photographs, of a group of college students, in the center section of the book.

"One of the students is shorter, more boyish, with knowing eyes set in a round country face. In his natty gray suit, he could pass for the first Snopes to struggle into a state university."

That referred to a photograph of Wallace with Johnson.

Raines liked the interesting juxtaposition; he wanted more of it than the author of the book supplied:

"But in only a few scattered passages has Mr. Kennedy's friendship with the judge produced information that cannot be gleaned from newspapers and magazine clippings. The result is a book that neither adequately defines Judge Johnson's role in modern southern history nor captures the fabled and compelling story suggested by the photograph."

Raines liked the several anecdotes at the beginning of the book that tended to show the brief friendship of Wallace and Johnson before they split and became deadly antagonists.

"Unfortunately, Mr. Kennedy abandons this lively material in favor of a plodding, disjointed analysis that clouds rather than clarifies Judge Johnson's achievements as a jurist."

But that wasn't all. Raines didn't like the structure of the book.

"Mr. Kennedy has ignored the orderly and dramatic march of history from year to year and case to case in favor of jerking the reader back and forth across the decades."

And he sensed omissions that he felt were egregious.

"There are oversights, too, that seem inexcusable in a biography, even allowing for the fact that this is a first book that had its beginnings as a senior thesis at Harvard. It is puzzling, for instance, that Mr. Kennedy, a member of a political family dogged by tragedy, does not mention the suicide of Judge Johnson's son and the erratic behavior of the judge's brother, both of whom are said in other accounts to have suffered terribly from attacks visited on the family as a result of Judge Johnson's stand on racial justice."

He sensed a political bias in the author's writing.

"It is probably unkind to mention, but nonetheless true, that Mr. Kennedy glosses over a key point in his analysis of the role of Federal judges in the desegregation of the South. Judge Johnson and other Republicans appointed by President Dwight D. Eisenhower generally pushed forward the frontiers of racial justice in the region with their rulings; however, Presidents Kennedy and Johnson appointed several southern segregationists to the Federal bench who at the time did their best to dismantle the progressive rulings of Judge Johnson, Judge Elbert Tuttle of Atlanta, and others appointed by Eisenhower."

In conclusion:

"Frank M. Johnson is a heroic figure, who, in his twenty years on the bench in the 'cradle of Confederacy,' towered over a political landscape populated all too heavily by small men of villainous motives. For such a large man, a larger book than this is in order."

In one sense, Raines is right. The early anecdotes about Johnson's youth and his early days in college, when he met Wallace, are excellent. After the initial massing of personal data and the delineations of Johnson's character, the narration does tend to glide easily into a case-by-case reconstruction of the judge's rulings.

Bobby's love of the South and its attitudes is obvious in the following passage, describing Sand Mountain Ridge:

"It was a different breed of man that was molded by this tough and hardy mountain region. This is not a terrain that allows a man to settle back and grow lazy. It is no place for mint juleps and magnolia blossoms, no place for reclining on the veranda under the lazy spell of heat, no place for patrician privilege. In this hill country the corn whiskey at 180 proof is more often than not drunk straight up. The emphasis is on getting the job done as quickly and efficiently as possible. There are no frills. The importance of one's tastes and comforts is sharply diminished by the preoccupation with survival."

That passage evokes a feeling for the country that produced Johnson.

However, his style occasionally lapses into clichés: "He was a friendly, fun-loving man," for example.

And some of the passages echo the diction of academic halls:

"Nine years after the *Plessy* v. *Ferguson* doctrine of separate but equal had been reversed by the Supreme Court, no effort had been made to rectify Alabama's dual school system. Despite the fact that *Brown* v. *Board of Education* demanded compliance in good faith at the earliest practicable date, the petitions of aggrieved parties had been buried beneath the monolith of official recalcitrance."

To be fair, Bobby's original paper *was* a college thesis. That he had been able to make it appear to be a biography at all is definitely to his credit as an author.

There is a theory that reviews kill or make a book. This is true only to a certain extent. Bestsellers make millions for authors who are treated odiously by reviewers. Conversely, authors have starved to death on glowing reviews that are unanimous in praise and exaltation.

Bobby learned one thing immediately. The real clout in book salesmanship is found not in the printed word but in the glowing lights of the television studio. Early on he was sent on the national rounds: the morning talk shows, the evening talk shows, the midnight-and-after talk shows, and the game and quiz shows in between for guest appearances.

He admitted at one point that plugging his book on television made him feel "a little mercenary," but he was realistic enough to understand that everyone who wrote and lived by writing had to do the same thing he did.

And so he appeared one night on "The Mike Douglas Show," dressed in sartorial elegance, exhibiting his lizard-skin boots to the audience, who wildly applauded.

He wasn't always applauded. One night he met a man in a bar who accused him of not writing the book at all but of hiring a ghost writer to do the job. Bobby blew his top. He responded in typical Kennedy fashion by getting into a fight.

Most on-camera interviewers didn't always play fair either, Bobby protested. "When I am introduced as Bob Kennedy who will talk about what it was like growing up as a Kennedy, and the book isn't even mentioned, well . . ." He became adept at leading the conversation back to the book. "If I could spend a minute out of an eight- or nine-minute segment talking about the judge, then I liked the show," Bobby concluded.

He finally had to concede that "My name opens doors for me. I admit I do some traveling on it." In fact, he had really learned to accept the problems his name brought up. "I decided the advantages definitely outweighed the disadvantages."

There was one other thing he learned from the experience.

"I learned it's going to be a long time before I write another book," he said with a grin.

In late 1979, when Uncle Ted announced for the presidency, Bobby was assigned Alabama, on the theory that he had already worked the territory.

Immediately he got into a scrap with Joe Reed, chairman of the Alabama Democratic Conference, and a noted southern black leader. Reed's organization had endorsed President Carter. Bobby claimed in a speech that "money" had influenced the group's decision to go for Carter.

What he said was: "Joe Reed's got a lot of money and he's passing it around."

Reed blew his top. He thought it sounded indecent if not scurrilous, meaning that he was supposedly being paid off to support Carter. He accused Bobby of "practicing a politics of deception and desperation."

But Bobby knew how to turn that charge the other way. He said that Reed was "just grandstanding." And he went on to explain: "I don't want to imply he is doing anything illegal. That's campaign funds. Everybody does that."

Bobby drew good crowds, particularly at the University of Alabama, where he was pictured in the press with a large group of Kennedy sympathizers on the campus.

But then, it was never hard to collect a crowd if one was a Kennedy. Crowds surrounded the Kennedys in New York,

Boston, Washington, Los Angeles and anywhere else they happened to be. Sometimes even a Kennedy look-alike would do.

A young woman from Mamaroneck whom we'll call Sally Norton decided that she would wait out one such crowd and see just what this young Kennedy was like. When the crowds thinned, she found that the center of attention was smiling at her.

They began talking, and soon Sally was being taken around to various restaurants and discos in New York by someone who called himself Bobby Kennedy, Jr. She had seen his pictures in the newspaper, and knew what a Kennedy should look like, and he did indeed look like a Kennedy.

She took him home with her to Mamaroneck and introduced him to her father. Her father and members of her family were pretty excited to be talking to a real Kennedy, but they took it in stride.

One night Sally and friend borrowed the Norton family car and took off for a spot in New York. When he dropped off Sally at home, he asked if he could borrow the car for the night and return it in the morning.

Sally didn't think it would be a good idea, but "Bobby" was persuasive. She let him take the car.

That was the last she saw of the car. And it was the last she saw of "Bobby." Her father was understandably enraged and called the police.

Meanwhile a dentist in Manhattan whom we'll call Dr. Mortimer Davidson gave said Bobby Kennedy emergency treatment on his teeth one day in early January. The dentist was shocked to see the condition of the young man's teeth. He had always thought the Kennedys took better care of their health than this young man.

He sent the bill and a letter to the Kennedy compound in Hyannis Port, recommending that the young man come in for a thorough dental examination and possible replacement of his lost teeth.

Meanwhile, reporters were tracking down a story that a Bobby Kennedy had slugged a girl on a sidewalk in Manhattan outside a disco. But they couldn't locate either the girl or Bobby Kennedy to ascertain the truth of the story.

Several restaurants—two of them exclusive ones—duly sent out bills to a Bobby Kennedy for large meals eaten during the long winter nights of 1979–80.

What was happening to the rational, maturing, and intelligent Bobby Kennedy? What had caused him to revert to his earlier days of youthful indiscretion? Had he undergone a personality change?

A couple of enterprising New York *Daily News* reporters tracked down Bobby in Alabama and asked him what was going on. Instead of being peeved, Bobby was affable and cooperative.

"He's an imposter," Bobby Kennedy told reporters Phil Roura and Tom Poster. "Look, you guys got to help me out. I haven't been in New York since November 7. All of a sudden I'm getting bills in the mail, and the cops are looking for me in Mamaroneck where this guy, who says he's me, took a girl's car. The girl's father is demanding $460 from me for the car. I also got a bill for $35 for emergency dental treatment. But there's nothing wrong with my teeth."

Bobby informed the reporters that he had opened his mail and found two bills that same day, both addressed to him but at "Compound No. 2, Sarasota, Florida."

"I've never been there nor do we have family there," Bobby complained. "The mail was forwarded to Hyannis Port, then to me, here in Alabama. Apparently this guy looks like me, acts like me, and knows a lot about me."

Bobby said he had called Mamaroneck and talked to Sally Norton's father. Norton had told Bobby that he had met him at the house and knew him.

"I've never been to Mamaroneck," Bobby told the reporters. "I can't even pronounce it. As for my teeth, the dentist claims to have given me emergency treatment on January 2.

He wrote a letter saying that he has never seen a mouth in such disrepair. He even said he could replace the teeth I lost. Well, I still have all my teeth so I don't know what he's talking about."

The reporters asked if people might be confusing him with his brother David.

"No way," Bobby said. "David is still at the Hyannis Port compound recuperating."

But the problem for Bobby was definitely a real one. He would be returning to New York after the Alabama primary campaign was over to work on the New York primary campaign.

And who was this imposter trying to get girls and cars and dental assistance by playing Bobby Kennedy, Jr.?

The business of being a Kennedy is always a difficult one. "There are a lot of advantages that other people don't have," Bobby admits. "And I wouldn't give them up." The obvious disadvantage is "celebrity."

Bobby Kennedy has gone through a lot in his lifetime already as animal-lover, college graduate, campaign worker, and author. At present he's a law school student, attending the University of Virginia Law School like his Uncle Ted and his father before him.

He seems to have settled down at least as well as most of his contemporaries. That in its fashion is a triumph in its own way for someone who has always had everything from the moment of his birth.

CHAPTER 7
David Anthony Kennedy

On June 5, 1968, David was twelve years old. He would be thirteen on June 15, and he was looking forward eagerly to that date, when he would at last be a true teenager.

The last few weeks had been stimulating indeed. David's father was running for president. Now, in California, the primary was being contested by his father; Hubert Humphrey, a friend of his father's in the Senate; Lyndon B. Johnson, president of the United States; and Eugene McCarthy, another friend in the Senate.

David knew enough about politics to realize that California was important. The family talked enough about it. He knew that if his father lost in California, he could pretty much say good-bye to any chance of being president like his Uncle Jack.

His father had lost a squeaker in Oregon, and some of the experts had him "down for the count," but the Kennedys were sure he could win California—and there were more delegates from that state than from Oregon anyway.

David and five of the Kennedy children had flown out with his mother to be with their father during the balloting on primary day. There was David, the fourth of the Kennedy children, Courtney, Michael, Kerry, Christopher, and Max. Douglas was only a little over a year old—just a baby. He was back in Virginia, at home.

David loved to swim. Like all the Kennedys, he knew how to manage himself very well in water, deep or shallow. And the Pacific Ocean was a lot more exciting than the Atlantic. The waves were bigger, especially at Malibu.

His father knew a lot of very important people in Hollywood, and one of them was John Frankenheimer, who was a movie producer and director. The family was staying overnight with the Frankenheimers at their beach home. The Frankenheimers were not used to the presence of six rambunctious children, but they seemed to be surviving it in pretty good humor.

It was misty and cold, but that didn't stop David and Michael from running up and down the beach after breakfast. They knew their father would soon join them. He always did. And then they would be able to go in swimming. He had warned them that there was an undertow in the surf.

David could see that it was rough out there. But he had been in rough water before.

Soon enough their father did come out, and the two older boys ran down into the water, plunging in. It was cold— freezing cold. But when David and Michael saw their father jumping in right after them, they kept up with him and tried to ride the waves.

By the time their father had swum back and forth a dozen times, and announced he was going to leave, the boys were just getting warmed up. As the senator toweled himself off on the beach, he watched them while they struggled with the waves. David could feel the strong pull of the water as the tide flowed back from the beach.

It was about two o'clock in the afternoon and the waves had changed appreciably. The pull out to sea was savage, a crosscurrent that almost pulled the two of them off their feet.

The girls didn't want to swim at all. They sat on the beach and watched.

David and Michael scoffed at them, yelling and challenging them to ride the waves in. But the others wouldn't budge off the sand. It was warmer now, although the fog had never really lifted.

David caught a wave, arched his body, and suddenly lost his balance as a huge surge of power pushed him down under the foaming surf. He glanced around and saw a mountain of swelling blue-green water about to fall on him from a tremendous height. A surge of water pushed him up from below, to meet the mountain of water smashing down on him from above. He waved his arms frantically, trying to catch the attention of his father who was talking on the beach to a writer who had come to interview him.

"Help me," cried David. "I can't stand up!"

He felt the wave hit and drive him down, and then before he could understand what had happened, he was scraping on the sand, the weight of the wave pounding him down and down and down.

The next thing he knew, he was being seized by strong arms and lifted out of the water which was foaming and roiling around him. He tried to open his eyes, but they were full of water. Then his vision cleared. His father had him in his arms.

"Let me down!" snapped David, and his father, smiling slightly, let him go. David coughed up water and hunched over on the sand, trying to get his breath back.

His father pounded him on the back.

"Let's try it in the pool, huh?" he asked with a grin.

Michael was standing there with him, looking a little scared.

David didn't want to admit he had been bested by the surf. But he didn't want to battle those waves again, either. After a moment's thought he said: "Okay, Dad. We'll use the pool."

That was when he noticed that there was a big red bruise on his father's forehead. It hadn't been there before.

"What's that bump on your head?"

Senator Kennedy laughed. "Nothing, David. Now get up to the pool and no more of this surfing today."

They went up to the pool, and the girls joined them. The senator spent some time with them tossing the little ones in the water while David and Michael played water polo with a beach ball.

Max, who was three, finally conned his father into walking down the beach with him to bury coins in the sand. Later they could come back and dig them up, like pirates recovering buried treasure.

David sneered at the thought of that little kid's game and stayed at the pool with Michael.

He never admitted it to anyone, but he was scared. He still could not breathe right. His body hurt where he had scraped the sand. And he still could feel that surge of power that had almost taken him away with it.

But he told no one how he felt. He had learned early in his life that no Kennedy ever gave voice to his fears. There were things bigger than he was, he knew, and whatever that thing in the ocean was, it had almost got him. His father had saved him. He didn't think he could have come up by himself. It was a frightening admission to make. But a Kennedy never flinched from danger. Yet death was close to him that day. He knew it, and he didn't want to think about it.

The rest of the afternoon passed quickly and it was night soon enough. That meant driving downtown toward Los Angeles to the Ambassador Hotel, a big palatial hotel on Wilshire Boulevard. David had never been there before.

When they arrived what he liked about the place was not the Ambassador Hotel at all, but a funny little restaurant across the street built in the shape of an old-fashioned hat. He had seen men wearing those strange hats in movies on the Late Late Show. His mother told him that the hat was a derby, and that the restaurant was a very famous one called The Brown Derby.

California was certainly a weird place. He wanted to eat inside the big hat. He knew they weren't going to, but he wished he could anyway. He knew that they were going to be spending their evening in the hotel suite at the Ambassador where his father was giving the campaign workers a big party at the end of the evening when the votes had been counted.

They would have a celebration if his father won, and a "wait-till-next-year" party if he lost, his mother told him.

"He'll win," said David stoutly.

His mother laughed.

David was dressed up in a flashy outfit for the occasion: blue blazer, striped tie, and gray slacks. Most of the time he didn't wear a tie, but this was a very special occasion, and he knew he had to.

Their hotel room was very posh—in fact, it was the Royal Suite, located on the fifth floor. David asked his mother what royalty there was in America, and she explained to him that there wasn't any, but that the hotel suite was called "royal" anyway.

There were bedrooms sealed off from the rest of the suite. That meant that the children could get to bed long before the party was over. The party would go on for some time after midnight. David knew he could stay up later than the rest of them. After all, he was going on thirteen, and he could wait up with the grownups until after the returns were in. "Returns" were what they called the result of the votes.

The children had dinner and then David went out to see what was going on in the rest of the Royal Suite. He found that it was pretty quiet now, but he knew it would be getting noisier and full of people later on.

He came back and stayed with his brothers and sisters for a few more hours. At about ten o'clock, he went out into the crowded suite and began walking through as he had been instructed, shaking hands with his father's friends. He had done it before at home in McLean and at other affairs where his father was present.

He found his Aunt Patricia—his Uncle Peter was divorced from her now—and he found his Aunt Jean, too. There were a lot of other people there, walking about holding drinks and cigarettes in their hands.

Pierre Salinger, who had been his Uncle Jack's press secretary when he was president, came up to him and shook hands and talked to him just as if he were already grown up. Finally David found Roosevelt Grier, the giant of a lineman for the Los Angeles Rams. The 320-pound football star knew David, and came over and talked to him for about five minutes.

Then Rafer Johnson, the Olympic Games champion from U.C.L.A., came up and joined the two of them. That was exciting, and David listened to what they had to say with great attention.

After that John Glenn, the first astronaut, who had been a friend of the Kennedy family for years, came up and began talking to him about politics. It was turning into a very exciting evening.

There were six television sets going full blast in various corners of the suite. David kept his eye on them as he circulated about. Every so often someone like Walter Cronkite or David Brinkley would appear and talk about the primary results.

The California primary wasn't the only one held on that day. There was another one in South Dakota. And soon the news came in that David's father had won hands down in South Dakota—almost fifty percent for his father against Humphrey and McCarthy. That was big news, and cheering news, because Humphrey was a native son who had been expected to win.

But at the same time, one of the networks predicted that McCarthy was going to get half the vote in California and beat Kennedy. People stood around and booed the set, and even his father came up and frowned at it.

After a moment or two the buzzing and talking started

again, and David went back to the bedroom where the little kids were already in bed. When he returned to the party, he found that the news had changed, and that it looked as if his father *would* win.

At eleven o'clock, his mother found him and steered him to the bedroom, telling him it was time to go to bed. There was a television set in the bedroom, and David asked if he could watch the party downstairs. After a moment or two, his mother said he could, if he kept the sound quiet for the other children.

Then she kissed him and left. A moment later his father came in, said good night to him, kissed him, and went out into the corridor. David undressed slowly and turned on the television set, keeping the sound down very quiet.

There was a Western series on, but in a few moments it ended and the news came on. David switched channels and finally found the one that showed the Kennedy headquarters in the Ambassador Hotel. The announcer was saying that the votes had been counted and that Senator Kennedy had won the primary.

A big cheer went up. David climbed into bed, propped his pillow up, and watched the people milling about in the room downstairs.

He was tired. He could still feel the bruises from his brush with drowning that morning. He had not really had time to think about it. He didn't want to think about it, actually.

The program went on, with reporters talking to Kennedy workers and visitors to the Kennedy party. David jerked his head, realizing he had fallen to sleep. He was having a hard time keeping his eyes open.

And then he was watching his father and mother standing on a small platform, hand in hand, with his father smiling out at the camera. There was a lot of applause, whistling, and yelling. Finally the crowd calmed down and his father gave a little speech thanking his helpers and inviting everyone watching to help out in the hard campaign to come.

"I think we can end the divisions within the United States. What I think is quite clear is that we can work together," he said. "We are a great country, a selfless and a compassionate country."

There were cheers and whistles.

"And so my thanks to all of you, and on to Chicago, and let's win!" he cried, holding up his fingers in the V-for-victory sign.

Everyone burst into applause. A lot of people waved the V-sign, and David saw his father wave at the crowd. And then his father and mother turned to leave the platform and the announcer took over.

David decided to listen for a few minutes before getting up to turn off the set. He knew there would be a lot of talk, chit-chat about the campaign, the margin of victory, and some comments on the voting. He had seen it all a dozen times before. But it still gave him a thrill to see his own father on the television set! Wouldn't it be great if he did win and did become president, like his Uncle Jack?

He closed his eyes, and let himself think about that for a moment. He dozed, and then shook himself awake. He had to get up and turn off the set. If his mother came in and found the set still on, and him asleep, she'd bawl him out good.

He crawled out of bed and heard a sudden shout over the television set. The announcer looked flustered and turned, looking at someone near the camera. There was a moment of tension, and then quite suddenly there was a flurry of movement. The camera waved sickeningly.

David was frozen in the act of switching off the set. Fear seized him. It felt just like that morning, when the wave had pounded him into the sand, when he had been afraid he would never breathe again. He could *feel* the closeness of death.

Stricken and unbelieving, the announcer suddenly came on again, and babbled out a few words of comment, asking his viewers to bear with him while he verified something that . . .

And then, quite suddenly he came back on and said in a

very concerned voice that Senator Kennedy had been hurt by a gunshot wound and was now being hurried to the hospital.

David felt his legs trembling. He had been only six when his uncle had been murdered in Dallas. And now someone had tried to kill his father! Suddenly Michael was awake.

"David, what is it?" he asked, rubbing his eyes.

"I don't know," David answered truthfully. He crawled back in bed, pulled the covers up over his chest and stared at the set. "I think something's happened to Dad."

Michael did not say anything, but watched dazedly.

Soon there was no doubt about the seriousness of the incident. The TV crews were soon at the Los Angeles Receiving Hospital, and the commentator was discussing the shooting. No one knew yet how serious the senator's wounds were.

The bedroom door burst open.

David hoped it was his mother, coming to tell him his father was all right, but it wasn't.

It was one of his father's good friends, Theodore H. White, a writer, in fact, the one who had been on the beach that morning.

White was covering the election for a book he planned to write. And now this!

In the midst of the excitement downstairs, White had suddenly remembered the children, and it crossed his mind that they might be watching the party on television.

He had dashed quickly up to the Royal Suite, trying to get to the set before the grisly facts were broadcast, but . . .

In a piece for *Life* magazine, White wrote about his feelings as he comforted David Kennedy in his room.

"One could not explain to the brave youngster, still awake, fighting back his tears at the horror he had seen on television. One could only hold the child, order hot chocolate for him, try to comfort him, fighting back one's own tears while recognizing the father's image in the good strong face of the child.

"And hope that he would keep the faith, as all his family had, in his country and people, hard now as it might be."

David could think only of his own skirmish with death that morning in the undertow off Malibu. His father had snatched him from the arms of death. He had cheated death with the strength of his arms and saved his son.

But death had refused to be thwarted. If it couldn't have the son, it must take the father.

He never said it to anyone. But somehow he knew that he had been spared, by his father's own strength, and had caused his own father to be taken.

He lay back and tried to sleep, but couldn't. He kept thinking of his father, fighting for his life. Somehow he knew what would happen.

In the morning they told him the worst.

It was his fault. He had caused his father to die. Yet he could never tell anyone the truth. No one would believe him. But he knew. He *knew*.

The nightmare soon faded.

But David's feeling of guilt did not. He never admitted it, never gave it any voice. It was simply something he always lived with.

Those powerful arms cradling him, saving him from the force of the sea. And then the sound of those gunshots in the television set, and the knowledge that his father was powerless to resist their force, even as David had been powerless to resist the force of the water.

He was never the same again.

Whatever trauma there was—if there was any—remained invisible. He was the same on the outside, but he was different inside. He had gone through too much to remain unaffected.

Only a month before, he and a neighbor friend had been arrested for throwing rocks at a car passing by on the street. David didn't get much from that run-in with the law except a scolding. He had always been an active boy in the tradition of the Kennedys. What he had done was put down as a childhood prank.

When he telephoned home, a governess rushed down to the police substation and drove him home. She phoned Capitol Hill, and that afternoon Senator Kennedy—who was just beginning his campaign for the Democratic presidential nomination—issued a statement from his Washington office.

"I regret to say that one of my sons in the company of another boy got into trouble . . . while my wife and I were away from home," he said. "He feels very badly about what he has done and has apologized to all concerned. He is a good boy . . . and never has been involved in any trouble whatsoever prior to this incident."

That was the truth.

Nevertheless, within a few days, David was in trouble again. This time he placed a cherry bomb in the mailbox of a neighbor in McLean. Senator Kennedy did not issue a statement from his Washington office.

He took David in hand himself. David understood that he had done wrong and shouldn't repeat the offense. Yet somehow the action was still considered part of his youth—in other words, another childhood prank. Of course, other kids *did* put cherry bombs in mailboxes, but they didn't get headlines for it the way David did.

Now, with his father gone, he tried to turn over a new leaf. He determined that he would change his life for the better. He was through with all that kid stuff.

Except for the obvious headlines in the world press because of his father's assassination and the fact that he had been with him on his last day, David kept out of the newspapers for at least five years.

They were not happy years for anyone in the Kennedy household. But somehow the members of the family made it through the difficult months of readjustment. Somehow they survived.

David's years in prep school at Middlesex School in

Concord, Massachusetts, were relatively quiet. He took part in the usual pranks his classmates indulged in, but nothing untoward occurred—at least nothing that was picked up by the press. He was glad of that. He did not want his mother bothered anymore over concern for him.

As he grew up he became more withdrawn, it seemed, more sensitive to everyone's reaction to him. What his aunt Eunice Shriver once called "intramural competition in a large and accomplished family" was obviously unnerving him, perhaps even breaking his spirit.

"There weren't any disadvantages being a Kennedy in my generation," Aunt Eunice said, "but for the children it may be difficult. It may be tough for them to acquire their own identity. If you have lots of kids, and one of them is going to law school and another has dropped out and another is in college but having a hard time and they hear about each other —that could be a disadvantage."

David was in Nantucket with Joe in 1973. Joe was having his own troubles. He had dropped out of Berkeley, quit a job in San Francisco, and had injured several people including David in a car accident in Nantucket. Why couldn't things settle down for the Kennedy brothers? Why was life so rotten?

David had wrenched his back badly in that car accident. The doctors put him on medication to relieve the pain. The drugs were powerful narcotics, reportedly the first that had ever been administered to him. One of the drugs was Percodan, a powerful painkiller.

He stayed in the hospital for some days before he was released. The horrors of Pamela Kelley's permanent paralysis affected him as much as they did Joe.

Once again death had been close to him. The fact that every occupant of the car had cheated death made no matter. It seemed to him that there was no way he could avoid an eventual confrontation.

A shadowy fear hovered over him—a fear that the accident that had almost killed him would be repeated, that it wasn't an accident at all but a part of the working out of his destiny. The Kennedy fatalism—the thought that a curse hung over the family—took a deep grip on him once again.

It recalled the day when he had cheated death in Los Angeles, only to have his father taken from him that same night.

If there was a curse, and if they were all intended victims, why did he try to fight it? Why should he not live the life he wanted to live, and suffer the consequences only when they came?

Fatalistic acceptance of fate was an old story to philosophers. A psychologist who later studied David said:

"An assassin had taken his Uncle Jack when David was eight. An assassin had taken his father when David was twelve. Death had almost taken him, had almost taken two girl companions when he was eighteen, and had permanently crippled one of them and left the other with a lifelong limp. If he was next, could he avoid death?

"It could have been the reason he took his responsibilities so lightly, the reason he began to suffer intermittent sieges of depression, the reason he tried to alleviate his emotional pain by living as high as he could."

And it may have been one of the reasons he continued to take painkilling drugs after he had physically recovered from the Nantucket accident. By that time the tranquilizers had begun to take care of his emotional doubts, fears, and insecurities, as well as his physical sufferings.

David was a more closed and ingrown person after the Nantucket incident. His inner sensitivity was sharpened. The slightest hurt seem magnified. He brooded over personal slights and was plunged into depression over his own inadequacies.

He enrolled in Harvard in the fall and tried to take on college life with all the enthusiasm he could muster. His outward appearance belied his inner psychological doubts.

The image of David at the time was that of a typically

active, aggressive, action-oriented Kennedy kid. He was strong physically, alert, and quick. He continued to keep himself in good shape physically. He loved all the sports the Kennedys always loved: sailing, swimming, skiing, football.

The winter of 1973 was to be David's breakthrough to a better life, the promised life he had always been building up to. He was going to knuckle down to his books at Harvard and make them proud of him. His older sister, Kathleen, who was a senior at Radcliffe, was being married in November, and that was one good sign in the future.

Then, quite suddenly, everything turned sour. Kathleen was married—but on the very same day David's cousin Ted had his right leg amputated because of cancer.

The Kennedy curse was not gone at all. It was simply waiting in the wings for the rest of them. In fact, David was beginning to experience returns of the physical pain he had suffered in his accident in Joe's car.

He was put under medical care, which frequently included the use of drugs. In addition to Percodan, which he had been given when he was in the hospital, he was sometimes given Dilauded. To counteract depression, he was also given Quaaludes.

It is not unusual for patients with depression to be put on Quaalude therapy. The drug was developed as an aid to depression. Nevertheless, the drug is a dangerous one when combined with other depressants like liquor.

The combination of the two can cause permanent physiological damage, or death. In addition, one can become "hooked" on Quaaludes, or, even worse, move on to a dependence on drugs more powerful than Quaaludes as a result of that type of treatment.

No one will say exactly what dosage was prescribed for David in those years just after the Jeep accident. Nor will anyone say exactly what kind of medical care David was subjected to—that is, if his care included psychiatric help.

His work at college was suffering. He seemed unable to

concentrate on books or attend classes. Although he had always been bright and intelligent, he could not seem to focus his intelligence on the pursuit of knowledge—at least the way in which it was set up.

Harvard was a tough grind.

David was a Kennedy, and a Kennedy learned to accept challenges and overcome obstacles. Yet somehow David was not able to leap in, confront the problem, and whip it.

He drifted in and out of class, drifted in and out of relationships with friends, male and female, and drifted through his days as if in a kind of dream. Only it was not a dream—it was a nightmare.

In the summer of 1975, on July 12, shortly after his twentieth birthday, David was out driving his Toyota on Interstate 81 near New Market, Virginia. A state trooper clocked him at 92 miles an hour, went in pursuit, and nabbed him after a long chase. He was taken to the Woodstock barracks.

And David was in the courts once again. He was charged with driving without a license. The trooper reported that he was driving in a "reckless fashion." Certainly, at a speed of 92 miles an hour, he was way over the limit. He was told to appear in court that September. He did so and pleaded guilty to a charge of reckless driving. The county judge fined him $50 which he paid immediately. He was released.

Once again David was in the newspapers. Once again his mother was angry with him.

The family held a council. David could feel the pressure on him. He knew he was doing badly, failing at what Kennedys did best. He offered no excuses. He promised to do better. So far the situation did not seem serious enough to put him under any kind of special care.

But his mother was worried. Uncle Ted was concerned. And David himself knew something was very wrong. After all, his cousin Ted had survived the amputation of a leg, and was doing very well learning how to walk, run, and do everything a normal person could do—without a right leg!

Everyone in the family was doing better than he was.

But his studies continued to baffle him. He simply backed off and tried to get by without working.

He made it through his sophomore year, not without difficulty, and finally began his junior year. Then, one spring day, David ran through a stop signal and was stopped by police. This time he was charged with driving without a license and running a stop sign. He was fined $20 and released.

A pattern was emerging. David's more-than-occasional brushes with the law, his inability to settle down and simply get a driver's license, his obvious contempt for the law, and his more and more frequent sieges of deep depression—all these facts proclaimed some deep-seated psychological problems.

Suddenly in March, 1976, David was admitted to Massachusetts General Hospital, suffering from what was diagnosed by doctors there as "pneumonia."

Pneumonia is a disease marked by inflammation of one or more lobes of the lung, attended with chill, elevation of temperature, rapid breathing, pain in the side, and cough. There are many varieties of pneumonia, and it is a diseased state that is usually reached through complications due to any number of lesser complaints.

David complained first of abdominal pain and was believed to be suffering from appendicitis, until explorational surgery revealed that he was actually suffering from an inflammation of the lymph glands.

He was kept in the hospital for several weeks and then released. When he got out he was still taking medication of one kind or another. He could not keep his mind on his studies. Everything seemed to be falling to pieces.

At first he seriously settled down to his college work and seemed to be doing all right, but then quite suddenly he seemed unable to attend classes, to take tests, or to read books.

David tried to face the facts—that he was coming apart inside, that he was simply unable to cope with life. But somehow he could not admit it to himself. After all, he was a Kennedy. A Kennedy met the challenge and bested it!

There came a day when he couldn't face going back to class again. He turned his back on school. He got in his car and drove away. He never went back. There was never any official record of the time he dropped out of school, but the fact of his dropping out was noted.

The winter of 1976–77 was a nightmare. He began hanging around in various places with friends and talking about what he was going to do. Reality and unreality were becoming fused in David's mind. He was bright, everyone knew that. He could certainly finish college if he put his mind to it.

But it was impossible to do so.

In February 1977, David was arrested and ordered to appear in court to answer four specific motor vehicle charges. The report said that he had run a stop sign in Arlington, Massachusetts, that he had been driving an unregistered car, that the car was also uninsured, and that he was driving without an operator's license.

He pleaded guilty and paid a fine.

He drifted about, played with his cousins and brothers and sisters, and seemed completely at loose ends. The pain continued, and he kept on his medication, sometimes getting drugs from doctors who did not report the prescriptions.

In April, 1978, he was once again admitted to Massachusetts General Hospital in Boston suffering from pneumonia. He was suffering so much that he was put in the Intensive Care Unit. He was soon reported to be in a stable condition.

By now it was obvious to his family and his doctors that he was exhibiting a dangerous degree of recklessness toward his own physical well-being.

One of the physicians who treated David during that period of his life was Dr. Lee Macht, a prominent Harvard psychiatry professor and chief of psychiatry at Cambridge City Hospital.

He later admitted that he had issued David at least fifty prescriptions over a two-year period for various drugs like Percodan, Dilauded, and Quaaludes. Since he did not, as the law required, notify the state mental health department of these prescriptions, no one knew David was getting them.

That David was taking drugs fairly regularly did not seem to be general knowledge among the Kennedys. It did explain his casual attitude toward the laws of the land, his inability to cope with the realities of college life, and his own personal problems.

Sometime after his release from the hospital in Boston, David packed up his things, and drove down to New York where he got a cooperative penthouse apartment on East 72nd Street and began making the rounds of town, looking for some kind of part-time job, looking into the college scene, and drifting into the night life.

Big city night life during that era was centered mostly in the discos in Manhattan. The two most popular were Xenon and Studio 54. Studio 54 became notorious when two of its owners were indicted for tax evasion and sentenced to three-and-a-half years in jail. They had "hidden" from $350,000 to $400,000 in receipts and avoided paying taxes on it, according to the charges.

In fact, it was at Studio 54 that Hamilton Jordan, chief of staff of the White House under President Jimmy Carter, had allegedly procured and sniffed cocaine in 1977.

David immediately settled into the excitement and stimulus of the disco life. He roared about the city in his $15,000 BMW sports car, meeting people, and occasionally getting together with any of his Kennedy cousins who were in town.

He loved the Saturday night fever of the discos, where the heavy sound of the disco music was amplified to head-splitting level. He liked the sight of the girls in their flimsy dresses and the men in their John Travolta suits.

Celebrities appeared everywhere, as much to view the scene itself as be seen by the gawkers. The losers lined up in the streets outside the discos, waiting for their chance to get in. Many of them never made it, but it was enough—they had been brushed by the known, the chic, the "in."

And David was "in." The disco bosses loved to have him at the scene. He was a Kennedy. The Kennedys drew in other people—people on the make and people on the way down. Most of them didn't mind a little pot, a little cocaine, perhaps a little morphine.

Rumor had it that you could get your own cocaine at any disco if you paid enough for it.

Whatever the drawbacks—David didn't really like to be seen in public; he was basically a shy, introverted young man —he liked drifting about the city. He liked the heady life of being with those celebrities and hearing the loud music and watching the dancers whirling about.

Yet he recognized it for what it was. It was a backwash, a stagnant pool in which the losers of life floated about aimlessly.

He drew back from it, as a man might who couldn't make up his mind whether or not to jump over a precipice, and enrolled in Boston College, using his earned credits at Harvard to get in.

Boston College accepted him—what third-generation Kennedy wouldn't be accepted?—and David started in the fall. He had made up his mind to be successful at B.C.

Somehow it didn't work out that way. After a few months of studies, he began to tire of the work load. Soon he was driving around again aimlessly and drifting with various friends here and there.

About this time a rumor surfaced that the district attorney's office of Middlesex County was making an investigation into illegal prescriptions of drugs in the county. David's psychiatrist, Dr. Lee Macht, was one of the targets.

The rumor was true.

The illegality was not in the prescription of the drugs, but in the psychiatrist's failure to notify the state mental health department of the dosage.

The effect of the investigation, however, apparently frightened David and may have been enough to keep him away from his source.

Whether or not that was the reason he dropped out of Boston College after a few months, he did leave Massachusetts once again and moved into the penthouse in New York.

He met a model named Rachel Ward and friends of hers in what has been described as a "very fast crowd." Xenon was her favorite hangout, and it became David's as his relationship with her grew. Xenon was run by a management that very wisely aimed its wares at the rich preppie crowd.

David Anthony Kennedy was a perfect advertisement for Xenon and for the crowd it was trying to attract.

Rachel Ward was a successful model some three years younger than David. She was friendly with many big names in show business and the arts.

At a touch football game in early 1979, David broke his left leg and appeared in town in a walking cast. When he visited Xenon with his leg in a cast, along with Rachel Ward and another girl named Sara Metcuff, he danced to the disco music and clowned around at a table along the wall.

A photographer named John Bardazzi took pictures of him and the girls, and these appeared everywhere in newspapers and magazines.

David's Uncle Ted had been analyzing his chances for seeking the presidency, and these publicity pictures froze his blood. The family was angry over David's antics. The pictures made David look freaky and absolutely decadent. The family leaned on him, and David promised to do better. He began going out to look for a job, and decided that he would eventually go back to college to get his degree. But for the present, he would write an article on Urban League director Vernon Jordan, whom he had heard a lot about and who was a family friend. Writing seemed a natural career for him to pursue.

In 1979, David's sister Kathleen was married, had a child and was studying law in Santa Fe, New Mexico. His older brother Joe had straightened out his life, had married, and was a lawyer and embryonic politician in Boston. His brother Bobby had written a book on Judge Frank Johnson, and was a student at the University of Virginia Law School after graduation from Harvard. His cousin Caroline had worked on a newspaper one summer and was on the staff of the *Harvard Crimson.*

All the Kennedys were doing something—all but David. He would get a job. He would shape up.

But it never happened.

"We smoked joints now and then," Rachel Ward said, "but there was no suggestion of heroin." She liked David. "He ate like a pig and didn't take good care of himself, but he was crazy, with a wonderful sense of humor, and he was always very merry. He talked about his cousin Teddy and his father and his family in a happy way."

Rumors surfaced about David once again. It was said that he had been having "psychiatric problems" and that he had left Boston College because of these problems. More rumors surfaced: that he had originally dropped out of Harvard because of "psychiatric problems." There was no indication exactly as to what kind of problems these were.

It was a long hot summer, the summer of 1979. David was on the outs with his mother, with his Uncle Ted, and with his aunts and grandmother. And he was at a loss as to what he could do to get back on the right track again. It was not impossible to go back to college, but it was hard to believe that he could go back to that kind of life and make a success of it now, with two strikes against him already.

David was twenty-four years old. He had enough money to survive and would always have enough. Maybe he had too much, but that was beside the point. Why should he battle school administrators, teachers, and his own inadequacies by going to class and making a fool out of himself every time he opened his mouth?

Who needed everybody second-guessing him?

He was still trying to get it all together once again when another big blow landed on him.

The authorities had been closing in on Dr. Lee Macht in Cambridge. The New York authorities had been closing in on several of the disco operators in Manhattan, too. The drug supplies were rumored to be drying up.

No one knows for sure what David Anthony Kennedy was doing on the night of September 5 at a ramshackle building in Harlem called the Shelton Plaza Hotel at 300 West 116th Street.

The Shelton Hotel was well known to police officers who worked out of the 28th Precinct in New York. It was being used and had been used for years as a place where illicit drugs could be procured and administered.

It was 5:30 P.M., or thereabouts. David was driving his BMW sports coupe along West 116th Street near Eighth Avenue. According to his story, he was suddenly "signaled" by two men from the sidewalk. The men were making beckoning signs with their hands.

David said he parked the car and joined the two men on the sidewalk. After a short conversation, the two men took David into the lobby of the Shelton, in front of which they had been standing.

Once in the lobby, David reported that the two tried to beat him up and steal the $200 he had. They only got $30 of it.

David was dragged onto a stairway and punched and slammed against a wall. He was bloodied and bruised in the altercation.

Meanwhile, someone outside must have seen the struggle. At one point it was thought that David had a companion in the car with him. Whomever it was, the caller dialed 911 and reported that there was a white man being mugged in the lobby of the Shelton. Soon after that, there was another call, repeating essentially the same information.

A patrol car sped to the hotel. The siren alerted the muggers and they fled. The police rushed into the lobby and found David bleeding there. They pulled him out into the street.

David told them that he had been lured into the lobby and beaten up. Meanwhile, the police investigating the scene found twenty-five decks of heroin on the third floor of the building. The muggers had escaped in that same direction.

They did catch one possible suspect, but David said the man was not one of the two muggers. Upon further questioning, David's story changed slightly. At one point, he is said to have confessed that he was trying to buy heroin at the hotel.

"I'm a stoned-out junkie," he reportedly said.

However, that part of the story did not get into the newspapers immediately. Sources inside the police department admitted that the facts given to the newspapers were carefully laundered so as not to offend the Kennedys.

"Police here know you don't mess around with Kennedys," one source said.

David was not arrested. He was sent home.

Police reporters immediately got onto the story and began combing the Harlem area. What they discovered cast some doubts on the story David had told to police.

Several witnesses reported that they recognized David Kennedy not as a Kennedy, but as a frequenter of the hotel. He had come to the area several times in the past, and was known as "White James"—a strange appellation, but one that made sense in Harlem.

"He was brought up to the area months ago by a black dude and said his name was James," one source of information said. "But they got so many Jameses up here they put the tag 'White James' on him for obvious reasons."

Reporters questioned the police as to why they had not asked David the reason for his presence in Harlem.

"We don't ask complainants who allege robbery what they are doing at the scene," one officer at the 28th Precinct explained.

As to why David ran into trouble, if indeed he was known

in the area and had been there before, it was speculated by police that "with the wheels, he was easy to spot. He ran into trouble last night because his usual tout wasn't out front, but somebody knew he had bread and figured he was a mark."

Others agreed that David was not new to the neighborhood. "I've seen him before, a few times in the past months," one told a *Daily News* reporter. "You can't believe what the cops say, that he came down here and just parked and followed the two guys into here."

And that was the way things were on Wednesday, September 5. David reacted as any Kennedy would react after an unfortunate incident. He got in the car and drove to Hyannis Port.

There, one source revealed, he was put to bed and placed under medication. However, even though security was very good, and the family was aware of the terrible strain under which he was living, he managed somehow to escape from the compound on Monday, September 10.

Meanwhile, police had been trying to reach him to patch up some weak spots in the story he had told on Tuesday night.

But David could not be found in New York.

On Friday a registered letter was sent to his East 72nd Street apartment, explaining that he was needed for further information on the Harlem incident.

The letter remained unclaimed at the post office.

Reporters were swarming everywhere, trying to track down leads on the story. "We're looking forward to hearing from him," the police told reporters.

Then, quite suddenly, David ran out of money. He had been wandering around trying to live "out of pocket." On Tuesday, September 11, he once again turned himself in to his family.

A curtain of secrecy immediately descended. Reporters and police got their information about David through spokespersons working for the Kennedys.

The information said that David was in a "metropolitan

area hospital" for treatment of a drug addiction problem. It also said that he had been missing for one and a half days.

"David turned himself over to the family and he will be receiving long-term 'treatment' for his drug habit," the statement went. It also said that the family was reporting the facts in order to help "hold down all the rumors."

The New York cops were miffed. "No one from the family told us he was missing," one inspector said, sounding like a TV cop, "and no one asked us to render any assistance either formally or informally in finding him."

But the saga of David Kennedy had not yet ended. On September 13, the press reported that David was suffering from bacterial endocarditis in Massachusetts General Hospital, where he had been admitted twice before suffering from pneumonia.

Bacterial endocarditis, the story went on to explain, is an inflammation of the outer lining of the heart. Physicians everywhere know that bacterial endocaritis is a heart infection that is quite often—more often than not, in the opinion of one physician—associated with narcotics addition.

David was being treated by antibiotics, and "other treatment" by a team of doctors.

Stephen Smith, who ran the multimillion-dollar Kennedy portfolio, suddenly became the family spokesperson. He estimated David would need to stay there "several weeks."

He pointed out that David was in "serious condition," according to hospital officials. He was "seriously ill."

The inflammation of the heart lining could affect vital valves and seriously threaten his life.

The inflammation could have been caused by the use of needles.

"David has had a serious medical problem in recent years for which he has required hospitalization several times. The family for a long time has been very much concerned about his condition, and has endeavored to help him in what is finally a long and hard personal as well as medical struggle."

David voluntarily gave himself up to the family after the "incident" in New York, the statement went on. "It is the family's hope that people will understand David's need for privacy as he continues this difficult effort to get well."

It didn't take the newspapers long to write their headlines.

The *New York Post,* a notorious afternoon tabloid owned by Rupert Murdoch, an Australian publisher and owner of the most outrageous of the London thrill papers, headlined the story:

"RFK'S SON IN DESPERATE BATTLE TO BEAT DRUGS."

The *Daily News,* with the biggest circulation of any local daily newspaper in the country (with the exception of the *Wall Street Journal* which is a *national* newspaper) said:

"DAVID KENNEDY'S SECRET LIFE."

Friends of the Kennedys chastised the two newspapers for their "yellow journalistic tactics."

But the editor of the *Daily News* responded: "The Kennedy story, whether we like it or not, is the story of a great national family and everyone is interested in how tragedy affects their lives."

He said nothing about the politics involved, nor did he mention the fact that Teddy Kennedy was about to announce running for the presidency.

While the public was titillated at the stories and the speculation about a member of the famous Kennedy clan, the clan itself was not insensitive to the situation. Immediately they began a search for someone to help David.

Dr. Macht was out of the question. The investigation into his activities had been concluded. After pleading not guilty to charges of prescribing drugs without notifying the state mental health department, he agreed to plea bargaining and wound up paying a $1,000 fine. His license to prescribe "Class 2" drugs was suspended for a year.

The Kennedy family finally decided on Donald Juhl, executive director of a California-based drug-abuse program called Aquarian Effort. The Aquarian Effort is funded by the National Institute of Drug Abuse. The organization operates three clinics in Sacramento and another in nearby Yolo County.

According to a source in California, the Kennedys selected Juhl over any number of other drug-abuse treatment professionals because he had been recommended by a high-ranking Democrat in California whose son had had a similar problem.

Dr. David Smith, founder and director of the Haight-Ashbury Free Clinic in San Francisco, said he had been approached by Dr. Larry Horowitz, a physician on the staff of Senator Edward Kennedy in Washington. Horowitz wanted an opinion on the Aquarian Effort "because it had offered to work with David Kennedy."

Dr. Smith told Horowitz that he had always been impressed by Juhl's tenacity and his "determination to hang in there in difficult circumstances."

When Juhl was summoned by the Kennedys, he moved in with David and began treating him on a one-to-one basis.

Dr. Smith, who has had experience treating addicts, said that David Kennedy was in a "very difficult spot," because this is the time when [addicts] hit bottom and make a serious effort to recover or they keep going down to self-destruction."

For a few weeks in November, David had spent some time in Palm Beach, Florida, where his grandmother Rose was accustomed to spend the winter.

Reporters who tried to get at him were unsuccessful. But there were always people who would talk about the Kennedys.

"He seems to be doing okay," one of them told a reporter, who duly wrote it up in a newspaper story. "He's not doing much of anything these days. However, the family is trying to get him a job in Tennessee on a local newspaper."

With his grandmother, he very soon returned to Hyannis Port, Massachusetts, where he spent the end of the year in the heart of the family at the Kennedy compound. It was there that Juhl took over his therapy work.

There was no question about it. David was a troubled individual. He was twenty-four years old and still drifting about like a teen-ager, having failed to finish his education—a prerequisite for any Kennedy in the rough-and-tumble modern world.

He was also making news in the tabloids like some kind of wastrel offspring of an aristocratic family. And that kind of news wasn't helping his Uncle Ted, who in November announced his run for the presidential candidacy.

One friend of David's with an understanding of him and the problems he faced was philosophical about his ordeal.

"He is an awfully nice guy," said Madeleine Fudeman, who met David at Xenon. "Maybe it's better he got caught now, before he is too far gone."

David staged a sudden return to New York on the weekend of March 8, 1980. On that Saturday evening he appeared, without fanfare, at Xenon with his kid brother Michael. It was his first public appearance since he had begun drug treatment.

Michael had been making the rounds fairly regularly without David, and this was one of his few recent appearances with his brother. In fact, Michael was sedately dressed, and, according to patrons of the disco, "he seemed to be keeping tabs on his older brother throughout the evening."

But David was the focus of all attention. "I think he looked a little bit heavier than he did when I saw him last," said one friend whom David had dated in the past.

He spent his time moving from table to table, talking to friends, and even taking a turn on the dance floor.

"I'm over the drug thing," he said to one of his acquaintances.

Michael kept bobbing up everywhere David was, acting for all the world like a chaperone.

"You back in town for good?" one friend asked.

David shook his head. "I'm only here briefly to visit my old friends."

Someone asked him where he was staying now—Hyannis Port, Palm Beach, or Virginia?

David told them that he was not staying in the East at all but was out on the Coast where he was working for a "publishing company." He said he had been there for the past three months.

"I just came in from Washington, where I've been visiting relatives at home," he said. He was planning to fly back to his job in California the first of the week.

To another acquaintance David confided that he was afraid his appearance at Xenon might lead everyone to think that he was going to be back on the disco scene for good. It wasn't true at all, David said. He was only in town for a brief visit.

Although he seemed to look all right, he complained later on in the evening that he was not feeling well. Quickly Michael appeared and the two of them left.

Ironically, they were exiting at exactly the same moment David's younger sister Mary Kerry came in. She was at Xenon to try to put together a list of well-heeled guests for a fund-raiser she was running for her Uncle Ted on the following Sunday.

Neither Michael nor David came back. New York City got nothing more out of it than a very brief look at David—the first sight of him after his troubles began piling up in the fall of 1979.

CHAPTER 8
Edward Moore Kennedy, Jr.

It was a cool day in November, 1973, and Edward Moore Kennedy, Jr. was in an unusual place. He was home in bed in the rambling old ranch-style house the Kennedys owned in McLean, Virginia, overlooking the Potomac River.

He was usually at school or out playing. Today, however, the Kennedy family governess had made him stay home from school again. He had been home Monday and Tuesday because he had a fever and the beginnings of a cold.

Besides that, he had been walking around with a sore leg for a couple of days already. He played football on the team at St. Albans School, where he was in the seventh grade. The sore leg could certainly have been a result of some play he had made. It was nothing new in his young life. Since his childhood he had been competitive and athletic, like all the Kennedys.

He sailed during the summer with his cousins off the Cape, had once rafted down the Colorado River with his father, played a tough game of tennis on the family courts, and skied at Sun Valley every winter.

Yet this sore leg was a little different. It nagged at him. It wouldn't go away. It hurt when he walked. There was a kind of hard, reddish lump, about the size of half his kneecap, three or four inches below his right knee.

Now, after two days of enforced inactivity, he was beginning to rebel against the enforced leisure. He had read most of the magazines and comic books in the house, and the television was boring with a lot of soap operas and game shows on during the day.

He was alone at home with the governess. His mother was in Europe attending an Austrian music festival. She played the piano and had once performed a concert with the Boston Pops Orchestra.

The senator was in Washington, preparing a speech he was to give later in the week in Boston. He was preoccupied as usual with the day-to-day pressures of his job. Ted's sister Kara was at school, and so was his younger brother Patrick.

When his mother was away, the governess was in charge. Everyone obeyed her. When she had first noticed the sore leg, she had thought it was a normal bruise. She had seen many of them, usually caused by football.

But when this one refused to go away she knew she should tell the senator, even though it might prove to be nothing at all. So that night Senator Kennedy was alerted to the bruise and promised to glance at his son's leg when he came in to talk to him.

Young Edward—called Ted just like his father—wondered why his father was bothering so much about his leg. But he answered him truthfully.

"It hurts a little, but I've had worse," he said.

"How did you get it?" the senator said.

"I don't really know. Maybe playing football at school."

His father studied the leg a little longer and then went out of the room. Later on that same evening, after Ted had spent some time with his sister, Kara, and Patrick, a man in formal evening attire came up into the bedroom with the senator.

It was Dr. Philip Caper, a member of the senator's Subcommittee on Health. Dr. Caper had been attending a formal dinner that evening, but had come quickly when he got the senator's call.

Dr. Caper asked Ted some of the same questions the senator had. He actually thought it was simply a bruise that would go away. However, he knew from his training that he had to be concerned about the possibility of something like a bone tumor.

"We'll want to keep a close watch on it, son," he told Ted and then got up to go. He turned to the senator. "If the swelling doesn't go down in two days, call me. If it does go down, there's no need."

The governess was told to keep watch.

Two days later she examined him and discovered that the swelling had not gone down. If anything, it might be a little worse. The senator was in Boston, giving an important speech. She put in a call to his hotel room, and he instructed her to call Dr. Caper.

When Dr. Caper heard that the bruise had not healed, he told the governess to drive Ted over to Georgetown Hospital for tests. The boy was brought over to the orthopedics section, where Dr. George Hyatt, head of the department, joined Dr. Caper and examined the leg.

Then he took X-rays of the leg.

Studying the X-rays, and comparing them with what they could see visually, the two doctors agreed that the bruise was suspicious. They watched Ted as he limped out of the hospital with the governess.

When the senator returned to Washington, Dr. Caper was waiting for him at the airport.

"That leg looks serious," he said without preliminaries. "We suspect it might be a cancerous bone tumor."

At Georgetown Hospital, Dr. Hyatt confirmed what Dr. Caper had told the senator. "We think that your son has a bone tumor of his right tibia. That's the inner of the two bones in the lower leg. I want to make several more tests, and call in additional consultants."

The senator agreed.

Ted was sent back to the hospital the same day, and through Friday and Saturday, teams of doctors from the Du-Pont Clinic of Wilmington, Delaware, and the Mayo Clinic in Rochester, Minnesota, probed and poked about at the leg. In the end, everyone agreed. A complete examination was mandatory. Then Ted was subjected to more X-ray treatment. His entire body was photographed to see if there could be any spread of the cancer spotted.

By Saturday, Ted knew that something must be up. He had never had so many examinations, or so many doctors asking him questions. The senator realized his son must be anxious. Of course, he couldn't tell him the whole truth, because the whole truth really wasn't yet known.

"There's still a rough spot on your leg," he told Ted, "and Dr. Caper and the other people at Georgetown want to examine it more fully."

Ted was up and out of bed by now, and the senator let him go to a party that night. On Monday Ted went back to school. That same day, his mother flew back from Europe after the senator had called her.

Tuesday a biopsy was scheduled to open up the leg and examine the tissues in the bruise under a microscope. Half a dozen specialists would be there to examine Ted.

And, in what seemed like a logistics exercise to equal anything since World War II, all Ted's cousins on the Kennedy side were flown in, driven in, or walked in to be with Ted.

Even Louella Hennessy, then seventy, a semiofficial "nurse" for the entire Kennedy family for forty years, arrived from Boston.

Up to now Ted had experienced only examinations and X-rays. Now he was slated for surgery. He was wheeled into the operating room, and Dr. Hyatt, assisted by three physicians, with Dr. Caper observing, gave Ted a general anesthetic.

The incision was made, and a slice of the suspected tumor removed. This frozen section was immediately examined by Dr. Kent C. Johnson, Jr., of the Armed Forces Institute of Pathology.

It didn't take him long to look at the frozen section and determine that it was malignant.

"It looks like a chondro," he said.

"Chondro" was the familiar term physicians use for chondrosarcoma, a fast-growing cancer of the cartilage. Actually, it was a very rare bone cancer, usually found in children. In spite of the bad news, chondrosarcoma was about the most controllable of the bone cancers. It had a 70 percent survival rate of ten years.

Had the tumor been osteosarcoma, or primary bone cancer, the chances of survival would have been much less, with only 23 percent surviving for five years.

The survival rate, of course, depended upon immediate amputation of the area affected by the tumor.

Back in his room, Ted was unaware of the diagnosis. In fact, he was still sleeping off the anesthesia. Nor did any of the Kennedys know of the diagnosis as yet.

Forty-five minutes after the biopsy had been performed, the medical team assembled in a conference room and were introduced to Joan and Senator Kennedy.

Dr. Hyatt, acting as chairman, explained that the biopsy had indeed proved malignant, and explained the medical facts about chondrosarcoma. One by one, the members of the team stated their opinion:

Ted's leg must come off.

Furthermore, they were equally sure about the details. Whether it should come off above or below the knee seemed obvious. The knee joint might well be infected. They were unanimous in stating their opinion that the leg should come off above the knee.

They were also unanimous that it must come off "as soon as possible."

There was a problem. Ted still had a cold, and the cold would be made worse by the anesthesia to which he had been subjected. The first day possible for the operation would be Saturday morning.

Ted's mother and father didn't want him to know immediately what was going to happen. It was decided to delay telling him until one day before the operation. But who was going to do the unpleasant job? The doctors at first told the senator that they felt they should do it.

But Kennedy said, "No, he's my son. *I'm* going to tell him."

Louella Hennessy, who was there when he made up his mind, said: "I think Ted grew 20,000 feet in my estimation during that time."

The press had recognized the importance of the operation by the number of Kennedys running around the hospital. They knew there was something in the works. It didn't take them long to find out what it was.

Richard Drayne, Senator Kennedy's press secretary, met with them and begged them to hold off on the story until Friday, when they could all break it together.

"We don't want him to hear on the radio or see in the paper that he has cancer."

The Kennedy clan began trooping in, one by one, two by two, three by three, for visits during Wednesday and Thursday. Even non-Kennedys sent their best wishes. President Nixon rang up and spoke with Ted and his father both.

Senator Kennedy was deeply touched by the president's thoughtfulness.

In spite of the press pledge, Ted found that his radio and television set had been removed from his hospital room. He knew there was a lot more going on than he could know about. He was frightened, but he never let on to all the cousins and aunts and uncles constantly by his bedside.

In spite of all the precautions, a London newspaper broke the story ahead of time, and that prompted its release in the

United States. But that was Friday, and by that time the senator, his wife, and Dr. Hyatt had broken the news to Ted.

"We know what's wrong with your leg," the senator told
him.

His mother was gripping his hand hard—harder than
she usually grasped it.

"What is it?"

"Your leg has a kind of cancer inside it."

Ted knew what cancer was. "Does that mean I'm going
to die?"

The senator shook his head. "The doctors are going to
stop the cancer from spreading into the rest of your body,
son." He took a grip on himself, and got the words out:
"They're going to have to take your leg off."

Ted glanced at his father and his mother. She was trying
to keep from trembling. "They'll give you another leg!"

"It's a kind of challenge," the senator said. "We all have
challenges and we try to surmount them."

Ted knew about his father's serious airplane accident,
in which several other people were killed and badly injured,
and which caused his father to lie for nine months completely
immobilized in an orthopedic Stryker frame, able only to move
his head, hands and feet, and be rotated from one side to the
other every three hours of the day to prevent bed sores—like
"a human rotisserie."

He knew about his Uncle Jack's battle for years with a
bad back. He knew about challenges generally, and what they
were.

This one would be a hard one to fight.

"It's another adventure to be mastered."

He saw that his mother was openly weeping now. "Don't
cry anymore, Mother."

The operation was scheduled for 8 A.M. the next morning. That night, Ted was put under sedation, and slept early.
The room was empty for the first time in days.

By a supreme and ironic coincidence—a typically Kennedyesque quirk of fate—Ted's cousin Kathleen was being married on that same day at Holy Trinity Church in Georgetown, only three blocks from the hospital. And Ted's father was giving the bride away!

At 8:30 next morning the operation began. Dr. Hyatt led the medical team that did the job. Incisions were made through the skin, muscle, tissue, and then a surgeon's saw cut through the femur—thighbone—above the knee. As soon as the incision was closed, Ivan R. Sabel, a bio-engineer who specialized in fitting artificial limbs, applied a rigid plaster cast around the remaining part of the limb.

The cast was to harden directly over the wound. The tight dressing would prevent postoperative swelling, and would minimize the pain. This would allow the healing process to begin immediately.

The plaster cast would then be removed and used to shape a temporary artificial limb called a "sach foot" so that this "instant prosthesis" could be attached.

The technique used here was a relatively new one, introduced less than a decade before by Dr. Marian A. Weiss of Poland. It was based on the theory that since the leg is four-sided—quadrilateral—rather than truly round, a limb would fit more snugly into a prosthesis made in that shape. Holding it in would be a phenomenon called "negative pressure," or what the layman calls suction.

Once the prosthesis was fitted to the limb, it would be held securely in place.

The sach foot, or temporary limb, would only be used until a permanent one, designed to fit the body, was fashioned.

By 10 A.M. the operation was all over. Learning that Ted was responding "uneventfully," in medical terms, the senator left the hospital to hurry for church. He arrived on time and at 11 A.M. gave his niece Kathleen away to David Lee Townsend. Then the senator rushed back to the hospital.

When Ted woke up, he was very groggy, not only from the surgery, but from the anesthesia. His father and mother were there, and so was Dr. Hyatt. And so was the temporary aluminum leg that he would learn to use, fitted into place on his leg.

Ted looked at the flimsy piece of metal and turned up his nose at it. He really didn't think it was much of a leg.

When the wound had healed enough Dr. Hyatt wheeled Ted into the physical therapy room on Ted's floor at the hospital. There he was introduced to Dr. Donald A. Covalt, a rehabilitation specialist.

Covalt got right down to business. "Now this is what you're going to have to learn. It's complicated, but once you catch on, you'll be able to do it automatically."

He explained patiently the various steps in using an artificial leg.

- First, Ted must learn to bend the flexors—the muscles used to pull the leg back.

- Then he must lift the artificial leg and swing it forward.

- When the heel of the foot touched the ground, he must reverse the action of the hip by using the extensors—the muscles that move the leg outward—to extend the artificial knee.

- Once he straightened the knee and locked it in place, he would be ready to rest his weight on the prosthesis and swing his good leg forward.

- From that point on, the process was simply a repetition of the same steps.

"Let's stand up and try it," Covalt said.

Ted held on tightly to the sides of the wheelchair and slowly began to rise. Finally he got himself up out of the chair and put his weight on both legs.

"Now take a step."

Ted straightened up. He was shaking. He was frightened. But he resolved not to cry out or wince in any way. The Kennedy courage seemed to charge through him.

"How does it feel?"

"It hurts," Ted admitted.

"It will hurt until it heals. You can do it," said Dr. Hyatt.

It was true. He could do it. He took a dozen steps to the parallel bars along the wall of the room. He grabbed them hard and grinned. He had done it. He had walked without his right leg.

Drs. Covalt and Hyatt sat him again in his wheelchair and wheeled him back to his room. From that moment on he had physical therapy sessions—sometimes as many as twice a day—and his progress was speedy.

Sometimes at night he could feel pain in the leg—when there wasn't any leg there! The doctors explained that it was "phantom" pain, a common medical phenomenon. Louella Hennessy was there now, and she rubbed his back, helping him through the painful moments.

All during Ted's convalescence, the senator stayed each night in the room with his son. He only went to the Senate for two or three hours a day. He ate all his meals with Ted, and accompanied him each time to therapy.

Louella Hennessy said of Ted's father: "It was so difficult for him to look down and see that the leg was not there. There'd be tears in his eyes."

The news of Ted's ordeal had broken around the world. Over 50,000 letters and get-well cards came to the senator's office for his son. Flowers poured in. And there were all kinds of gifts.

The next day Ted found it wasn't quite so hard to put on the obnoxious aluminum leg, and stump about the room. It was, just as his father had explained, a "challenge." And he accepted the challenge. He could stand for fifteen minutes by Monday.

At the end of the week, he was walking the distance from the room all the way down the hall to the elevator by himself. Kara and Patrick were always with him when he walked down the corridor.

The wound was healing, too. Now it didn't hurt anymore. He spent more and more time out of bed.

To answer all his well-wishers, Ted wrote a note in his own handwriting and had it duplicated and mailed so that everyone who had written to him would have a reply.

He continued to improve rapidly. His doctors kept him under close observation, both at the therapy unit where he worked out on the bars, and in his own private room.

"Listen, Teddy," his father told him one day, "I've got a ski instructor with one leg lined up, and I guarantee you if you get through your therapy and get strong, you're going to be the best skier!"

And he made the promises come true.

On Friday, November 30, exactly thirteen days after the operation, Ted Kennedy, Jr., walked out of Georgetown Hospital through a crowd of people outside, without help.

Although he used a pair of crutches, he was well able to control the sach foot that was attached to his right leg.

Gripped in one arm was a football that had been given him by the coach of the Washington Redskins professional football team, George Allen. Allen had taken the football to him when he learned from news reports of the operation that Ted was a Redskins fan.

Once he got home, he started immediately to dig into the books to make up for the three weeks of school work he had lost. And he continued to take the therapeutic exercises to learn to walk on the artificial limb which had been fitted.

His sister and brother helped him, along with the cousins nearby who came around to help. His last X-ray pictures at the hospital had indicated that the cancer which had attacked his leg had been arrested.

A week before Christmas his father took him to the Senate office. Ted was overwhelmed by the magnitude of the piles of gifts. There were hundreds of packages piled against the wall. It took him an hour just to open the boxes. From these gifts he selected only a few, and then gave the rest of the toys to kids in the local hospitals. Most of them went to Children's Hospital in Washington to help the needy with their Christmas.

Next step was the substitution of an artificial leg for the aluminum and rubber sach foot. At Capital Orthopedics in Washington, Dr. Covalt took charge of Ted and showed him how to use the regular prosthesis. Called an "AK" model, it was an above-the-knee semisuction limb which was the simplest kind to wear.

The prosthesis, the latest in artificial legs, consisted of an articulated metal-and-wood knee which bent with the same resistance as a human knee, a leg section made of plastic, and a foot of molded rubber. The leg weighed 7½ pounds and cost about $1,000.

Although the AK generally is held in place by suction, Ted was such an active boy that a leg was temporarily attached to the limb by means of a belt fastened around his waist.

At first he walked with a pronounced limp, but as he continued to use the leg, he began to lose that.

In spite of the tremendous progress Ted was making, it was still only the beginning of his treatment. Amputation had been simply one step in the process of arresting the cancerous growth that had been found.

Now came the anticancer treatment. Led by Drs. Caper and Hyatt, a group of doctors met with Senator Kennedy and his wife at the Kennedy house overlooking the Potomac.

The group included Dr. Hugh H. Fudenberg, from the University of California at San Francisco; Dr. Emil Frei III from Boston; Dr. James F. Rolland from New York's Mount Sinai School of Medicine; Dr. Kent C. Johnson, Jr., of the Armed Forces Institute of Pathology; and Dr. Joseph Ballant of Georgetown University Hospital.

The point of the discussion was to make sure the treatment initiated would ensure that the cancer would not recur.

A four-hour discussion followed, outlining the therapeutic methods available. Some of these were rejected outright because of their experimental nature. Others were scrapped because they were needed only if the patient had active cancer, which Ted Kennedy did not have.

Finally a twenty-four-month course of treatment involving the powerful anticancer drug methotrexate was decided upon.

This was Dr. Frei's innovation. He had pioneered the use of methotrexate. They found that many drugs could keep cancer cells from multiplying, finally killing them, but these drugs could also harm normal cells. An antidote called citrovorium factor, closely related to folic acid (a vitamin), was used.

Dr. Frei and a colleague, Dr. Norman Jaffe of Children's Hospital, had used the drug-plus-antidote for two years on twenty-one children, and in only two cases had the cancer spread. None of the children had had serious side effects.

In addition to the methotrexate and antidote, a special backup treatment was held in reserve. This treatment was composed of a "booster" compound obtained from the blood of Ted's mother and the Kennedy family governess. Called a "transfer factor," the compound was supposed to help the body resist further cancer growth, if such occurred.

The compound was derived from normal persons exposed to a cancer patient who have not come down with the disease. These persons are usually household contacts.

"Transfer factor" is exceedingly powerful. Only a small amount is ever necessary to transfer immunity. The compound was not used, but only held in reserve if there was a sudden growth of the cancer.

"We don't know for sure if we are doing the right thing," Dr. Caper admitted. "We may have been better off doing nothing. But decisions in medicine are made that way. We tried to balance the benefits to Ted against the risk."

The chemotherapy treatment was given under the supervision of Dr. Jaffe, and involved three consecutive days of extreme unpleasantness, scheduled every three weeks. And so, beginning in February 1974, every third Friday afternoon Ted and his father or his mother flew up to Boston to admit him to Boston Children's Hospital. It was there that experiments with methotrexate were developed.

Louella Hennessy was always there to watch over him in his room.

First came six hours of massive, painful injections of the drug, 2,000 times the normal dosage. The toxic substance killed cancerous as well as healthy cells.

Then, massive doses of an antidote were administered a few hours later, then periodically for three days. The methatrexate level in his bloodstream was constantly checked to make sure the antidote was taking effect. There was little pain but a very sick feeling that very frequently caused vomiting. And it sometimes was difficult to get to sleep.

Ted had lived a healthy young life, and had experienced very little sickness during his twelve years. He wasn't used to feeling nauseated and sick. Now he became accustomed to it.

But he gritted his teeth and didn't let it get him down. Even though he was impatient to be done with the course of therapy, he only occasionally let himself become irritable and make life miserable for those around him.

Senator Kennedy learned how to give injections of the antidote at home. Ted left for Boston on Friday afternoon after school and returned to Virginia Sunday night in time to go back to school the next day.

One hardened doctor on the staff at Children's Hospital summed up the institution's feeling about Ted Kennedy, Jr.:

"That kid's terrific."

He was that.

In fact, he had always been "terrific."

Edward Moore Kennedy, Jr., was born on September 26, 1961. He was the second of Ted Kennedy's three children. His father was the youngest of the seven Kennedy children. Wherever the Kennedys went, Ted, Sr., was always called "the baby."

Because so much attention was focused on the six other brothers and sisters, "Teddy" managed to grow up doing pretty much what he wanted. Yet he was instinctively a Kennedy at heart. He loved athletic endeavors. He loved sailing. He loved doing the good things in life.

Ted, Sr., inherited his father's interest in attractive women, as well. He was married to Virginia Joan Bennett, a quiet, unassuming, very beautiful young woman who had been born and bred in Bronxville, New York.

She had studied piano from an early age and she was a good student at school and college, taking courses in sociology and American history. For a short period she became a model, represented by a top modeling agency in New York City.

It was during this period of her life that she met her future husband. After their marriage, Joan tried to fit into the Kennedy mold—that fast-moving, energetic, pace-setting mold that was typified by Kennedys like John and Robert and by Kennedys-by-marriage like Ethel.

But it never worked out. She was too quiet, too private a person. She tried to be a good wife to Teddy and looked forward to having his children, but she was unable to form any warm personal relationships with any of the Kennedy women.

She did like Jacqueline Kennedy the best of the Kennedy clan women. Liz Smith wrote: "Joan admires Jackie's bright culture, taste, and most of all her witty bitchery." Once when Joan was sick, Jacqueline brought her books to read. She got them from the library, and they were sent back when Joan finished with them. Jacqueline didn't believe in spending money on anyone outside her immediate family.

It was into this atmosphere that Ted, Jr., was born. Joan had developed a hormonal deficiency which made her pregnancies precarious. She was forced to spend most of her pregnancy with Ted, Jr., in bed on doctor's orders.

Ted grew up in a much quieter atmosphere than did his cousins nearby at Hickory Hill. But he and his sister Kara were always instructed in current events and the political happenings of the day. Ted grew up watching news on television and explaining and discussing the events afterward.

Then his mother and father would explain to him and his sister what they did during the day. When his father was elected senator from Massachusetts in 1962, the family moved to McLean, Virginia, near Ted's brother Robert.

Ted went to ten o'clock Mass every Sunday at Holy Trinity in Georgetown. His mother was not a daily communicant like Rose Kennedy, his grandmother, or Ethel, his aunt.

Ted grew up to be a good athlete. He loved to swim and played tennis. His two main occupations, however, were sailing and camping. He was never a boisterous youth, but had a certain shyness of his own. His looks suggested those of a typical Kennedy, but he spoke in quiet tones, and his eyes looked away when he talked to strangers. He was the only Kennedy, one observer said, ever seen to blush at a compliment.

Lester David wrote that the Ted Kennedy children were "quieter, more like their cousin Caroline, in sensitivity."

They grew up polite and unspoiled. Joan once explained that she and her husband worked hard to develop their children's manners. "We're always reminding them how fortunate they are to be able to have the best of everything."

That included telling them exactly how much they were paying for their rooms when they were staying overnight at a hotel, or living in a rented place on the ski slopes during winter vacations.

Another time-honored Yankee trait of frugality entered into their training, too. If they were to lose anything they owned, like a toy or a piece of clothing, they were supposed to pay for its replacement out of their own allowance. And, Joan told a writer, their allowances weren't very big.

Nevertheless, all was not well in the Kennedy household as Ted grew up. His mother seemed to be unable to bear up under the tremendous pressure of her life. Most of the trouble stemmed from her effort to conform to the Kennedy mold and her basic inability to do so. She visited psychiatrists to find the answer to her dilemma.

After her visits the pressure seemed to abate some, but then it always returned with renewed vigor. There were pills and alcohol. And finally came the straw that almost broke the back of the already tenuous marriage.

The incident at Chappaquiddick Bridge on Martha's Vineyard has been retold so many times it would be redundant to say a word about it here. But the fact that a young woman was dead, and that the incident itself occurred, brought into the scrutiny of the public the freewheeling social life of Senator Kennedy, which only added pressure to the already unsupportable problem of Joan's life.

Yet she rallied and became an ally of her husband's, trying to brush off the fury of the public against his actions. Her unexpected strength in the crisis helped him through those bad days, but eventually the strain began to show once again. She went to psychiatrists and rest homes.

Even before Ted's problem with his leg, there were rumors of a separation. The husband and wife spent little time together. Ted's ordeal brought them together for a brief moment at least. Everyone hoped it would last.

In the summer of 1973, when the rumors of a breakup were at their height, Ted went with his father out West to ride the Colorado River in a raft with a group of the senator's Washington friends and their sons.

Joan took Ted's sister Kara to Europe. Kara returned home, but Joan continued traveling in Europe, visiting Salzburg, Austria, and attending the Volpi Ball in September. With six hundred revelers she danced to 6 A.M. at the Venice palazzo of Giovanni Volpi, an Italian financier and "most eligible bachelor." She was photographed dancing with Giorgio Pavone, a Roman publicist. At one bash she was found dancing with Prince Rainier.

It was at the end of this extended trip through Europe that she heard about her son's trouble and flew home.

By early January 1974, Ted was in Palm Beach, Florida, visiting his grandmother Rose's house. He got hold of an old tricycle in the garage that some of the Kennedys had used before, and was pedaling up and down the road with his crutches in a wire basket behind him.

Then, barely four months after the initial operation, photographers took pictures of him skiing in Vail, Colorado, with two additional miniature skis attached to his ski poles for balance. His instructor said that he was doing well with it. There were pictures of him in the newspapers, being accompanied by his brother Patrick.

One month after that he traveled along with his parents to Russia, touring the museums, churches and public markets in Moscow, like any other tourist. He shook hands with Communist party chairman, Leonid Brezhnev, and even sat in Czar Nicholas' easy chair in the Kremlin museum. Afterwards, the group went to Leningrad and to southern Russia for more sightseeing.

At the beginning of summer, he flew to Ireland for a month-long minibus tour with five other boys. One was his cousin and friend, Joey Gargan; another was Teddy Tunney, the son of Senator John V. Tunney of California. Senator Tunney was Ted's godfather. Accompanying them was twenty-seven-year-old Rick Van Nuys of Boston.

In Ireland at the same time was his sister Kara accompanied by Aunt Pat and the three Lawford girls.

En route to Dublin Ted began sniffling with a head cold. He stayed indoors one day to try to get rid of it, and then after that they traveled to Carrick-on-Shannon, 90 miles northwest of Dublin, for a cruise along Ireland's famed River Shannon.

Three days after he had arrived in Ireland, Ted learned that his mother had been sent to Silver Hill Foundation, in New Canaan, Connecticut, for treatment. This attack had apparently been brought on by the pressure of Ted's ordeal.

She had been in a private psychiatric hospital in May,

and at that time the press had reported that she was under "continuous strain because of the serious illness of the Kennedy's son Edward, Jr., which required the amputation of his leg last November and has required regular treatment since that surgery. She was also very fatigued when she returned from the trip she took with the senator and two older children to Europe and the Soviet Union. Her doctor strongly urged that she take a complete and prolonged rest."

After their return to Dublin, Ted began feeling sick once again, this time with nausea he had experienced in Children's Hospital during his treatment.

He wound up in Saint Vincent's Hospital in Dublin. Doctors found that he was suffering from the side effects of his anticancer treatments. He stayed over the weekend at the hospital, and on Monday his father flew to Ireland to join him. He was soon discharged and left with the senator to spend several days fishing off the Aran Islands in Galway Bay.

It was the only time Ted ever had a bad reaction from the therapy he was required to take.

Next May, Ted accompanied his mother and father on a tour of the Mideast, starting with Saudi Arabia, where they were received by King Khalid, and then on to Jidda, the Red Sea port, and to Iraz, an Arab socialist country that had no diplomatic relations with the United States since the Seven Day War in 1967. After that, the itinerary included Iran and Israel.

Shortly after that tour was completed, Ted went back for treatment at Children's Hospital and got good news. He had been tested and watched for eighteen months, and no evidence of cancer had appeared. The physicians in charge of his therapy said that he did not need to take any more treatments.

"Because of good progress, treatment was ended in eighteen months," the official report stated. "There is no evidence of a recurring malignancy at the present time."

The worst part of the ordeal—the treatment—was over.

He would have to be tested regularly, of course, to be sure the cancer had not reappeared, but he did not have to go through the nauseating treatment by methotrexate.

When he had first been operated on, Ted had started a correspondence with Steve Southerland, the fifteen-year-old son of a Miami policeman. Steve had lost a leg for the very same reason Ted had. Their letters had begun with a mutual complaint:

"I don't have any friends who are amputees."

Now a new spirit was reflected in them.

"Things are going pretty well," wrote Ted.

Steve answered: "I am beginning to adjust well to my artificial leg and I know how great it is to be off therapy."

That was the key: to be off therapy.

Things began to settle down for Ted. He went back to school and renewed his attack on the books. He spent the summer of 1976 with his cousins and family. In 1977 he earned $2.35 an hour directing cars onto ferries going over to Nantucket and Martha's Vineyard from Cape Cod.

The next year he determined to get himself a better job. He applied for a number of them, selecting the position of recreation assistant on three cruise lines that operated in the Mediterranean—a British, an Italian and a French line.

The British responded with regret: the labor unions wouldn't stand for hiring an American, the Italians also would not hire him. But the French decided to take a chance on him.

Obviously, the firm of Croisiéres Paquet understood the magic of the Kennedy name and realized that this was the son of a possible U.S. presidential candidate.

Ted's job took him to the Mediterranean and the cruise ship *Azur,* where he was made assistant to the recreation director. His instinctive reserve was beginning to change a bit as he grew up. The Kennedy verve was never much below the surface.

The women tourists, in particular, were attracted to the

handsome young man. His missing leg seemed to add an aura of allure to his smiling, casual all-American visage.

"Un beau garçon," muttered one Frenchwoman from Alsace-Lorraine.

A beautiful Parisian, eyeing him with calculating appraisal saw the leg and bit her lip: "Quel dommage!" (What a pity!)

The cruise ship sailed from Toulon and stopped at ports in Greece, Yugoslavia, Turkey, Egypt, Israel, and Italy. Ted's jobs included any number of duties like playing deck games with the guests, decorating the ship for Bastille Day, and entertaining in show biz style at night. He even imitated Maurice Chevalier at one point, and got a rousing cheer when it was over.

In Egypt, small children ran up to him and wanted to touch his artificial leg. "They'd never seen anything like it," he said in surprise.

At one point he was giving scuba diving lessons in the pool of the cruise ship. When he swam, Ted removed his leg, and astonished the guests by the way he could glide through the water.

An instructor said: "He's like a big clumsy albatross hopping around on deck. Then he gets into the water—and transforms himself into a fish! And I'll tell you something else. That boy even smiles underwater. I never saw anyone do that."

He had a companion from school named Adam Randolph rooming with him. The captain of the ship was appalled at the housekeeping of his American employees. He called them into his cabin and bawled them out. But Ted charmed even him.

"I've never met a Kennedy before," Captain Jean-Marie Guillou said, "but if they're all like this young man, it is easy to see why the family is so exceptional."

After the excitement of the trip, Ted returned to the

United States and enrolled at Wesleyan University in Middletown, Connecticut, for his freshman year.

But even Ted Kennedy made mistakes, as if to prove that he was still a Kennedy in spite of all the positive publicity he had gotten. One night in New York he visited Studio 54, the city's famed disco. Plenty of Kennedys went to Studio 54— that wasn't the problem. The problem was that he let a photographer take his picture there. When the photo hit the papers, Senator Kennedy was enraged. But he finally cooled down when it became obvious he could do nothing about it anyway.

In 1979, Ted was nominated for the Valor in Sports Award given in London. He traveled there to receive the award, if he turned out to be the lucky one, but he lost out to Naomi Vemura, the thirty-seven-year-old Japanese man who crossed the Arctic Sea alone and reached the North Pole.

He spent some quiet months working with his cousin William Smith for a summer stock company in Stockbridge, Massachusetts. There he helped make scenery, acted in several bit parts and sold tickets.

In the fall things livened up a bit when his father declared for the presidency. After threats on his life had surfaced, the government assigned Secret Service guards to every member of his immediate family. That meant that Ted was now escorted about the campus by two guards in the same manner John and Caroline Kennedy had been.

It didn't bother him any. He had gone through a great deal of personal hell and survived. The challenge awaiting him if his father did run for office was just another obstacle he would encounter and somehow master.

In fact, even during the time his father was working the hardest on his primary campaign, in March 1980, Teddy was back in the newspapers as he qualified for competition in the Special Olympics for the Handicapped held at Winter Park, Colorado.

It seemed that nothing could keep him down when he

wanted to be up and going—not even the lack of a leg. He was and is a doer in the Kennedy tradition.

His mother once said of him:

"He skis like crazy. I can't even keep up with him. And he loves sailing. When you think at age twelve he had to go through the amputation of his leg because of cancer! He was a wonderful little boy before that, but that tragedy only made him, I think, better.

"I know I sound like a mother bragging, but he is an exceptionally strong boy at sixteen, and he is mature, because he has had to go through an inordinate amount of suffering."

She summed it up: "Ted is a natural, cheerful boy, always thinking of others, a really wonderful child."

More than that, he had been through one of the toughest ordeals ever faced by any third-generation Kennedy, and he had weathered it with dignity, courage, and panache. He was, unquestionably, the bravest of the astonishingly brave Kennedy kids.

CHAPTER 9
A Kennedy Sampler

Not every Kennedy makes the headlines continually. There are even some Kennedys among the twenty-nine Kennedy children who have never been involved in bad press.

This does not mean that these "other Kennedys" are any less charismatic or singled out for fame or infamy than the rest. It simply means that statistically not all twenty-nine Kennedy children are going to get the same amount of space in the newspapers, or the same amount of personal attention from the public.

Seeing the mass of Kennedys assembled at Hyannis Port or in McLean where many of them live can be an unnerving, somewhat awesome experience. Each of these Kennedys is an individual, yet at the same time, each is somehow stamped indelibly with the Kennedy image.

Ethel Shakel Kennedy, who is by temperament even more a Kennedy than some blood-relations, once said that all Kennedys are recognizable as such.

"If any one of them strayed out of the compound or got lost, somebody would find him, put a stamp on him, and mail him back."

Art Buchwald went her one better, saying that with all the Kennedys together, no one could tell the difference between any two of them.

Ethel's energy is legend, as is her record of motherhood. Eleven children in seventeen years!

It is she who rides herd on the twenty-nine Kennedy kids —even those who are grown up and married. She wields her power not only on the estate in McLean but at the Kennedy compound, where she shares the scepter with Rose Kennedy.

Action swirls about these two nonblood-relations but still very Kennedy Kennedys. Barbara Gibson, a private secretary who worked for Rose Kennedy, once kept a diary of her days at the Kennedy compound. It gives the feel of the activity and the energy of the place.

Rose was constantly annoyed at the Kennedy children and thought they were spoiled. One entry of Barbara Gibson's says: "Grandchildren just won't use plastic glasses! Mrs. Kennedy told me: 'I will *not* take that sort of gas! They will drink out of plastic glasses or go thirsty! There is no reason to take good glasses to the swimming pool and tennis court.' She shut the four-dollar glasses away in a cabinet."

Another entry suggests the tone of life at the compound:

"Pat Lawford is here with her children. So is Jean Smith. They brought their own maid and cook! Jeannette [Rose's cook] refused to cook for so many people without help and Mrs. Kennedy refuses to 'waste money' on more help. Jeannette is mad and is staying at home until the Lawfords and Smiths leave."

The younger generation was a trial to Rose Kennedy, as is noted in this entry:

"Mrs. Kennedy told me that at dinner her grandchildren had been discussing abortion, talking about the 'fetus.'

" 'These children are so advanced for their age—I hardly knew what the fetus was until about two years ago!' "

But at the same time, she was very definitely anxious to have them grow up healthy:

"Mrs. Kennedy had me send a memo to all the grand-children telling them to drink milk: Jack drank milk and that's why he always had such white teeth."

Although untoward things were always happening to in-dividual Kennedys, sometimes they happened to groups of Kennedys, as reported in this item:

"Ethel's sailboat sank with twenty people aboard—the whole Moveable Feast! Too many people for that boat, it seems. The police called me at 2 P.M. The boat was not too far from shore and everyone was floundering around in the water with the hampers of food!

"A $65,000 boat! It went right to the bottom. (It was later retrieved and repaired.) Buddy Hackett, the comedian, who was visiting, didn't go; he hates boats and was in Ethel's kitchen making chili at the time of the accident!"

At Rose's house in Palm Beach, one entry sums up the explosive energy of the Kennedy kids:

"Thanksgiving turmoil. Five Lawfords, Joe Kennedy, and five guests.

"By Monday morning the house looked like an aban-doned bomb shelter."

Action. Sports. Games. Movement. Excitement. They make the world go around for the fantastic twenty-nine.

It was Ethel's husband, Robert, who set that pattern for the RFK children some years ago.

"I think that life for them must be an adventure," he said. "Young people must be shown a way to escape from the mold they live in, in a responsible way, and to get out of them-selves, and get interested in other people. That is the important thing. You can always find other people with bigger prob-lems than you have. You know the story of the man who had no shoes until he met the man who had no feet."

All eleven of the Robert Kennedy kids look out for the needy, see the way the less affluent live, help others. Each Kennedy child does so by different degrees, but each follows his father's precepts.

"I enjoy [my children] a lot and try to stimulate their interests in many different areas," Robert continued, "whether in the fields of poetry, interest in other countries, sports, politics, or any area in which they have some special interest. A couple of my children are very interested in animals . . . Some of the older children are interested in other areas. I suppose Ethel and I want them to have as wide a range of interest as possible."

Once he was asked in 1967 what he wanted for his children in the years ahead, say in the 1980s.

"Well, I think there has to be trust in individuals. At the same time we have to feel that society needs something more than personal aggrandizement. If material wealth is emphasized, then I think we are going to have estrangements and difficulties in this country."

A year later he was murdered.

But his values have been absorbed by his children. Naturally, there are contradictions, and there are lapses. But, generally speaking, his children *are* following in his footsteps.

Mary Courtney Kennedy, to take up with the next of Robert F. Kennedy's children after David, was born on September 9, 1956. She spent some years after graduation from college in teaching kindergarteners and first graders in California.

Then she returned East and got a job with the Children's Television Workshop in New York. When her Uncle Ted declared his candidacy for the presidency, she went on the road for him.

She had been dating a number of men in New York, but in December 1979 she suddenly announced her engagement to Jeffrey Robert Ruhe. Ruhe is assistant to Roone Arledge, president of ABC-TV News and Sports.

The two planned to be married in McLean, Virginia, on June 14, 1980. She had asked her Uncle Ted to give her away, and he had agreed, campaign problems or no campaign problems.

As to who would be the maid of honor, Courtney was undecided. However, she announced that her close friend, Vicki Gifford, daughter of ex-football great and now ABC-TV sportscaster Frank Gifford, would be one of the bridesmaids.

"It could turn out to be a huge family reunion," the *Daily News* reported, "with most everyone expected in from the campaign trails."

It would be the third marriage in the third Kennedy generation.

Michael LeMoyne Kennedy, the sixth of Robert Kennedy's children, was born on February 27, 1958. The "LeMoyne" in his name refers to K. LeMoyne Billings, of course. He has led a life similar to his brothers and sisters, traveling all over the world with them and with cousins and friends.

He had one early brush with the law when he pleaded guilty in New Hampshire in 1976 on a speeding charge. He was fined $35.

In 1979, while a student at Harvard, Michael spent part of his winter break in Colombia, with two of his brothers and a sister—Bobby, Jr., David, and Kerry. They all took part in a whitewater raft expedition.

After their raft trip down the Atrato River, they were riding on a sightseeing bus in Medellin, an interior city, with Blake Fleetwood, the free-lance travel writer whom Bobby knew from an earlier skiing trip in Chile.

"My arm was sticking out a window," Fleetwood later recalled, "and suddenly one of Medellin's hundreds of street thieves yanked off my expensive wristwatch. I yelled and jumped off the bus, followed by Michael Kennedy, who passed me as we ran after the thief."

Michael was obviously in better shape than Fleetwood. He pursued the thief for nearly five blocks, and wore the man out. Finally the thief surrendered, laid the watch down gently in the middle of the street, and vanished.

There Michael picked it up.

"As he and I walked back, holding the watch up," Fleet-wood wrote, "we were applauded and cheered by the people, who had no idea who Michael was, but were apparently impressed with a young gringo who had gotten the best of one of Medellin's thieves."

In spite of the fact that he is an action-oriented Kennedy in the tradition, life is not all derring-do and outdoor action. He has recently discovered the beautiful people in New York. At least he has been visible in Manhattan dating Tatum O'Neal, who seems to have become a favorite of the Kennedy clan.

None of this goes down too well with Uncle Ted—or any of the aunts or Grandma or Mother.

But Michael has been behaving himself at Harvard recently, so all seems to be going well. Lately he's been seen around New York with his sister Courtney's good friend, Vicki Gifford, of whom the Kennedys approve.

Mary Kerry Kennedy is next in line, born September 8, 1959. She followed her sister Kathleen to Putney School and then distinguished herself in college first by crashing her car into a snowplow in the winter of 1976–77, and then the next year by jumping out of her college dorm window into a four-foot snowbank and breaking her leg.

She is a well-built, bouncy, and energetic girl, loves to get about with her peers, and is usually present at kickoffs for events like Kennedy celebrity tennis tournaments. She also shows up at benefits like the one for the Whitney Museum, in Wilmington, Massachusetts.

She also appeared in New York working for her Uncle Ted's campaign for the presidency in the big New York office along with her cousin Steve Smith, Jr.

Christopher George Kennedy, who shares a Fourth of July birthday with his older sister Kathleen, was born in 1963.

At the age of sixteen he had developed a real eye for beauty and publicity, and was seen with Tatum O'Neal in

New York, trying to steal a page from his brother Michael's book.

Matthew Maxwell Taylor Kennedy was born on January 11, 1965. Named after one of his father's favorite people, General Maxwell G. Taylor, Max grew up in the limelight just like his brothers and sisters. Writer Robert S. Bird described Max at the age of three in a report on the Robert Kennedys in *The Saturday Evening Post*.

"In toddled the second youngest of the Kennedy children. The senator addressed the youngster with the razor-sharp voice of a drill instructor of Marines addressing a boot on Parris Island," Bird wrote.

"Matthew! Maxwell! Taylor! Kennede-e!" Senator Kennedy shouted.

"What, Daddy?" Max asked.

"Stand up!" snapped Kennedy. "I want to introduce you!"

With a grin Max did so, and put out his hand to shake hands with his house guest.

"Matthew!" shouted Kennedy. "Say how old you are!"

"You mean on my *next* birthday?"

"Yes, on your next birthday."

"Three."

"Show with your fingers how old you will be!"

Maxwell did so, "having the time of his life," so the writer said.

Four years after his father's murder, Max was playing one day during the fall in front of the Hyannis Port home of his grandmother, Rose Kennedy. Some of the Kennedys had come in from sailing, and had hauled the wet sail up a flagpole in the front yard to dry it out.

A strong wind came up suddenly, filled the sail, and the pressure of the wind snapped the pole. Max was hit by the flying top of the shaft. The force of the blow was sharp enough to break his leg. He was taken to the hospital, the bone was set, and he was given a walking cast.

Later on, when he and his sister Rory were with their mother at the site of his father's grave, Max threw everyone into a tizzy by suddenly fainting dead away. Shortly after he revived, his sister Rory also fainted.

It was never made clear why either incident occurred.

Accidents seemed to go around looking for Max. Six years after the incident of the broken leg, he was playing with his cousins in the Shriver home in Maryland when another weird mishap occurred.

The Shrivers have a small elevator which moves up and down a stairwell. It was installed when one of the Shriver children had to wear a cast. Max and his cousins were playing near it when suddenly the elevator moved down and caught Max. It slammed into his head and knocked him unconscious, but stopped immediately once it had hit him.

Nevertheless he was out cold and had to be taken to the hospital in Bethesda, where he was put in the Intensive Care Unit. X-rays showed that there was no fracture of his skull.

Finally he was released with a clean bill of health.

Douglas Harriman Kennedy was born on March 24, 1967, named after Governor Averill Harriman of New York, an old family friend of the Kennedys. He was just over one year old when his father was killed.

At that time, in June, 1968, Ethel Kennedy was three months pregnant with her eleventh child.

Louella Hennessy, the nurse who presided over most of the Kennedy children's births, wrote how Senator Edward Moore Kennedy, the self-appointed surrogate father for both the John Kennedy and the Robert Kennedy offspring, had reacted when the time of hospitalization for his sister-in-law Ethel approached.

"I remember he called me after Robert Kennedy was shot in Los Angeles and Robert's wife Ethel thought she would have a miscarriage. He said, 'Louella, you've got to come right away. What would ever happen if we lost that baby?' So I came to be with Ethel and in due time she delivered Rory all right."

Rory Kathleen Elizabeth Kennedy was born on December 13, 1968, over six months after her father's death.

According to Hennessy, Uncle Ted would stop by to visit Ethel and the children every single day.

"Sometimes he'd come on his way home, sometimes he'd come after dinner with Joan. I can still see him. He'd walk in and stand in the front hall and clap his hands and call upstairs. 'Well, who's here? Come on down and see Uncle Teddy,' and they'd all come running and cling to him.

"His heart was broken, but he never showed his true emotions. He'd just act like everything was normal."

The last of the Kennedy brothers had his own children to take care of, and a wife who had problems of a special kind.

Kara Anne Kennedy is the oldest of their three children. Now nineteen, she is enrolled at Trinity College in Connecticut. From the beginning her life has been a troubled one.

Some of the trouble comes from the physical constitution of her mother, Joan. After Kara's birth and her brother Edward's, Joan had two miscarriages. One source close to the family says that Ted Kennedy had always wanted a big family, just like his brother Robert's—ten kids at least.

It was not to be.

Joan was forced to stay in bed most of the time before her third child, Patrick, was born. She was pregnant once again in 1969, awaiting the birth of her fourth child, when the incident at Chappaquiddick Bridge took place.

Joan suffered a third miscarriage shortly after.

None of this anguish and desperation was lost on young Kara, who was a child then. Following Ted, Jr.'s, bout with cancer and the amputation of his leg, Kara saw her mother slowly begin to lose her grip on life. She knew her mother was drinking too much.

Her brother Ted's amputation had had a deep effect on her. Before the operation, when his leg was only bothering him slightly, their relationship was not at all serious. After the amputation, she began to understand what it was to have tragedy close at hand.

During the vacation in Ireland that followed Ted's recovery, Kara was traveling with her Aunt Pat and the three Lawford cousins, Sydney, Victoria, and Robin, when Ted was suddenly felled by after effects of his anticancer drug treatment and was hospitalized in Dublin.

Shortly afterwards, Aunt Pat and the girls went out in a horse-drawn carriage called a jaunting cart just outside the village of Adare, southwest of Limerick in County Limerick. As the creaking cart maneuvered along a narrow lane next to a stone wall, Kara got her foot caught between the carriage and the jagged rock surface.

She could barely walk afterward. Her aunt took her to an orthopedic hospital in Croom nearby. She was kept there for several days, during which time her injury was watched closely. No one wanted to take a chance that it might develop into a serious problem like her brother Ted's leg injury.

It proved to be not serious, and she was released after a few days. There were no after effects, but her parents and the doctors kept close watch on the foot for several months.

Kara was going to public school in Washington during these years of turmoil, and witnessed the gradual disintegration of her family. It was small wonder that her own life began to take on the same kind of detachment from reality that her mother's had. By the time she was in high school, she was already exhibiting some signs of what friends simply called "adolescent problems."

These problems took the form of typical alienation. She vanished from home once, and police had to be summoned to locate her. She could never explain why she had gone off that way.

The incident was repeated later, with the same results.

A close friend says:

"Kara is a rebel. While the rest of us rebel against the establishment, she rebels against the Kennedy lifestyle. Who'd want to do that? She wears sloppy jeans, smokes pot whenever she can, and goes for the counterculture types."

Kara's rebellion against the Kennedy lifestyle is quite different from the rebellion of her cousin Kathleen. Kathleen's revolt includes affecting a kind of antichic style of dress; but Kathleen believes in helping the poor and in the liberal ideals all Kennedys espouse.

"I can't see Kara walking down a dusty Indian reservation street and pausing to chat with the natives," one close associate of the Kennedy family says.

When she finally graduated from high school, her school grades weren't good. She rarely saw her mother, who had left home in Washington and was living most of the time in Boston. Nevertheless, Kara had applied to Trinity College in Hartford, Connecticut. She was accepted and started there in 1978.

"She has always been a good student and now is off this September to college," her mother Joan was quoted in a magazine article. Actually, Joan was overlooking the fact that Kara's grades were never very good.

In the summer of 1979, Kara moved to Boston to be with her mother, who after several bouts of alcoholism and depression, was feeling and looking better and teaching at the Heath school there. Kara took up photography for the summer.

At Trinity, Kara tried to settle down to an ordinary college student's life. However, in her second year there, a deranged woman broke into her father's office in the Senate building wielding a knife, threatening to kill him.

The senator decided that he had better put guards on his children. Kara acquired two bodyguards, exactly like Caroline and John before her. They stay in the background, but it is not easy for Kara to continue a normal school life.

One schoolmate at Trinity said: "Kara has her problems. She has her own friends. I wouldn't say she's an easy person to get to know. She keeps pretty much to herself and a small clique. I guess every Kennedy does that."

Lately, though, Kara hasn't been all that much alone in her favorite little Cinderella corner. She's been hitting the night spots in New York—both the "in" places for the beautiful people and the *boîtes intimes* which are so popular with the Kennedys and their circle.

And she hasn't been alone. She's been on the arm of John Florescu, termed simply a "journalist" by the other journalists who write the gossip columns in the newspapers

At Magique, an elite watering place in Manhattan, the press cornered Kara and questioned her about her relationship with Florescu.

"We're very close," Kara replied—"shyly," according to the *Daily News* scribes who reported the item.

The youngest of the Ted Kennedy family is Patrick Kennedy, who is twelve years old now. Of all the Kennedy children, it is Patrick who takes the most after his mother Joan.

One writer described him as "a cross between Peter Pan, a leprechaun, and Huck Finn," with a "thatch of strawberry blond hair, innocent emerald eyes, and freckles."

When younger, Patrick was always Joan's "little shadow." He would run around the house after her begging: "Mummy, please teach me how to play the piano the way you do."

Joan never did.

Once Art Buchwald visited the compound when Patrick was there. In typical Buchwald fashion, he took a bunch of the Kennedy children to a nudist colony at Martha's Vineyard.

"I'm never going to trust *you* with my children again!" Patrick's Aunt Ethel told the columnist.

When Ethel asked Patrick Kennedy, then eight years old, if he'd looked at the people, Patrick said, "No, I kept my hands over my eyes!"

Patrick and his father usually begin each day at 7:15 A.M. jogging in the driveway for at least fifteen minutes before eating breakfast together.

Patrick goes to Potomac School, a private institution in Washington. His father tries to appear at every school function, including midday events. And he tries to be home with Patrick for dinner each night, hard as it is with his almost impossible campaign schedule.

"I spend as much time with him as I can," says Ted Kennedy. "In the evening in winter we try to play as much outdoors as possible. He likes Frisbee, tennis, and soccer, and he's a very good card player—crazy eights—or we play backgammon or Ping-Pong." And they play pool or try the pinball machine that is located in the basement of the house.

Patrick has had his share of accidents, too. One winter when he was in the second grade he was playing on a jungle gym at school when he lost his balance and fell. He put out his hand to break his fall, and fractured his wrist.

He was sent to the hospital where hospital attendants reduced the fracture, put it in a cast, and sent him back home. He was in school the next day, cast and all.

But his life has been mostly a normal Kennedy one. He too has been swept up in the current campaign excitement.

Typical of a recent afternoon during the Kennedy campaign in Massachusetts was a race between the senator and his son Patrick down the double fiber glass track of the 3,200-foot alpine slide on Mt. Tom. Father beat son.

"Patrick, we had a real match," his father said. "That's a challenge for tomorrow." Next day would be the slide at Jiminy Peak.

All this activity has taken place in spite of the fact that Patrick has had bronchial asthma from birth and is still allergic to animal hair. He cannot be in a house where a dog has been. He carries a Medihalor with him at all times.

As in all Kennedys, a flash of the patriarch's shrewdness occasionally surfaces. As the campaign for his father got under way in 1979, Patrick accompanied him on many of his visits all over the country.

In Nashville, Tennessee, he was approached by reporters as he stood with his father in what looked like a "forest of Secret Service agents," according to one writer covering the story.

When Patrick was asked what he was doing there with his father, he replied: "I took three days off from school so I could come along. I'm writing a journal about it to take back to school. I've written about three pages so far."

The reporters asked him might he sell his journal for possible publication?

Patrick thought about that a moment. "Maybe. How much could I sell it for?"

There were no takers.

About the fatherless Kennedy children—for whom Senator Ted Kennedy is the surrogate father after double tragedies left their indelible mark on two families—he says this:

"I find the children a source of warmth and happiness. They're a job—lively and full of mischief at times—but I find that time spent with them is a source of enormous pleasure. They're all good friends and the cousins that have grown up here together continue their relationship in the summer. We spend vacations and Christmas together, so we're all one extended family."

Jean Kennedy, the eighth of Joe Kennedy's children, married Stephen E. Smith in 1956. Smith was "old money," born with an excellent business and managerial sense. From the beginning he was put to work by the patriarch managing the Kennedy oil interests. He now handles the entire Kennedy portfolio of investments, amounting to almost half a billion dollars.

He also manages the Kennedy political campaigns and has an excellent average up to this point. He once tried to enter politics, but it didn't work out. He is now quite happy to stay exactly where he is, in the business end of the Kennedy fortune, where he can manage the money and help the other Kennedys attain the power positions.

As if the name Smith isn't enough of a shield to effect invisibility, the Stephen Smith family believes in maintaining the lowest profile possible in the news media.

The Smiths are definitely the Kennedys that the public doesn't know. They ignore reporters and shun the limelight.

At the age of fifty-one, Stephen Smith seems to have accomplished the rare feat of becoming a Kennedy by association. As a *Washington Star* reporter once wrote: It was an honor unconferred on most in-laws; denied Lawford, taken from Jackie, elusive to Joan.

Smith never speaks of the patriarch as anything but "Mister Kennedy." His origins are in Brooklyn, where his family lived for a number of years. The Smith money comes from tugboats.

"My family had money way before the Kennedys had money," he once said with a twinkle in the eye. "After all, we were over here a long time putting up with just what the Kennedys put up with. Smith is an Irish name, you know."

And it is the badge of anonymity.

Smith has a chameleon-like ability to vanish before the public eye.

"He likes being a bit mysterious," an associate confides. "Although of course now he'll be as public as necessary with Ted Kennedy running for the nomination."

Interviews?

"There's no purpose in my looking for or granting interviews," Smith says, his voice stern, his diction correct. "I mean there are some people who like to read about themselves, but that's not one of my problems."

Smith's life has not been all that smooth or empty of typical Kennedy mini-scandals. Five years ago, in New York, a cab driver had him arrested over a quarrel regarding a fifty-cent fare.

"The driver hadn't put his flag down!" Smith told the police.

Comedian Alan King, who is a close friend of Smith's, uses the anecdote to illustrate a point about Smith. "A matter of principle," he says, "not a matter of money. Steve Smith doesn't like to be stuck."

From his office in the Pan American Building in New York, Smith operates the Kennedy empire, flying to Washington, Chicago, Los Angeles, and other points of the globe on demand.

He also attends to a number of other Kennedy family chores. For example, it was Steve Smith who made the hospital arrangements for young David Kennedy when his drug problem surfaced recently. It was also Smith who called the press conference at which the official information about David and his rehabilitation program was released.

His wife Jean Kennedy Smith usually sticks to the New York environs and appears at all kinds of fundraising affairs with great frequency, many times in the company of her sister Patricia Kennedy Lawford. She is a Kennedy par excellence.

In fact, it was Jean who introduced Ted Kennedy to Joan Bennett and Robert Kennedy to Ethel Skakel. And it was she who dropped hints of Bobby Kennedy, Jr.'s, thesis in range of the proper ears in the New York publishing industry.

Stephen E. Smith, Jr., is the oldest of the four Smith children, is aged twenty-three now, and is out of college. He suddenly appeared full-blown in the media in January 1980, after having been appointed head of the Senator Ted Kennedy local campaign headquarters at 15 East 41st Street.

At that date, Steve, Jr., had just come back from the Iowa caucuses, where he was working for his Uncle Ted. To kick off the opening of the new campaign headquarters, Steve's father flew back from Washington, where he was masterminding the nationwide Ted Kennedy campaign, and helped open up the shop.

"It's Little Steve's first fling at big-time politics," said a story in the New York *Daily News.* "After the opening, Big Steve flew back to Washington to continue managing the national campaign, confident that his lad had everything under control here. But daddy is only a phone call away."

Liz Smith wrote about Steve, Jr., at a fundraising party given by Lauren Bacall, mentioning that he was with his mother, Jean Kennedy Smith, and calling him "her super good looking son, Steve, Jr."

When Liz asked Steve, Jr., if he objected to being in the limelight, Steve, Jr., responded:

"No, I kind of like it!"

The Smiths are Kennedys, all right, but they aren't totally dedicated to the physical culture ethic. Steve, Jr., once wrote about his grandmother, Rose Kennedy:

"One of the things I've always thought was really amazing about Grandma was that she'd go swimming out in the Sound every day like up to and through Thanksgiving. It'd be fifty degrees out—I mean in the air, and the water could be colder. And Grandma would have her towel over her shoulder and would be going down the dune to go swimming.

"It would just freak out all the kids, all these tough little kids throwing footballs and climbing all over the roof and stuff. They wouldn't dream of going into that cold water. They couldn't *believe* it; but there goes Grandma, eighty-something years old, right into the ocean."

Next in line in the Smith family is William Smith, who's nineteen and usually called "Willie" in the clan. Now enrolled at Duke University, he often appears at festive events or on vacations with other Kennedys. During the New England primaries for Uncle Ted, he appeared with his brother Steve in Syracuse, Rochester, and Buffalo to whip up enthusiasm for the candidate.

Third in the Smith clan is Amanda Smith, now twelve years old. Amanda is adopted, and joined the Smith family over a decade ago.

"To start with," Jean Smith says, "I love children—well,

I think we all do. We had plenty of room for other children. And I felt I was in a position to do that."

True to her word, after Amanda the Smiths adopted another child. The fourth Smith, Kym Maria, joined the clan six years ago as a tiny baby.

And that's the four Smith children.

In 1973 the Smiths suddenly put the house Jean had been given by her father in the Kennedy compound at Hyannis Port on the market for sale. Eventually it was bought by a widow who lived in McConnelsville, New York. The sale price was reported to be in the neighborhood of $210,000.

There was never any reason advanced for the Smiths' sudden decision to sell the house.

Eunice Kennedy, the fifth of the patriarch's children, met a *Newsweek* editor named Robert Sargent Shriver at a New York party in 1947. Shriver was fascinated with the Kennedys. On his first visit to their home in Palm Beach, the dinner guests were a Harvard dean, Supreme Court Justice William O. Douglas, and a motion picture company president.

"Conversation whipped around like world-class tennis," Shriver said. "You'd have to be a stupid flibberty-jibberty kid not to get a charge out of that."

He and Eunice were interested in one another, but they did not rush out to get married the same day. Shriver began working for the family when Joe Kennedy hired him away from *Newsweek* and put him to work in New York first and then Washington, after which he sent him to Chicago to help manage the Merchandise Mart.

Eunice was engaged in social work at the time, moving to Chicago in 1950. She and Shriver were married in 1953. Eunice continued with her social work, eventually plunging wholeheartedly into helping the mentally retarded.

"She is a striking-looking woman," wrote Pearl Buck in *The Kennedy Women,* "forthright, vigorous, honest, and highly intelligent without being an intellectual in the theoretical sense. She has the Kennedy directness, the Kennedy energy, the Kennedy accents."

The author found Shriver a pleasant, intelligent man, relaxed in his humor, and a good foil to his high-strung wife. There was an "air of understanding between the Shrivers," she noted. They had a mutual consideration and respect for one another.

There are five Shriver children. The family makes its main headquarters in Washington, where all seven Shrivers live at a Maryland estate called Timberlawn. Shriver was one of Jack Kennedy's right-hand men during his brief presidency.

It was Shriver who planned and initiated the Peace Corps, a brand-new idea at the time and one which has long outlived the Camelot years of John F. Kennedy. Shriver himself was selected as candidate for the Democratic vice presidency in 1972 when Senator Thomas F. Eagleton was dumped after reports surfaced of his medical treatments for depression. The McGovern-Shriver ticket suffered at the polls, whipped decisively by the Nixon-Agnew ticket.

In 1976 Shriver decided to try for the presidency himself, but found himself buried in the primaries in New Hampshire. He pulled out graciously.

It is Eunice who fascinates many pundits. One writer opined that Eunice could be president, if she weren't a woman. "She is the one who looks the most like her brother, Jack. She is the one who is closest to her mother, Rose."

Oldest of the five Shriver children is Robert Sargent Shriver, Jr. He was six years old when his father was tapped by President John F. Kennedy to head the Peace Corps. He was nine when Uncle Jack was murdered, and fourteen when Uncle Bob was killed in Los Angeles.

Although named Shriver, he is remarkably Kennedylike, with most of the Kennedy traits and some of the Shriver characteristics as well.

Like all Kennedy children, he learned to hold his own

intellectually at the breakfast and dinner tables. Whether his father or his mother instituted this time-honored Kennedy tradition is unknown.

Nevertheless, Bobby (although his name is exactly like his father's, his father is "Sargent" and his son is "Bobby") grew up discussing all kinds of social, moral, political, and religious issues at dinner.

Early in his young life, his father promised him that if he never touched hard liquor until he was twenty-one years old, he would get some kind of an award. Shriver was following a precept laid down by old Joe Kennedy, who promised the same thing to his male heirs.

Shriver explained to his son that he shouldn't be a teetotaler. "If you go to a wedding and they're drinking toasts, obviously you ought to feel free to join your friends and have a taste of champagne."

Shriver felt old Joe Kennedy's influence all along. "All the family has self-confidence, which principally came from Mr. Kennedy, who said many times that his mother developed it in him."

Bobby certainly always had it. And along with it, he had another Kennedy essential: "All the Kennedys have an acute sensitivity to people."

In an article published in April 1970, Shriver stated with some prescience that he believed his son had had the opportunity to use marijuana at Exeter, the fashionable prep school which he attended. Bobby lived there in a dormitory with about 150 boys.

"In the first six weeks," Shriver noted, "six boys were thrown out of school for smoking marijuana. Bobby knew them. I'm sure he could have been one of them, but he's not so much attracted by drugs or liquor. He's more interested in girls."

In fact, Bobby's early training was paying off. When he went to see *Hair* in New York—an early example of frontal on-stage nudity—Bobby reacted with typical 1960s "cool."

Bobby's strict upbringing and his adherence to the Shriver code made it all the more surprising when suddenly, in August 1970, he and his cousin Bobby Kennedy, Jr., were arrested at Hyannis Port for possession of pot.

Ironically, his father had only recently addressed a California audience on the generation gap, saying:

"It is not easy today for parents to think about the future of their children. What do you do when your children go with a group in which marijuana or other drugs are beginning to be used?"

Nevertheless, both Shriver and his wife Eunice were there standing behind Bobby when he appeared in court.

"He has never been involved in any such situation before and we trust he never will again," Shriver annnounced. "We love him and for all of his sixteen years he has been a joy and a pride to us."

After the arrest, Bobby Shriver managed to keep out of trouble for the allotted thirteen months of probation—unlike his cousin Bobby Kennedy, who became involved in a spitting incident.

In fact, if anything, the drug experience was a turning point in Bobby Shriver's life. He buckled down, studied hard, graduated from Exeter, and entered Yale.

In the summer of 1972 he found a job with a motion picture company planning to film a version of *Jesus Christ Superstar*. The movie was to be shot on location in Israel. Bobby got a job driving a truck, hauling people and props about from one place to another.

He was working just outside Jerusalem one day in August, and had dropped in at his hotel to pick up some work clothes. As he passed through the lobby he overheard a couple of tourists from New York talking about somebody named Shriver.

Bobby knew the name wasn't all that common, and he paused to listen. It was then that he learned that his father had been decided on by the Democratic presidential nominating committee as a new vice-presidential nominee. R. Sargent Shriver II would be voted on by the delegates the next day.

He telephoned home, learned that the tourists were speaking the truth, and got a ticket to Miami. A stringer from *The New York Times* found him and asked him what it was like to be the son of the vice-presidential nominee.

"The news still hasn't sunk in yet," Bobby admitted.

Next day, when his father was approved unanimously by a roll-call vote as the vice-presidential nominee, he was there in the crowd. Bobby then went on to help out in the election as much as he could.

He weathered his father's loss in the election as well as he could, and returned to Yale where he graduated in 1976. He is now enrolled at Yale Law School, where he rooms with his brother Timothy.

During the summer of 1978, he got a job as a feature writer on the *Los Angeles Herald Examiner*.

Second of the Shriver children is Maria Owings Shriver, who is twenty-three and a television producer in Baltimore. Maria has charm and good looks. When she was twelve years old her grandmother Rose wrote about her:

"Maria is regarded as quite a beauty, with her regular features, rather piercing blue eyes, and, for a young girl of twelve, showing promise of having quite a good figure, now that she has lost weight."

Rose's prediction was right on the target.

Maria has led a very mild life for a Kennedy child, and the only time she did anything to upset her parents was fairly recent. She began dating Arnold Schwarzenegger, the muscle-man, and ex-Mr. Universe and Mr. Olympus. The Shriver family did not appear entranced when they learned the news from the press.

It was particularly annoying to read about Maria in Pat O'Haire's column in the New York *Daily News:*

"Must be the real thing: Arnold Schwarzenegger and his

best girl, Maria Shriver, made it look official. They were at the Stage Deli, occupying a window table looking out over scenic Seventh Ave. for all showbizland to see. Incidentally, Arnold had a double-cheese omelet heaped high with extra orders of cottage cheese, which was so fascinating looking, nobody noticed what Maria had."

Third of the Shriver children is Timothy Perry Shriver. He quietly grew up third in line, attended the exclusive St. Albans boys' school in Washington, graduated, and went on to Yale University where he is now in his second year.

During the summer of 1979 he worked in the advertising department of *Diplomat* magazine.

As for Mark Kennedy Shriver, the fourth in line, he grew up quietly, too, going to Georgetown Prep and sometimes spending his summers with his family at Hyannis Port. He is an avid sailor and tennis player.

Mark has always been the sensitive one, according to Shriver. All the Kennedy hustle and bustle sometimes disconcerts him.

"I don't want to be in the race, Daddy," he told Shriver once at a swimming meet. When he wanted to pull out, Shriver finally let him. He didn't like to lose, and he always seemed to.

After his Uncle Robert's murder in Los Angeles, a staff member remarked that "Mark's very sensitive. He talks a lot about death these days."

That talk passed over, and Mark is now a fifteen-year-old teen-ager who likes to play quietly. Competition in the Kennedy fashion is not his style.

Anthony Paul Kennedy Shriver is fifth. Now fourteen, he goes to Potomac, a private school in Washington. He is a quiet boy, respectful to his family, and quite responsive to decent treatment.

Their father once explained how difficult it is for his children to grow up in the Kennedy image, knowing that such a great deal is expected of them.

"I consciously try to play it down," Shriver said. "I tell them that they don't have to be upset if they don't get only A's and B's in school. I make it clear that I didn't get straight A's. Neither did their Uncle Bobby or their grandfather, who reportedly failed economics at Harvard. I don't think you ought to demand arbitrary levels of performance from people. I make it clear to them that if they do conscientious work, if they apply themselves, I'm much more interested in that. I want them to do whatever they do as well as they possibly can. If that means that they have a C average and that's as well as they can do, that's as satisfying to me as if they made B averages."

But it has always been hard. When the Shrivers lose to the Kennedys, they generally tend to feel bested.

Shriver has always been amazed at his wife Eunice's competitiveness. "I'd never been with a woman who really tried to beat the hell out of a man on a tennis court," he said. "I used to say, 'What's the matter with her?' "

Nothing.

She is simply a Kennedy.

Patricia Kennedy Lawford was the sixth of Joe Kennedy's children. Attractive, feminine, least dominating, most yielding and gentle, she grew up to be a Kennedy at heart, but not totally in attitude.

The man she married was an Englishman, although most Americans think of him only as a movie and television actor, probably best known for his role as Nick Charles in the television series "The Thin Man."

Peter Sydney Ernest Lawford was the only son of Lieutenant General Sir Sydney Lawford and Lady Lawford.

Lawford had come to America in the 1940s and met Pat

Kennedy's brother Jack at the home of Gary Cooper in 1964, shortly after Jack had been mustered out and returned home. The two of them got along well together.

It was in 1949 that Patricia met Lawford, when she was working for NBC and Kate Smith in Hollywood.

The romance pleased only the two principals involved. Lady Lawford thought her son's taste in women was "execrable." She would rather have had Peter marry an Englishwoman and live in England.

From a jewelry shop in Manhattan where she worked for $50 a week, Lady Lawford intoned:

"We would have liked Peter to pick a bride from court circles."

Joe Kennedy thought his daughter's taste in men was just as bad. He loathed Lawford before he even met him.

"If there's anything I think I'd hate worse than an actor as a son-in-law, it's an English actor."

To that, Lady Lawford responded: "I'm English and he's Irish, and we don't see eye to eye, and that's about that."

Finally Joe Kennedy ordered a one-thousand-dollar-a-month stipend and a chauffered limousine to be given to Lady Lawford if she would leave the United States and not give press conferences. She refused.

Parental reservations aside, Patricia Kennedy and Peter Lawford were married in New York at the Church of St. Thomas More in 1954.

That Christmas the patriarch met Lawford for the first time. Lawford had gone to an English public school—we would call it "private school"—was taught partially by tutors, and was shy and introverted the way only an Englishman could be. He was wearing bright red socks, with ice-cream striped pants and a blue blazer when Joe Kennedy saw him in Palm Beach at the Kennedy mansion.

Joe flinched, bit his lip, and murmured his impressions sotto voce. He thought Lawford was something that had escaped from an early Mack Sennett comedy.

For a while it seemed that the Lawford-Kennedy liaison would succeed. Lawford was a bouncy person, with a definite charm of his own. He had managed to get in with a group of young Hollywood stars of the period. The press called Frank Sinatra's entourage the "rat pack." It included Dean Martin, Sammy Davis, Jr., among others, as well as Lawford.

Even so, the Kennedy family kept the alien from over the Atlantic at arm's length. Nevertheless, in 1960, when Jack needed the Nevada delegation to swing its votes for him so he could beat Adlai Stevenson in his bid for the presidential nomination at the Democratic Convention, Lawford called on his friends in the rat pack and got help through some movers and shakers in the Las Vegas nightclub circuit.

And so Jack owed Lawford one.

In the Kennedy entourage, Lawford became the offbeat brother-in-law. He and Pat lived in a neo-Spanish beach home in Santa Monica, once owned by the late Louis B. Mayer. And Lawford frequently golfed with the president. His sobriquet in the rat pack was "Charlie the Seal." Pretty soon the Kennedys began calling him that.

When Jack was president, the distance grew between the two. On a presidential plane to Palm Beach, Lawford was once sitting with his brother-in-law. Finally Jack sighed and said:

"Peter, disappear."

Lawford moved off. On landing, brother-in-law Jack came up to Lawford and asked him where he was staying.

"Where you stay," Lawford responded.

"You're not staying with me. Let me know and I'll call you."

Lawford nodded. "I won't hold my breath."

"No, don't."

And Lawford found his own lodgings. It wasn't the first time they argued. And it wasn't the last.

One day in August 1963 he taught Caroline Kennedy a poem that was relayed through Lawford's son Christopher to the president.

The poem contained a word that Jack Kennedy would have smiled at had it just involved his brothers or other men. Since Caroline was involved, however, he was obliged to blow his top. He called Lawford and had it out with him on the phone.

"Being related to the president of the United States is a very great honor," Lawford once said. "But it is not and never will be a career."

One of the troubles for Lawford was the cloying closeness of so many Kennedys at the Hyannis Port enclave.

"The rough-and-tumble of a large gregarious family," bemoaned Lawford, "[is] completely foreign to me, and I became—by marriage—an outsider in an almost overwhelming situation."

The overwhelming situation did not last for too long. Eleven years after they were married, Lawford and Patricia Kennedy were divorced. It was the first divorce in the Kennedy family. The four children produced by the marriage went with Pat Kennedy in the settlement.

"When the Kennedys take you to heart," Lawford said, "you become one of them all the way. My four children will never be loners. They are full-fledged members of the Tribe."

Indeed they are.

First of the Lawford children is Christopher Lawford, now twenty-four. He grew up on the West Coast and in New York, although most of his life was spent in Manhattan.

He went to school for several years with John F. Kennedy, Jr., but did not follow him to Collegiate when John was transferred out of the Catholic school.

Later Christopher attended St. David's, a prep school, where he roomed with his cousin Bobby Kennedy.

He was always close with the cousins—especially John and Caroline, who lived not far from him in New York. He was frequently invited to Greece when Onassis became his stepuncle.

The Kennedy training has been strict. He was taught by his mother and other Kennedys that he was born with advantages that he should use to help people who were less lucky.

"I have grown up with that belief," he said. "It's something so much a part of me I don't have to think: it's what I have done and expect to do."

He worked on behalf of underprivileged people in several communities when he was a teen-ager. Among those he has helped are the mentally retarded in schools and at the Shriver Day Camp, run by his Uncle Sargent. Christopher was a counselor there for two summers.

A great deal of his strong humanitarian sense comes from Rose Kennedy.

"There's no baloney with Grandma," he once wrote. "She often reminds me that life is not a bowl of cherries, and that you have to do a lot of things you don't really want to do. And that often you don't get to do what you want when you want. And there are plenty of times when you're going to have to put your head down and just get through it. And she's right."

Christopher enrolled at Harvard, where he roomed with his cousin Bobby Kennedy, Jr., after graduation from St. David's.

He once called his grandmother Rose at Hyannis Port to gossip with her and discuss his roommate's political activities. It was at a time when Bobby was beginning to take a serious interest in politics.

Rose said to tell Bobby that if he wanted to be in politics he should practice charisma, like his Uncle Ted. His grandmother was being funny.

Shortly after he had hung up, Christopher was startled to have the phone ring. It was Rose's private secretary.

"What's the matter?" asked Christopher, alarmed and thinking his grandmother might be suddenly ill.

"Mrs. Kennedy says that the next time you telephone long distance, call at night. It's cheaper."

Christopher and Bobby had a good laugh over that one.

Most of Christopher's life involved other Kennedys. During one summer he worked for his Uncle Ted in Washington. And, like all the Kennedys, he was usually present when groups of them went on world tours.

Much of the time he has managed to stay out of the newspapers, unlike his cousins Caroline, John, Joe III, Bobby, Kathleen, David, and Ted, Jr.—but not all the time.

In January 1980, he was ordered to appear in court for arraignment in Aspen, Colorado, on a charge he obtained a prescription for a narcotic by fraud or deceit. Conviction on the misdemeanor charge would carry a fine of up to $1,000 and a jail sentence of up to one year.

The second Lawford is Sydney Lawford, named after her paternal grandfather. Sydney was very close to Caroline Kennedy during Caroline's youth. The two went to the Convent of the Sacred Heart together. Later she transferred to a private school and attended college uneventfully. She appears frequently with her mother at social events in New York.

Now twenty-two, she has managed to keep out of the newspapers and the public eye except for causes, such as her Uncle Ted's run for the presidency. She has appeared with her Aunt Joan several times in that capacity.

Third of the Lawford Kennedys is Victoria Lawford, who is nineteen.

Fourth of the Lawfords is Robin Lawford, who is eighteen. She is in her first year of college at Sweet Briar in Virginia.

CHAPTER 10
The Kennedy Promise

That's the lot of them.

Twenty-nine Kennedys.

Twenty-seven Kennedys by blood, and two Kennedys by legal adoption.

They are a formidable lot.

They are a fashionable lot.

They are a photogenic lot.

They have triumphs, and they have tragedies.

Some of their triumphs are so small as to be minuscule: retrieving a wristwatch from a would-be thief, or challenging a whitewater rapids or a mountain.

Some of them are large and memorable: living an action-oriented life on an artificial leg, or writing a publishable book on a national figure.

Some of their tragedies are infinitesimal: falling off a jungle gym, or getting arrested for smoking marijuana.

Some of them are large: amputation of a leg to cancer, or falling prey to drug addiction.

The details of these triumphs and tragedies become magnified because they happen to Kennedys. If they happened to Joneses or Smiths—which four of them, ironically enough, are—they would be ignored by the public.

But they happen to Kennedys and they become part of the everyday reading and viewing matter of the American public.

Why?

America discovered the Kennedys—discovered them through the means of the various communications media. They discovered the beautiful people and selected the Kennedys to place squarely into the epicenter of the gilt-edged aristocracy of the day. That is the reason we see them today as larger than life.

Our lives today have become humdrum and pallid. The eternal struggle for the dollar, the involvement in red tape and bureaucracy, the fight against the ever-encroaching power of the state—all these appalling pressures on us tend to make our lives a dull gray, a grayness without beauty, without faith, without hope.

America is mired in the principle of egalitarianism, by definition. The motto over the front door of one of the country's largest-circulating newspapers reads:

"God must love the common man because He made so many of them."

Yet we all have an inherent hunger for the uncommon. Our needs are not fulfilled by the pale gray bureaucracy in which we live.

Instinctively Joe Kennedy knew this. He understood America and the American people more clearly than many others who had read more and studied harder than he did.

Joe Kennedy created the Kennedy dynasty, and he created the myth that made the Kennedys exceptional people.

Where is it going from here?

There is an interesting general pattern that begins to emerge about this generation of the Kennedys.

Whereas the sons and daughters of Joe Kennedy sought fame and fortune in politics and in social services, the grandchildren of Joe Kennedy seem to have staked out an entirely different area for exploitation: communications.

Notice how many Kennedy children are interested in print journalism:
- Caroline with her summer job on a newspaper
- Bobby, Jr., with his thesis turned into a book
- Kathleen with her articles for law journals
- David with his work at a "publishing house"
- Bobby Shriver with his job on a Los Angeles paper
- Timothy Shriver with his job on a magazine

Look at this list of Kennedy children and their television ties:
- Caroline and her work with a documentary crew
- Joe III and the "American Sportsman" for ABC-TV
- Bobby, Jr., and his narration of an animal series
- Courtney and her Children's Workshop job
- Maria Shriver as TV producer in Baltimore

One other aspect of communications is drama. And that's where it seems John Kennedy, Jr. is headed.

Can it be that the Kennedys now instinctively feel that there is more clout and more power in communications than in politics? In Joe Kennedy's day it wasn't true, but today it may well be true.

Observing the frustrations and aggravations of the president and the Congress in their extravagant efforts to make the wheels of the country go around, one can see that perhaps the real power is being wielded by the typewriter and not by the gavel.

Joe Kennedy's dream was to build a bridge to the power center of the realm, which was called in the past the First Estate. Maybe the country has changed so that the power now lies in the Fourth Estate.

"Once the fortune is established and the family becomes aristocratic," an observer of the Kennedy fortunes says, "the blood line thins out. There aren't any more big money-makers among the Kennedys, no heavy movers. And pretty soon all that's left is a bunch of empty-headed playboys and playgirls, running around from discos to beaches to yachts. That's where the Kennedys are headed. Just look in your newspaper from day to day."

At the end of *The Candidate* Robert Redford, having won the election resoundingly, meets the men who put him there on the throne, and asks with a faint smile:

"What do I do now?"

Never forget that the triumphs and the tragedies of the Kennedys are *our* triumphs and tragedies. The Kennedys are our selected surrogates. Their lives are acted-out versions of the psychodrama of our own lives. And these triumphs and tragedies appear each day in the American media.

Even as we write these words. . . .